The Legal Determinants of Health

From Incarceration to Accessibility

Edited by Brian Dolan and Juliet McMullin

© 2025 University of California Health Humanities Press

University of California
Center for Health Humanities
Department of Humanities and Social Sciences
UCSF (Box 0850)
490 Illinois Street, Floor 7
San Francisco, CA 94143-0850

www.UCHealthHumanitiesPress.com
This series is made possible by the generous support of the Dean of the School of Medicine at UCSF and a Multicampus Research Program Grant from the University of California Office of the President. Grant ID MR-15-328363 and Grant ID M23PR5992.

Designed by Virtuoso Press

ISBN (pbk): 979-8-9926888-4-9

Printed in USA

Contents

Preface

Juliet Mcmullin

The inspiration for this book originated from a collaborative research project that responded to the stark inequities revealed by the COVID-19 pandemic, climate-related disasters, and a series of Supreme Court rulings that have reshaped patient autonomy. The project—Abolition Medicine and Disability Justice: Mapping Inequity and Renewing the Social—was designed by a group of scholars and community partners from five University of California campuses (Irvine, Los Angeles, Riverside, Santa Cruz, and San Francisco). Our proposal argued that health inequities are co-created by a complex web of policies, ethics, and narratives, that govern everything from immigration and incarceration to housing, education, and accessibility. By mapping these intersections, we can identify recurring patterns: laws that criminalize mental health issues, statutes that allow discriminatory medical practices, barriers to accessing disability accommodations, and regulatory gaps that leave communities vulnerable to toxic exposures. We also identified promising reforms, including the abolition of race-based medicine and the incorporation of restorative justice principles into health governance. We combined archival research with oral histories, ethnographic fieldwork with performance-based inquiry, and quantitative mapping with creative "anachronism"—applying contemporary disability concepts to historical texts to reveal hidden biases. It is our hope that the work of collaboration will point toward a more equitable future.

For the 2024 UCSF conference, our goal was to go beyond the usual focus on "social determinants" and highlight the *legal* structures that sustain or dismantle systemic racism, ableism, and other forms of systemic oppression. We aimed to show that the law is not just a background to public health and medical practice; it is a powerful force that influences who gets sick, who receives care, and who is granted the dignity of a healthy life. The two-day conference provided a chance to hear from the authors whose work you will read and to participate in a shared learning process where ideas and experiences fostered both understanding and actionable insights. In addition to the authors published in this book, graduate students played an active role, presenting their work and receiving support as they advance in their careers. The pages that follow capture the conversations at the conference, blending insights from legal scholarship, health humanities, and disability studies to show how statutes, regulations, and court decisions can become, for better or worse, determinants of health outcomes.

Why, then, does a book on legal determinants of health belong on the shelf of anyone interested in public health, medicine, law, humanities, or social justice? Because the legal landscape is not a static set of rules; it is a living, contested terrain that can either reinforce entrenched hierarchies or serve as a lever for transformative policy. Understanding the mechanisms by which law influences health—whether through zoning ordinances that dictate exposure to pollutants, immigration statutes that limit access to care, or judicial precedents that shape consent—offers a roadmap for focused advocacy and reform.

The journey from a grant proposal to a fully developed body of scholarship has been a collective effort, made possible by the dedication of faculty mentors, graduate an medical students, community advisors, and the many individuals who shared their stories and expertise. Their voices resonate throughout this volume, reminding us that the pursuit of health equity is intertwined with the pursuit of justice. We thank all the contributors to the Legal Determinants of Health edited volume and the members of the Abolition Medicine and Disability Justice project: Brian Dolan, Rachel Lee, Megan Moodie, Fuson Wang, Carla Mazzio, Matthew King, Helen Deutsch, James Lee, Candice Taylor Lucas, Roy Cherian, Micayla Wilson, Reelavioleta Botts-Ward, Nicholas Freeman, Lesley Thulin, Caitlin Flaws, Alisa Keesey, Fernando David Márquez, Kelly Dong, Mustafa Baqai, Katherine Peeler, Yajaira Ceciliano-Navarro, Leonora Naser-Saravia, and Bonita Dyess. The Abolition Medicine and Disability Justice Project received funding from UCOP Grant ID: M23PR5992.

It is my hope that readers will find here both a rigorous analytical foundation and an invitation to act—to examine the laws that govern our bodies, challenge the statutes that sustain inequality, and reimagine a legal ethics that genuinely protects health and wellbeing for everyone. May this work inspire new collaborations, ignite bold policy initiatives, and ultimately help reshape the legal determinants of health toward a more humane and inclusive future.

Introduction:
From Structural Harm to Legal Redress—Charting the Legal Determinants of Health

Brian Dolan

This volume gathers six original essays that together chart the contours of how law and legal systems – not just medical interventions – profoundly shape health outcomes. By illuminating both historical and contemporary case studies, the authors collectively reveal that legal institutions often function less as protectors of well-being and more as conduits of structural harm. From the prison infirmary to the disability accommodation office, from immigration detention centers to the courtroom, these contributions demonstrate how the interplay between law, health, and power creates unequal burdens—and suggest new legal and ethical frameworks for confronting them.

Several of the essays center on incarceration as a paradigmatic site of legal health inequity. Jennifer Elyse James and colleagues open with a searing analysis of how prison healthcare – particularly reproductive care – subverts bodily autonomy through coercive structures that dispropor-tionately harm Black and Brown women. The authors critically examine the ethical failures in healthcare decision-making for incarcerated women, particularly focusing on forced sterilizations in California prisons. Through interviews with formerly incarcerated women, clinicians, and legal experts, the authors explore how the prison healthcare system undermines informed consent and bodily autonomy, especially for Black and Brown women.

Despite legislative reforms following public revelations of non-con-sensual sterilizations, the article reveals that coercive medical practices persist. The authors present a conceptual framework demonstrating how interpersonal, structural, and systemic barriers – such as clinician pater-nalism, limited treatment options, surveillance by correctional officers, and the trauma-laden carceral environment – collectively suppress incarcerated individuals' ability to make autonomous healthcare decisions. James and colleagues argue that structural factors, including racism, security priorities, and dehumanizing prison conditions, make genuine informed consent nearly impossible in carceral settings. Even well-intentioned healthcare providers are often constrained by punitive institutional cultures and security protocols that override medical ethics.

The article concludes by asserting that incremental reforms are insufficient to protect the autonomy of incarcerated patients. Instead, it calls for an abolitionist bioethics that recognizes incarceration itself as a form of structural violence incompatible with ethical healthcare. The authors propose that bioethicists must not only critique coercive practices but also advocate for the dismantling of the prison-industrial complex as a necessary step toward achieving reproductive justice and true medical autonomy.

In a related register, Keramet Reiter and co-authors dissect the conceptual slippage between "harm reduction" and genuine health promotion in solitary confinement, showing how institutional metrics can obscure the profound existential damage caused by extreme isolation. The authors explore how health and harm are defined, measured, and often misrepresented in studies of solitary confinement. Drawing on nearly a decade of research in Washington state prisons, the authors argue that most frameworks confuse harm mitigation with actual health promotion. They critique earlier influential studies – particularly the 2013 "Colorado Study" – for failing to detect psychological harm and for shaping legal interpretations of solitary confinement's constitutionality. In contrast, the authors describe their own robust multi-method research approach, incorporating psychological assessments, medical record reviews, and in-depth interviews with both incarcerated individuals and correctional staff. This triangulated methodology, they argue, better captures the breadth of harm, including the systemic, cumulative, and existential forms of suffering experienced in solitary confinement.

The second half of the article focuses on the structural and policy implications of how harm is measured. Reiter's team reveals how standardized tools like the Brief Psychiatric Rating Scale often fail to capture the psychological toll of isolation, missing symptoms unique to the solitary confinement environment. They emphasize that meaningful reform must move beyond mere harm reduction strategies like vitamin supplements or "positive behavior reports," which may only legitimize ongoing structural violence. By including staff experiences and examining reforms inspired by Scandinavian prison models, the article situates solitary confinement within a broader critique of carceral logic and palliative governance. Ultimately, the authors call for a reconceptualization of what counts as health and harm, warning that reducing suffering without altering its structural causes risks making solitary confinement more palatable, rather than obsolete.

Yajaira Ceciliano-Navarro extends this carceral lens beyond prison walls, examining how deportation, detention, and incarceration function as compounding social determinants of health within vulnerable families and communities, particularly among mixed-status immigrant households. Ceciliano-Navarro applies the Legal Determinants of Health (LDH) framework to examine the emotional, financial, and health consequences of family separation due to deportation, detention, or incarceration in vulnerable Houston communities. Drawing on survey data from 343 participants with affected relatives, the study finds that both men and women – regardless of immigration status or family structure – experience lasting stress, anxiety, and financial instability. These legal processes are shown to not only disrupt family structures and increase emotional distress but also create chronic barriers to education, employment, and healthcare access, deepening long-term health inequities in communities already facing systemic disadvantage. Women often assume new caregiving and financial responsibilities, while men are forced into premature maturity, with many reporting shame, stigma, and depression.

The study highlights the compounded burdens on families – especially in mixed-status households – where legal and immigration systems intersect to produce overlapping forms of surveillance and vulnerability. For women, these burdens often manifest in housing instability, emotional trauma, and intergenerational financial stress, sometimes leading to suicidal ideation or the need for psychiatric medication. For men, the pressure to assume the role of provider results in early abandonment of educational or personal development goals, and their emotional responses are often suppressed due to gendered expectations. Both genders report persistent mental health consequences that outlast the period of removal. The article concludes that deportation, detention, and incarceration are not just legal or criminal processes—they are social determinants of health that perpetuate inequality and require structural policy reform at local, state, and federal levels.

The legal legacies of these carceral structures are further explored in Brian Dolan's historical case study of early IRB governance at UCSF, where questions of informed consent, investigational drug use, and institutional self-interest converge in ethically fraught prison research. His narrative underscores how health harms are not merely accidental or administrative failures, but often the predictable outcomes of ambiguous legal regimes, scientific ambition, and bureaucratic complicity. Dolan offers a detailed case study of the UCSF Committee on Human Experimentation (CHE) as it grappled with the ethical and legal challenges of overseeing human research during a pivotal era. Focusing on the use of investigational new drugs (INDs) in prison-based studies, the article reveals the committee's struggle to define "informed consent" when even investigators lacked knowledge of drug toxicity—often due to trade-secret protections. It highlights tensions between institutional prestige and ethical oversight, especially when researchers resisted disclosing drug data or insisted that oral assurances to participants sufficed over written documentation. The article juxtaposes local review processes with national developments such as the Belmont Report, demonstrating how UCSF's CHE had to navigate murky regulations, limited transparency, and mounting legal risks during a time of expanding bioethical awareness. Ultimately, the article underscores how early IRBs faced both structural and epistemic limitations in protecting vulnerable populations, especially when commercial interests, institutional power, and scientific ambition collided within ethically ambiguous spaces.

Similarly, Katherine Macfarlane's essay on "self-accommodation" demonstrates how individuals with disabilities navigate legal protections that exist more in theory than practice. Her analysis reframes inaction not as ignorance but as a rational strategy of self-preservation in hostile or indifferent systems. She explores how individuals with disabilities often forgo requesting legally mandated accommodations and instead self-accommodate—personally managing or funding adaptations that enable access to work, education, or healthcare. Through detailed examples, Macfarlane challenges the prevailing assumption that such individuals simply lack awareness of their rights. Instead, she argues they are rational actors avoiding invasive disclosure, bureaucratic obstacles, ableist stigma, and retaliation. Whether it's a new attorney with Lupus buying her own ergonomic chair to avoid judgment, a patient negotiating with unmasked doctors, or a student with panic attacks navigating inflexible academic deadlines, self-accommodation emerges not from ignorance but from a desire to avoid humiliation, rejection, and punishment.

Macfarlane frames this phenomenon as a civil rights failure that undermines the ADA's vision of dismantling societal barriers and shifting the cost of accessibility away from individuals with disabilities. She illustrates how self-accommodation violates both the spirit and structure of disability law, redistributing burdens that the law was designed to relieve. Moreover, self-accommodation can result in punitive outcomes—ranging from job discipline to termination of healthcare to threats of academic misconduct. To reduce its prevalence, Macfarlane calls for structural reforms that prioritize confidentiality, transparency, and ease in the accommodation process, including shifting negotiation burdens away from disabled individuals. Ultimately, she urges a recommitment to the social model of disability, warning that the current climate of political hostility toward perceived "difference" only intensifies the reluctance to disclose and seek support.

Beth Ribet's concluding piece proposes a doctrinal evolution in tort law to account for "disabling torts"—those harms that not only cause impairment but generate enduring vulnerability to social and legal discrimination. Ribet's call to recognize disablement as both injury and injustice anchors the book's broader argument: that law must be accountable not only to its formal doctrines but also to its lived consequences. Her article proposes a radical rethinking of tort law's approach to disability. Traditional torts frame disability as tragic damage inflicted by a tortfeasor, a view that diverges sharply from the civil and human rights framing in disability rights law, which sees harm not in disability itself but in the discrimination and structural barriers disabled individuals face. Ribet introduces the concept of "disabling torts," inspired by Robert Rabin's notion of "enabling torts," to argue that tortfeasors who cause or escalate disability should also be held liable for making individuals vulnerable to subsequent discrimination and social subordination. This idea draws on critical disability theory and the concept of "disablement," which encompasses both the physical or psychological impairments caused by violence or inequity and the social consequences that follow.

Ribet explores how integrating these concepts into tort law can expand its capacity to address structural injustice. She proposes that the legal system recognize not only the immediate physical harm but also the long-term, foreseeable social consequences of disability caused by tortious acts. These include discrimination in employment, housing, and other domains, especially for individuals already marginalized by race, gender, or class. Ribet outlines how such an approach could enhance damages calculations and policy interventions, especially by focusing on "disablement" as a socially constructed and inequity-driven process. Ultimately, she calls for a more nuanced tort doctrine—one that captures the complexity of lived experiences and systemic injustice, offering a path toward greater equity for disabled individuals harmed by negligence or violence.

Together, these essays urge readers to confront how legal and regulatory frameworks often perpetuate the very inequities they purport to solve. They invite new thinking across disciplines—bioethics, disability studies, legal history, public health—about what justice looks like when the law is itself a determinant of harm. But they also chart possible paths forward. Whether through abolitionist bioethics, reconceptualized tort frameworks, or reformed IRB procedures, the contributors each propose structural transformations—not just policy tweaks—to align law with equity. In doing so, they advance a vision of health justice grounded in both critique and possibility.

1

Structural Limitations on Autonomy in Prisons and Jails: Incarceration as a Bioethical Crisis

Jennifer Elyse James, Vrindavani Avila, Shalila De Bourmont,
Leslie Riddle, and Aminah Elster

Abstract
In 2013, it came to light that hundreds of women incarcerated in California prisons had been sterilized without proper informed consent. While public outrage led to legislation aimed at preventing this practice, there is little evidence to suggest that the root causes of forced sterilization have been eliminated. Drawing on interviews with formerly incarcerated people, clinicians working in prison and jail settings, and experts in law, policy, and reproductive health, we center forced sterilization to explore structural barriers to medical autonomy and informed consent in carceral contexts. We introduce a conceptual framework to illustrate how the interpersonal, structural, and systemic context of prison healthcare, can serve as an extension of state violence and the control of the reproduction and autonomy of Black and Brown women's bodies. We consider the role of bioethicists in addressing structural limitations on care, and center healthcare decision-making in prisons and jails as key bioethical domain. Finally, we advance the concept of abolition as an important theoretical and practical intervention to the crisis of autonomy and consent in carceral settings.

* Author affiliations: **Jennifer Elyse James** is an Associate Professor in the Institute for Health and Aging and the Department of Social and Behavioral Sciences at the University of California, San Francisco. **Vrindavani Avila** is a graduate student in the Cultural Studies Graduate Group at the University of California, Davis. **Shalila De Bourmont** is a graduate of the Medical School at the University of California, San Francisco and a current resident physician in obstetrics and gynecology. **Leslie Riddle** is a staff research associate in the Department of Humanities and Social Sciences at the University of California, San Francisco. **Aminah Elster** is the cofounder and executive director of Unapologetically HERS, Healing Experiences through Research Solutions, and a co-organizer with the California Coalition for Women Prisoners and Survived and Punished.

Introduction

On September 14, 2020, Dawn Wooten, a nurse working for the Irwin County Detention Center in Georgia, came forward with allegations that physicians working for ICE had forcibly sterilized women held in the facility (Treisman 2020). Many across the country were shocked and outraged to learn that healthcare providers might be sterilizing women without consent. Yet, this practice of sterilizing women who are under state control is not novel. Legal sterilization of incarcerated people dates back to at least 1907 and as recently as 2017 a Tennessee judge offered reduced sentencing in exchange for permanent or temporary sterilization (Perry 2017). Over this time, the incarceration rate has grown exponentially in the United States, increasing more than five-fold since 1975 (Pettit and Western 2004). Specifically, the number of incarcerated women has grown eight-fold since 1980, with more than 200,000 women incarcerated or detained in the US (Aday and Krabill 2012). Despite this dramatic increase, comparatively less attention has been given to women's unique health concerns and the health consequences of the rapidly-growing penal system in the U.S. (Massoglia 2008; Braithwaite, Treadwell, and Arriola 2008). Even less research has focused on the bioethical crisis that lies at the intersection of mass incarceration, health care decision-making, informed consent, and reproductive justice (Hayes et al., 2020; Sufrin et al., 2015; Sufrin et al., 2023). Ms. Wooten's report and subsequent investigations have highlighted a practice that many thought had been eliminated across the country. However, those who have lived or worked in California State Prisons know that the legacy of forced sterilizations as a part of 20th century eugenics programs has continued into present day.

California had the most far-reaching eugenics program in the United States. By the time the program was ended in 1979, over 20,000 people had been sterilized, approximately one third of the total eugenic sterilizations that occurred in the U.S. (Stern and Stern 2016). Anti-sterilization laws were finally enacted in California after a group of Latina women filed a class-action lawsuit alleging they were forced to undergo tubal ligations in a county hospital in Los Angeles, drawing the attention of a state lawmaker, who pushed to end the practice (Stern and Stern 2016).

More than two decades later, judges in another class action lawsuit, *Plata v. Schwarzenegger*, found that medical care in California state prisons violated Eight Amendment protections against cruel and unusual punishment (Bradley 2006). The 1976 U.S. Supreme Court case Estelle v. Gamble established that incarcerated people are entitled to care for diagnosis and treatment, a professional medical judgment, and administration of the treatment prescribed by the physician. Yet, research and numerous lawsuits, such as *Plata*, have demonstrated that the quality of care received by people who are incarcerated is often poor, with lack of access to adequate care, treatment delays and staff shortages (Aday and Farney 2014).

After the *Plata* decision, California state prisons were mandated to improve their care. When it was deemed that sufficient change had not occurred, a receivership was established in 2006 to provide additional oversight to the medical care in the California State Prison system (Bradley 2006). As a part of this oversight, several health care procedures, including tubal ligations, were deemed "excluded" under the California Code of Regulations. These procedures could not occur without the approval of the Receiver's Office and a prison committee. Yet, in 2013, the Center for Investigative Reporting issued a bombshell report asserting that, despite this regulatory oversight, two prisons in California sterilized at least 144 women between 2006 and 2010 without the approval of a medical review committee (Johnson 2013). This was corroborated by a report from the California State Auditor in 2014 which found that not only were 144 tubal ligations performed without proper consent or institutional oversight, in total nearly 800 sterilizing procedures were performed in those years, often without evidence of proper consent and many without clear medical necessity (California State Auditor 2014).

In a damaging interview, one prison physician, Dr. James Heinrich, noted that the money spent on sterilization procedures was minimal "compared to what you save in welfare paying for these unwanted children – as they procreated more" (Johnson 2013). This quote implies that these sterilizations were in fact an extension of the California eugenics program. Yet, many health providers working in state prisons asserted they had alternative rationales for flouting these regulations; they stated these rules were unfair, limiting, and potentially damaging to the women who were incarcerated. The implication was that they bypassed the regulations as a way to help women in need of reproductive health care and that the oversight limited the decision-making capacity of incarcerated women, thus highlighting an ethical tension between state regulation and personal autonomy. The California State Senate passed Senate Bill 1135 in 2014 which prohibited any means of sterilization for people who are incarcerated, "except when required for the immediate preservation of life in an emergency medical situation or when medically necessary" (Jackson 2014). However, sterilizing procedures have continued in the state, including tubal ligations which are expressly prohibited.

While incarcerated patients are entitled to many of the same deci-sion-making rights (such as the right to refuse care) as non-incarcerated patients, little is known about how women make routine healthcare decisions to manage their health while incarcerated. While there has been research focused on surrogate decision-making (Tobey and Simon 2019; Scarlet, DeMartino, and Siegler 2019) and advanced care planning (Enders, Paterniti, and Meyers 2005; DiTomas, Bick, and Williams 2019), little research has focused on decision-making in chronic illness and routine care. Research has shown that incarcerated women are more likely to have serious health problems than incarcerated men and seek health care in prison more than twice as often (Fearn and Parker 2005). For many women, incarceration is the only time they have access to comprehensive medical care (Fearn and Parker 2005). However, numerous barriers such as co-pays, poor perceptions of prison health care staff, and security protocols may dissuade women from seeking health care while incarcerated (Wahidin 2006). Further, medical care and medical decision-making inside prisons occur under the shadow of the complex entanglement of historical injus-tices, regulatory oversight, and state violence.

Over the last four years, our team has interviewed more than 50 for-merly incarcerated people, correctional health care providers, and experts in policy, reproductive health, and incarceration; conducted hundreds of hours of participant observation; and used media analysis and archival research to elucidate how such a massive failure of consent and autonomy occurred in California and to better understand if it is possible to support a model of shared decision making and informed consent in the carceral context. Participants in our study have described hysterectomies performed under false pretenses (e.g., patients were misled to believe they had cancer) and without proper informed consent, including a lack of discussions of alternative treatments, expected side effects, or risks of procedures (Riddle, James, and Elster 2022; Elster 2021; Madrigal 2023; Henderson 2023). Yet, participants also described going without needed reproductive and gyneco-logical care and even the weaponization of legal protections in discussions of care options.

In this chapter, we will describe the structural barriers to medical autonomy and informed consent in the prison context. We introduce a conceptual framework to illustrate how the interpersonal, structural, and systemic context of prison healthcare, can serve as an extension of state violence and control, diminishing the reproductive autonomy of incarcer-ated women, who are disproportionately women of color.

History of Incarceration and Health: The Bioethical Crisis of Confinement

The U.S. Supreme Court established in the case *Estelle v. Gamble* that the Eighth Amendment protections against cruel and unusual punishment included protections against deliberate indifference to serious medical need (Rold 2008). This ruling, however, did not create a consistent standard for healthcare, nor establish what constitutes a serious medical need (Turnbull, Bouhassira, and Saloner 2023). Compared with people who are not incar-cerated, incarcerated people have higher rates of chronic illness, before, during, and after incarceration (Binswanger, Krueger, and Steiner 2009). While incarceration can offer an opportunity to intervene and offer treat-ment for chronic conditions (Wang et al. 2017; Oser et al. 2016; Nijhawan et al. 2010; Bai et al. 2015; Maruschak, Bronson, and Alper 2021), this vulnerable population persistently faces worse health outcomes than their non-incarcerated counterparts (Binswanger, Krueger, and Steiner 2009; Wang et al. 2017; Brinkley-Rubinstein 2013; Garcia-Grossman et al. 2023; Wang, Wang, and Krumholz 2013). Healthcare in correctional settings can be explicitly rationed with many barriers to access (Peteet and Tobey 2017) and the health disparities present during incarceration persist post release. In the months following release from a correctional facility, patients experience higher hospitalization rate and all-cause mortality compared with the general population (Sankaran 2023). One study found that every year of exposure to incarceration is associated with a 2-year reduction in life expectancy (Patterson 2013).

The disparate impact of mass incarceration on Black and Indigenous People of Color (BIPOC) in the United States and massive racial disparities in rates of incarceration have been well documented (Neills 2021). Focusing on the location of our research, state data shows that, of those who are incarcerated in California state prisons, 28.3% are Black, 44.1% are Hispanic, 21% are white, and 6.6% are other races, with approximately 19.4% born outside of the U.S. (California Department of Corrections and Rehabilitation 2019). For comparison, the population of California is 36.5% white non-Hispanic and only 6.5% Black (U.S. Census Bureau 2024). These numbers are even more stark in the context of San Francisco, where Black people make up 5.7% of the county population and 43% of the population of the county jail (San Francisco Sheriff's Department 2024).

It has been well established that incarceration can have serious negative health consequences. High levels of communicable disease, exposure to violence, and decline in socioeconomic status after incarceration can all lead to lifelong poor health (Hogg et al. 2008). Mass incarceration thus serves as a "key component of structural racism that creates and exacerbates health inequities" (LeMasters et al. 2022).

Bioethical Crisis of Autonomy and Decision Making

While this chapter began with a focus on clinicians who abused their positions of power, we are more interested in the *structural* limitations on care that shape patient-provider relationships and decision making. There are phenomenal clinicians who chose to work in prisons and jails precisely because they want to care for a vulnerable patient population in need of excellent healthcare. Yet, in our research, we've heard from clinicians who struggle to navigate shared decision making in carceral settings and worry if they are providing ethical care. Here is an example from a provider who realized that, despite her best efforts, informed consent with a patient was not adequately obtained:

I had a patient who came to see me for a method of contraception.... I thought it was very open-ended, non-directed counseling session. At the end she decided on an IUD. I said 'ok great, let's go through the consent form.' We went through the consent form. And then she was getting undressed behind the curtain and said very casually, 'hey so doc, do I have to get this?' And I was like mortified. Because I thought I was being so kind and open ended and non-coercive. And she just casually internalized or assumed that this conversation meant she had to do something and had to do an IUD.

This quote is from a healthcare provider recalling an experience caring for a patient in a county jail. In many ways, it is a positive story. The provider went on to describe feeling horrified that she may have performed an unwanted or coerced procedure. She did not place the IUD that day and, in fact, worked to revise the policy at her institution so that there was one visit for counseling and another visit to place the IUD as a mechanism for safeguarding against coercion. She acknowledged that this change in policy could mean that some patients go without a wanted form of birth control; people often leave jail quickly, sometimes with little warning. But this provider felt that it was better for someone to go without needed medical care than to have a procedure without proper informed consent.

This example raises important questions about how autonomy in medical decision-making is conceptualized and how respect for autonomy is practiced. Autonomy is typically defined as an individual's capacity for self-determination. Respect for autonomy - usually understood to mean allowing capacitated individuals to make decisions about and for themselves- is a central tenet of U.S. bioethics, yet bioethicists have increasingly realized the difficulty in reconciling autonomy with unjust contexts in which serious constraints and coercive structures influence patient choice. Healthcare professionals may reasonably ask whether informed consent is possible in these contexts, or whether practices of medical decision-making and informed consent actualize respect for autonomy in practice.

Most people who are incarcerated maintain their capacity and right to make medical decisions. (While decisions to remove capacity – in both institutional settings and the free world – is a critical topic, it will not be explored here). However, their freedom to make medical decisions according to that autonomous capacity can be limited. The structural and systemic obstructions on freedom created by incarceration affect both the internal constitution of the autonomy of incarcerated patients and the external availability of what they might choose. Here we describe some of the mechanisms of oppression of incarcerated patients making medical decisions to highlight the tensions impacting autonomy in this context.

Structural barriers to communication and patient-clinician relationships
     Across a series of studies, we have elucidated patterns in communication and barriers to clinical decision-making between incarcerated patients and providers (Jeske, James, and Joyce 2023; James 2023; James, Riddle, and Perez-Aguilar 2023; James 2021; Avila and James 2024). Like many other vulnerable and marginalized groups, effective health communication with incarcerated patients can be challenging. Patients and providers have different knowledge of disease and often approach decision making and consent differently. This is heightened by the communication barriers and power asymmetry in carceral healthcare (Pierce 2016). Further, and especially in the context of women's prisons, patients are often survivors of trauma (Lehrer 2021; Courtney and Maschi 2013; Jewkes et al. 2019; Levenson and Willis 2019; Auty et al. 2022; Law 2015; Harner and Burgess 2011), which, as we've demonstrated through our preliminary research, can make

informed consent and shared decision making even more challenging, due to lack of trust and fear of asking questions (Jennifer E. James 2021; Jeske, James, and Joyce 2023; Jennifer E. James 2023; McCauley et al. 2020).

The harms perpetuated by individual healthcare professionals in carceral facilities, particularly in reproductive health, have been well documented (Law 2015; McCormick 2021; Rayasam 2024). Yet, even in the absence of overt harm, formerly incarcerated patients have described a culture of lack of options and information. Many patients described feeling like their clinician only offered one treatment option, or as one formerly incarcerated participant noted, "Your other option is no care at all." Another patient described a nurse advising her to take the recommendations of her doctor to undergo a sterilizing procedure by saying, "Either you are going to want to do what he says to do, or he's not going to want to help you."

Many participants described being offered only a hysterectomy, for example, as treatment for heavy periods or fibroid tumors. As one patient with painful periods described:

> And so really the only option that was given to me was get a hysterectomy…. I didn't feel like I had another option because no other options were given at the time. It felt helpless and hopeless. I also didn't even question it at the time due to my trauma.

When asked to say more about the role of her trauma in this decision-making process she said:

> I was still fairly new in my time [in prison] and I hadn't yet gotten the tools or I hadn't yet taken my power back to stand up for myself. And being for me that it was another male that said 'no, this is what you're supposed to do,' I just went with it without question because I didn't want to cause… To me standing up to a male GYN or just a male period at that time, if I would've said no or opposed it, it would've, in my mind at the time, it would've resulted in violence. And that scared

me because I didn't want to go through another violent episode with another man.

This patient described being offered only one care plan, which alone is a violation of informed consent. However, importantly, this patient is describing that, due to both her own history of trauma and the structural violence in the prisons system, she did not feel safe to refuse or question this option. Even if more options had been provided – and even despite an implied option to refuse care – this patient did not feel safe to express concern or her preference. She was sterilized at a young age because she felt it would be unsafe to question the care plan from her prison doctor. While the clinician involved in this story likely could have used better communication techniques to understand the patient's goals of care, describe her options, and allow space for questions and alternatives, this story also represents a structural barrier to care. This woman, due to the conditions that *led* to her confinement, in combination with the confinement itself, did not feel she had autonomy over her body or her decisions.

Healthcare professionals we interviewed also described worry about patient autonomy, though at times it stemmed from internal conflict between a desire to protect patient autonomy when the option the patient wants feels like it's not within the patient's "best interest." As one provider who sees patients during incarceration described:

I sometimes will see patients in very difficult circumstances who actually want pro- reproductive changes in their birth control or their health. So they want to have an IUD removed or a Nexplanon removed and they are actively using [drugs], they just got out of psychiatric hospitalization, they already have children who have been born with physical disabilities because of drug abuse during pregnancy. And it's really hard as a human to not... Those are the ones that are ethically the hardest for me to not... To just feel... I can feel my own thoughts and opinions coming through... I want to do what the patient truly wants. But ...

This provider is describing feeling conflicted about supporting patient preferences and choices, despite advocating strongly for incarcerated people to have the right to access contraception and abortion. She wants to protect patient autonomy, but worries about patients making decisions that providers believe may not be in their best interest or in the best interest of potential future children. As another provider described, they have to maintain a "really difficult balance between knowing if someone can consent to a procedure versus being paternalistic and making a decision for them or making a delay for them that will lead to, you know, them not getting what they ultimately desire." While this tension – particularly around advocating for long-acting birth control and ideas of pregnancy intention – exists in many contexts (Dehlendorf et al., 2024), the structure of prisons and jails means that nearly all patients will be in a circumstance which a physician may judge to be a less than ideal times for "pro-reproductive" decisions. The structural realities of prison and jail, including separation from family, loss of employment and housing, disruption of parental rights, and potentially violence, abuse, and addiction, all present rationales that a clinician could use to deny autonomy. While this could be viewed as a classic example of clinician paternalism, the structure of carceral environments can surface and centralize these concerns. Further, patients are structurally prohibited from seeking other care options if a clinician is.

Structural limitations of care

The second jail I worked at, IUDs and Nexplanon were not available because they were considered too expensive. Because it [the jail] was run by a for-profit corporation.

—Jail Clinician

The carceral healthcare context affects both patients and providers in unique ways that can negatively impact the clinical encounter, by prioritizing the goals of the jail/prison over those of healthcare. While medical care in some institutions is run by the state or county and in others is contracted out to a for profit company, in general, healthcare in prisons or jails runs as an insular health management system, which both delivers the healthcare and sets the policy on what care is covered. A culture of what often feels, to patients and clinicians alike, like restrictions on available care, coupled with interpersonal communication challenges between patients and clinicians and a general sense of lack of autonomy and choice in prison can lead many incarcerated patients to feel that they do not have any choices in their care. Among those we interviewed, this was often interpreted as a punitive feature of the prison system itself.

Patients have quite commonly described tooth extraction as the only care option for a toothache or cavity. Others describe going without medication because of side effects of the only available medicine in the prison formulary; one patient described her options when she was unable to continue a medication saying, "it's either that or nothing. So I think you do have a choice, and the option is just no help at all." However, even the choice to refuse care is complicated as it can, from the patient perspective, be interpreted within the system as refusing all medical care. One participant, *Ms. Legacy*, who is in substance use recovery, reported that when she refused narcotics for pain to protect her sobriety that the response was "when you refuse that, then they say you are refusing medical attention."

Despite the legal right to refuse care, many patients reported facing forms of retaliation or punishment for refusing care. That is, what could be an individual decision (to refuse care) or an issue of interpersonal communication (negotiating care options with one's clinician), in the carceral context operates as a structural issue by the nature of how refusals are documented. Further, many patients expressed a worry that a documented refusal could become a justification for punishment. One woman, *Isis*, reported that she was sexually assaulted by a nurse while incarcerated. For a period after this, she refused to go to medical appointments. She described this time saying,

> I was threatened if I didn't go to my medical appointments—because I became very fearful of going to medical, I didn't trust them no more and I didn't want to be there—I was threatened to get written up. I

would get in trouble. I've gotten written up a few times for refusing to go so, yeah, that was definitely a form of retaliation.

Both sexual assault and not being believed or feeling like one has no recourse following assault in prison are, unfortunately, all too common (Fedock et al., 2016, 2019; Wolff et al., 2006). While survivors of custodial sexual abuse have used legal remedies, such as class action lawsuits, to draw attention to harm and seek injunctive relief (e.g., institutional changes) both abuse and disbelief remain common. Isis was justified in her fear of retaliation.

Reporting abuse often results in being placed in administrative segregation. But, even if one does not report and, like Isis, refuses care, even something as small as a "write up" can become a reason for a praole denial. While this is the story of only one person, these types of stories circulate the prison and perpetuate the idea that "medical" is not a place for healing or a source of care. For some it can serve as a site of violence, but in general it can feel like a place where disagreeing with one's clinician could potentially lead to more time behind bars. This is coupled with the pervasive perception that the system does not want to help them; this perception extends to healthcare. Another participant said,

You see people so sick. I've seen people die in their rooms because they won't go to medical. [My friend] died in her own room because she wouldn't take medical, she's like, 'why, they're not going to do nothing. They're not going to do nothing.' She died in the room three nights later. Because you don't want to go. You don't want to deal with it. You just want to be like, okay, I can handle this.

Correctional officers as gatekeepers to care

You need custody to bring patients to you and you need custody to bring patients to the hospital. And to help provide care you need custody's eyes and ears to see how patients are doing... You need to work as a team and you need to be really separate.

—*Prison Clinician*

Perhaps the most common sentiment expressed across dozens of interviews about numerous types of healthcare experiences, was patients being told "Nothing's wrong with you." There was a consistent perception that, in the eyes of the institution and its agents, incarcerated patients are not to be believed, are manipulative, or should not speak up to advocate for themselves. Months, years, or decades of being told that one's perception of their health is wrong weighed on those we interviewed. Many participants described not feeling like they should or could articulate their symptoms or needs when receiving community-based care either. While some participants described this sentiment as coming from healthcare providers, others described being disbelieved by correctional staff, who often determined if or when someone could access care for the acute onset of illness.

One woman, who asked to be called *Second Chance,* described the importance of demonstrating one's character while in prison. According to Second Chance, she was known as the "Church Lady" while she was inside due to her involvement in faith-based activities. She expressed that she felt she was lucky because she was incarcerated when she was in her late 30s, a bit older than most are when they first go inside, and knew to be "respect-ful" and how stay out of trouble. She said the guards thought of her as "one of the good ones." Second Chance said, "If you don't have that type of character in you to let them see, they're not going to show you any type of caring, any type of sympathy. They're not going to show you anything. They just feel like you don't deserve it." According to Second Chance and others, women who are incarcerated have to prove their worth and humanity before they are afforded access to healthcare when ill. In the view of Second Chance and others, if the guards didn't see you a certain way, you wouldn't be believed when you got sick.

In this sense, correctional officers act as gatekeepers to healthcare. Barriers to care are not unique to carceral environments. Many patients in community settings face barriers such as insurance status, transportation, wait times, language barriers, and more. Yet, healthcare operates differently inside prisons where an individual needs permission from a security officer to avail themselves of medical service. Many formerly incarcerated women understand why the system works this way; they note that there are "fakers," who as one participant described it, "pull shenanigans" and fake illness at times. However, there is a severe cost to this, especially to those who may have not demonstrated "good character" in the past. As Second Chance described, "a lot of ladies have died in there because of the lack of care, because they didn't believe them. Absolutely. I've had quite a few friends that died in there from cancer and stuff like that because when they got sick, they just didn't believe that they were sick like that. And they waited until the cancer got to phase 3, phase 4 and then they died." Second Chance herself noted that despite her own good reputation, despite being "the Church Lady," when she became sick, the officers still "thought that [she] was just trying to get attention."

Correctional officers also play a key role when incarcerated patients are transferred to hospitals or other community-based care settings. Research shows that the presence of correctional staff changes how care is delivered, with healthcare providers noting that the presence of law enforcement officers in the room challenges their ability to develop patient-provider relationships, discuss treatment plans, spend time with patients, and maintain privacy (Kaiksow, Williams, and Haber 2023)(Haber et al. 2019; Tuite, Browne, and O'Neill 2006; Zust, Busiahn, and Janisch 2013; Harada, Lara-Millán, and Chalwell 2021). Incarcerated patients are still entitled to privacy (Kaiksow, Williams, and Haber 2023) and HIPAA protects the health information of people who are incarcerated (Scarlet and Dreesen 2019; 2017). However, the enforcement and protection of the right to privacy is materially different for incarcerated patients, who may often be accompanied or surveilled by correctional staff. Practices like shackling and the presence of armed guards limits privacy and has the potential to discourage patients from sharing information with their clinicians, which may in turn limit autonomy and self-advocacy (Scarlet and Dreesen 2021). Most clinicians have not received training on how to interact with correctional staff. In several studies, providers described guards and correctional staff as "intrusive" (Zust, Busiahn, and Janisch 2013; Harada, Lara-Millán, and Chalwell 2021). Overall, clinicians express uncertainty about whether to request that correctional officers remove shackles or leave the room (Sankaran 2023). Physicians and nurses have been reported to interact differently with corrections staff and with security protocols, with nurses more likely than physicians to discuss the reason a patient is incarcerated with a correctional officer and less likely to ask correctional officers to step out for exams (Brooks, Makam, and Haber 2022).

The provision of care to incarcerated patients presents several ethical challenges. Healthcare providers may be obligated to follow reasonable rules set by correctional officials. While clinicians can challenge these rules, often the decisions ultimately lie with the correctional officials (Kaiksow, Williams, and Haber 2023; Kaiksow, Patel, and Fost 2023) heightening the potential for moral distress among clinicians and raising the need to center power in analysis of autonomy, consent, and decision-making.

Prioritization of security

When you leave the institution to go out for medical care…they parade you and take you in the back. You're shackled at your waist, your hands and your feet… It felt like it was implied that, you know, this is public enemy number one, we're going to do as little as possible. Yes, we have to treat them, but we don't like it. I felt like a spectacle.
                                                                —*Optimus Prime*

Prisons and jails offer a varied range of health services, depending on the capabilities of the facilities. This can range from small jails with limited clinical staff and capabilities, to prison hospitals capable of performing operations and tertiary levels of care. In all cases, when the healthcare needs of an individual surpasses the level of care that can be provided at a correctional institution, patients are transferred to offsite hospitals or clinics for care. While discussion of forced sterilization often centers on California prisons, it is important to remember that these surgical procedures took place in community and academic hospitals. The structural limitations on autonomy that shape care inside prisons and jails, also manifest in community contexts when patients are transferred to hospitals or clinics for care. In general, we heard from both patients and clinicians a perspective that security policies often override the medical needs and priorities of patients and providers. This is true both inside and outside of carceral facilities, but it often felt more acutely in care delivered at community hospitals and clinics where security staff, weapons, and shackles become a feature of the delivery of care.

Correctional officers play a key role when incarcerated patients are transferred to hospitals or other community-based care settings. Research shows that the presence of correctional staff changes how care is delivered, with healthcare providers noting that the presence of law enforcement officers in the room challenges their ability to develop patient-provider relationships, discuss treatment plans, spend time with patients, and maintain privacy (Kaiksow, Williams, and Haber 2023; Haber et al. 2019; Tuite, Browne, and O'Neill 2006; Zust, Busiahn, and Janisch 2013; Harada, Lara-Millán, and Chalwell 2021). Incarcerated patients are still entitled to privacy (Kaiksow, Williams, and Haber 2023) and HIPAA protects the health information of people who are incarcerated (Scarlet and Dreesen 2019; 2017). However, some health systems policy manuals have been found to include wording that erroneously states that HIPAA does not apply to incarcerated patients (Junewicz 2014; Goldstein 2014) and the enforcement and protection of the right to privacy is materially different for incarcerated patients, who may often be accompanied or surveilled by correctional staff. In several studies, providers described guards and correctional staff as "intrusive" (Zust, Busiahn, and Janisch 2013; Harada, Lara-Millán, and Chalwell 2021). Physicians and nurses have been reported to interact differently with corrections staff and with security protocols, with nurses more likely than physicians to discuss the reason a patient is incarcerated with a correctional officer and less likely to ask correctional officers to step out for exams (Brooks, Makam, and Haber 2022). Many participants described having intimate examinations, hearing devastating news, or even giving birth with a correctional officer in the room, aware of all that was said. When asked to describe what good care looks like in the hospital setting, one participant told us about a provider who asked the staff to step out of the room. Just that simple step of ensuring they could have a private conversation, made the participant feel like they were treated with respect.

Hospital policies regulating the care of incarcerated patients can vary. Often, these policies are a patchwork of local, state, and federal law, with conflicting directives from hospitals, law enforcement, and correctional institutions. These policies, including the default usage of shackles and police presence in the room, may have the consequence of relegating incarcerated patients to second-class status (Junewicz 2014) and have the potential to discourage patients from sharing information with their clinicians, which may in turn limit autonomy and self-advocacy (Scarlet and Dreesen 2021).

While at least some policies and guidelines for the care of incarcerated patients exist at most hospitals (Smith 2016) they are highly variable and often focus on security requirements, and not the unique vulnerabilities of this patient population (Suh and Robinson 2022). Further, importantly, research has shown that providers are often unaware of policies or guidelines for the treatment of incarcerated patients, with one study showing that out of 184 surveyed physicians,180 had cared for an incarcerated patient but only 3 were aware of any guidelines in place for their care (Tuite, Browne, and O'Neill 2006). Overall, clinicians express uncertainty about whether to request that correctional officers remove shackles or leave the room (Sankaran 2023).

When in the hospital, the majority of incarcerated and detained patients are shackled for most or all of their hospitalizations – regardless of their conviction status, alleged crime, or risk of violence or flight (DiTomas, Bick, and Williams 2019; Junewicz 2014; Scarlet and Dreesen 2017; Haber et al. 2022; Douglas et al. 2021; Grundy, Peterson, and Brinkley-Rubinstein 2022; Hernandez 2022; Courtwright, Raphael-Grimm, and Collichio 2008). The First Step Act of 2018 prohibited the use of shackling during labor and delivery for people incarcerated in the federal system, and 39 states have similar laws restricting the use of shackles during birth (Kramer et al. 2023), however, these laws are not always enforced and apply to only a fraction of hospitalizations and acute care events experienced during incarceration. Even in the case of labor and delivery, which has the clearest laws and guidelines, a study of U.S. perinatal nurses' found only 7% correctly identified whether their states had shackling laws and only 3% correctly identified the conditions under which shackling may ethically take place (Goshin et al. 2019). In one survey, 65% of medical residents noted caring for a patient who remained shackled during surgery and 45% reported witnessing patients shackled while intubated and sedated (Moin and Sisti 2019; Douglas et al. 2021), despite it being "extraordinarily unlikely" that any escape or other attempt would happen after a patient is sedated (Beyer and Applewhite 2022).

It has been well established that the use of shackles during hospitalization compromises care (Junewicz 2014; Zust, Busiahn, and Janisch 2013) and influences how providers view and interact with patients (Harada, Lara-Millán, and Chalwell 2021). Visible restraints may exacerbate stigma (Scarlet and Dreesen 2021) and has been reported to influence the quality and type of care delivered by both physicians and nurses (Beyer and Applewhite 2022; Harada, Lara-Millán, and Chalwell 2021; Haber et al. 2022). Shackling during procedures and examinations is a violation of autonomy that can erode trust and potentially reduce the efficacy of therapies and interventions, including delaying recovery through restricted ambulation (Beyer and Applewhite 2022; Scarlet and Dreesen 2017).

In sum, the provision of care to incarcerated patients in the hospital presents several ethical challenges. Healthcare providers may be obligated to follow reasonable rules set by correctional officials, but it can be unclear which rules or restrictions are reasonable. While clinicians can challenge these rules, often the decisions ultimately lie with the correctional officials (Kaiksow, Williams, and Haber 2023; Kaiksow, Patel, and Fost 2023) heightening the potential for moral distress among clinicians and raising the need to center power in analysis of autonomy, consent, and decision-making. Participants in our study who underwent sterilization procedures reported signing a consent form, which no one reviewed with them, while shackled to a gurney and in the presence of an armed correctional officer. Coupled with limited options for care and feeling unable to refuse a doctor's recommendation, signing consent while restrained and surveilled raises critical questions about the possibility of true free and informed consent.

Structurally Diminished Autonomy

The structure of care delivery in prison, which includes limitations on the number of medical problems that can be presented, types of medications that can be offered, and correctional officers acting as gatekeepers to care, can create a punitive care environment. The perceived punitive nature of care is magnified by those who, often due to perceptions of their race, gender, and class, are perceived to be aggressive, assertive, or unworthy of care. This creates interpersonal, structural and systemic restrictions on autonomy, with even those clinicians who strive to offer patient centered care being limited in their ability to build trusting relationships by a structure that prioritizes institutional safety and security, diminishes personal autonomy, and presumes that patients are not to be trusted.

When incarcerated, one's body becomes the property of the state. Individuals lose the right to determine what they eat, where and when they sleep, and how they spend their time. Control over one's health and wellbeing are deeply infringed upon, and this lack of autonomy extends to the healthcare context. While patients have a right to access healthcare, their ability to make decisions about their care, let alone pursue health and wellbeing, is structurally stripped away by the punitive nature of carceral facilities. While protections for medical informed consent exist, at least in the law, for people who are incarcerated, the right to personal bodily autonomy is fundamentally disrupted and challenged by incarceration.

Autonomy is a bedrock principle of healthcare and bioethics in the U.S. and there are explicit laws to protect the autonomy of incarcerated patients (e.g., right to refuse, the existence of consent forms). Yet the system is designed to constrain and limit choice in nearly all areas of life. These limitations on choice allow for both bad apples – doctors who may be motivated to provide negligent or abusive care – and poor practices of consent and autonomy to flourish, even when clinicians have the best intentions. When a system limits autonomy in all other areas of life, that can easily slip into the healthcare system and – intentionally or unintentionally – allow for people to be subject to procedures they don't really want or to refuse medical care out of fear or mistrust, which can lead to more harm and complications. Even for rights that are protected by law (e.g., the right to refuse medical care), threats of harassment and retaliation persist, and the right to seek care remains conditional on the structural and punitive conditions of incarceration.

As described, refusals of care can result in a write up or be documented as refusal of any treatment for the condition. Similarly, just as in the free world, patients can lose wages or be reprimanded for missing work for a medical appointment and may face incredibly long wait times for appointments. Importantly, security protocols often require invasive strip searches for patients coming in and out of the facility for outside medical appointments. Patients may refuse needed outside care to avoid a traumatizing ritual. In these scenarios of refusal, patients are making a choice that should be honored and respected. Yet, it is not a choice free of constraints.

In order to better articulate this problem, we developed a conceptual framework to describe the process of health decision-making for people who are incarcerated within the complex healthcare and carceral policy landscape (See Figure 1). Our goal with this framework is to further categorize the limitations on autonomy and decision-making to elucidate priority areas for further research and advocacy. It is essential to understand the structural forces driving not only who is incarcerated but the interests of the state in both criminalizing and providing custodial care for this population (James 2022; Valles 2023; James 2023). This model is driven by six key assumptions, based in our research.

First, we place decision making and informed consent within the individual sphere, under the umbrella of interpersonal relationships, noting that patient values should drive health decisions. This is based in a U.S. model of healthcare decision-making which assumes that autonomy and

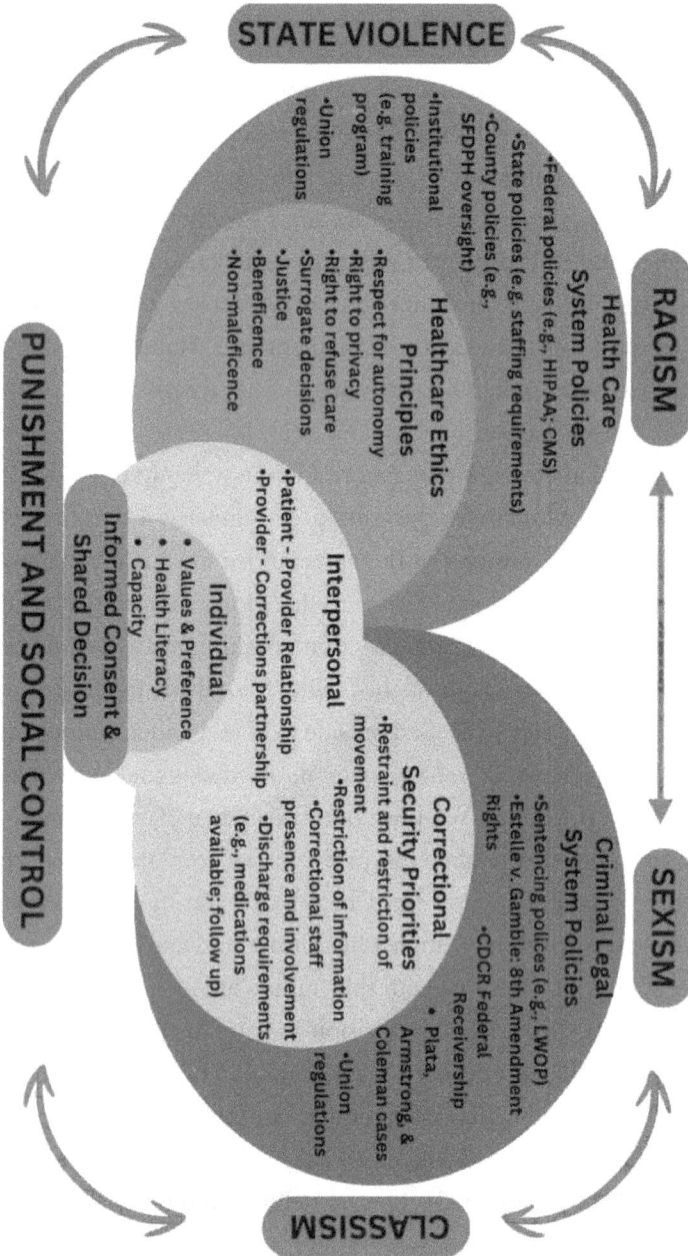

Figure 1: Conceptual framework for hospital-based health decision-making during incarceration

informed consent is central to the provision of ethical healthcare. In order for a patient to make an informed choice about their care, they must be informed of the risks, benefits, and alternatives to any intervention in a language they can understand, in a conversation driven by their values and preferences. Of note, this model does not include family or community as central. While this is somewhat aligned with a U.S.-based ethical framework, it also speaks to the explicit exclusion of family and community from most carceral healthcare spaces.

Second, as in the free world, these decisions occur within the context of the patient-provider relationships. However, third, the model clarifies that the carceral health care system, via limited choice and the presence of correctional officers, complicates both this relationship and the possibility for patient autonomy. Clinicians, in both carceral and hospital settings, are required to collaborate with correctional staff to deliver healthcare, whether through Cos bringing patients to medical appointments, or through negotiations on the presence of COs or other security measures in clinical spaces.

Fourth, this model assumes that healthcare ethics principles, such as the right to privacy and respect for autonomy, may at times come into conflict with correctional security priorities, such as the presence of correctional officers and restrictions on care delivery. We argue that, whether necessary or not, the presence of correctional officers limits both privacy and autonomy, both of which compromise the right to refuse care. One cannot make as free of a choice about their healthcare when they are not free to leave, when their jailer is in the room, or when there is an implicit threat of violence (via the presence of weapons) if their actions are viewed as threatening or even disrespectful. Further, institutional restrictions on care, including limitations on medications (e.g., opioid pain medications may not be permitted), communication (patients may not be told when follow up care will be provided), and living conditions (e.g., diet, bunk beds, work requirements) may all drive what care is offered, rather than the clinical judgement and beneficence of the clinician. Finally, research has demonstrated that involvement of surrogate decision makers in the case of incapacitated patients is often limited; correctional staff, rather than loved ones, are often tapped to make medical decisions. This may be in cases where there is no family or family cannot be reached but also occurs when correctional staff refuse to call family, often not allowing their involvement until the end of life (Batbold et al. 2023).

Fifth, this model assumes that judicial oversight, policy, and regulations directed at criminal legal systems intersect with healthcare system policies and may play a particular role in shaping the delivery of care. Much of this is not dissimilar to all of healthcare; staffing requirements, local, state and federal law, specific institutional norms and regulations, all play a large role in shaping how care is delivered. The carceral settings adds unique tension here. First because criminal legal system policies dictate factors such as who is incarcerated in the first place, for how long, and in what type of setting. But, further, because factors like sentencing may dictate the type and condition of care; for example, being incarcerated in a maximum security facility may mean more policing is necessary for accessing care. Or, for example, a patient receiving care in a skilled nursing facility under a medical parole program may have restrictions put on them as a condition of parole (e.g., restriction on visitation or the right to leave the facility) that are in direct contact with CMS regulations for residents of nursing homes (Mendelson and Yu 2022). There is a deep complexity in trying to integrate two highly bureaucratic and hierarchical systems to collaborate when their primary missions may be in tension.

Finally, this model elucidates that issues of patient-provider relationships and decision-making must be viewed through an intersectional lens. We must examine the oppressive forces of racism, sexism, and classism as the impetus for a system of punishment and social control, which is enacted via state violence and influences the interpersonal and individual domains. Specifically, in the case of forced sterilizations, we center obstetric racism, which has seven key dimensions: diagnostic lapses; neglect, dismissiveness, or disrespect; intentionally causing pain; coercion; ceremonies of degradation; medical abuse; and racial reconnaissance (Davis 2019), all of these have been documented occurring to people while incarcerated in California. We center prison industrial complex (PIC) abolition and, in particular, abolition feminisms in our approach, highlighting that incarcerated people must be centered in any analysis of state violence (Davis et al. 2022).

Conclusion: An Abolitionist Vision for Bioethics

The criminal legal system is a violent system based in racism and social control. Like other similar systems, including slavery and segregation, incarceration requires a deeply embodied othering. For society to accept and be comfortable with the idea of incarceration – the idea of locking people in cages and depriving them of liberties – we must believe they are fundamentally different from ourselves. It is challenging to maintain humanity within a system that relies on dehumanization to function. As Ruth Wilson Gilmore describes, racism makes it possible "to become so detached from another human being that another person with a different skin color might not even seem human" (Gilmore 2022). The criminal legal system has extended and legitimized this detachment. That is, the idea of incarceration continually reinforces itself. We create the "criminal" as a violent and dangerous other in need of incarceration for the safety of the public. This danger means that incarcerated individuals are deserving of punishment, and a loss of autonomy feels both necessary and legitimate. The loss of autonomy naturally and necessarily translates to a loss of bodily autonomy, which despite laws aimed at protecting rights in healthcare, has meant a lack of autonomy in medical decision-making and an erosion of informed consent.

Yet, in parallel, medicine is also a structure of control, one that can violently enact force over patients (Davis 2019). While distinct from the label of "criminal," being hailed as "patient" similarly creates subjects. Within highly medicalized systems, people are always, already patients (Joyce et al., 2020); yet patienthood is constructed based on intersecting oppressions and identities. Patienthood is materially different in the context of incarceration. While patienthood may be presumed to be potentially *protective* identity, our research has shown that, often, it is not able surpass the primary identity of "inmate"(James, 2023). Violence or loss of autonomy that may be experienced as a patient is magnified in this setting. Any forms of protection that being a patient may offer (e.g., a presumed need for care), may not be sufficient to ward off the structural realities of incarceration or the concerns of safety and security that rule day-to-day life. The patient journey is marked by disbelief and denial of care (Jeske et al., 2023), creating, for some, the feeling that healthcare is another form of punishment enacted by the state. We argue that due to this complex transformation of patienthood, true informed consent is not fully possible in carceral settings; the structural limitations are too great, diminishing autonomy even when clinicians have the best intentions. This presents a moral imperative to intervene.

Abolition, as a vision, a movement, an idea, is in closer grasp than it's ever been. The racial reckoning of 2020 led, for perhaps the first time, to a broader awareness of and interest in the tenets of prison industrial complex (PIC) abolition. The idea of defunding the police became a part of mainstream conversation, if not reflected in law and policy. In the last decade, the U.S. has begun to see a decrease in incarceration for the first time in 50 years. In California, after decades of tremendous advocacy, there has been a 70% drop in the number of people incarcerated in women's prisons, moving from 12,688 people incarcerated in women's prisons in 2010 to 3699 in 2022 (Mitchell and Piatt 2023). We see for the first time the possibility that the safety and community of California is not dependent on incarceration.

Bioethicists should play a leading role in the call to limit incarceration in our society. We must recognize that even the most fervent attempts to protect autonomy are grounded in changing how decisions are made, rather than changing the social context in which people make decisions. As described earlier, healthcare professionals may worry that even in cases where patients demonstrate full informed consent, respecting individual autonomy in the context of social or distributive injustices can perpetuate the conditions of injustice. There seems to be no good answer to how to respect a marginalized individual's (possibly diminished) autonomy. Over the last decade, as a response to concerns about diminished autonomy and the abuse of incarcerated people, California has taken steps to protect these patients, but often at the cost of their autonomy. For example, take California State Senate Bill 1135. This legislation, passed in 2014 after the forced sterilization came to light, prohibited sterilization for the purpose of birth control for anyone incarcerated in California. This law was seen as a necessary step to guard against abuse, however the result has been violation of autonomy in the name of protecting patients. While harm and reproductive injustice have not stopped in prisons, some women may be unable to access wanted or planned sterilizing procedures. We must ask why violations of individual autonomy are seen as the remedy for exploitative and abusive practices. Further, we must contend with the possibility that efforts to protect autonomy through policy, rather than with a fundamental transformation in the goal and reality of incarceration, may never be fully realized.

We argue that reforms are not sufficient to solve the problem of diminished bodily autonomy in carceral settings. There is no training on informed consent for providers, no plain language summary of a consent form, no hotline for patients to ask questions that can overcome the trau-magenic nature of prison, the structural violence embedded into carceral facilities, and the dehumanization that begins the moment someone is arrested. Prisons and jails put structural limitations on autonomy. Bioethics has a duty to name this as an afront to the bedrock principles of the field and to seek abolition as a way of enacting justice in our society.

Works Cited

Aday, Ronald, and Lori Farney. 2014. "Malign Neglect: Assessing Older Women's Health Care Experiences in Prison." *Journal of Bioethical Inquiry* 11 (3): 359–72. https://doi.org/10.1007/s11673-014-9561-0.

Aday, Ronald H and Krabill, Jennifer J. 2012. "Aging Offenders in the Criminal Justice System." *Marquette Elder's Adisor* 7 (2). https://scholarship.law.marquette.edu/elders/vol7/iss2/4/.

Auty, Katherine M, Alison Liebling, Anna Schliehe, and Ben Crewe. 2022. "What Is Trauma-Informed Practice? Towards Operationalisation of the Concept in Two Prisons for Women." *Criminology & Criminal Justice*, May, 17488958221094980. https://doi.org/10.1177/17488958221094980.

Avila, Vrindavani, and Jennifer Elyse James. 2024. "Controlling Reproduction and

Disrupting Family Formation: California Women's Prisons and the Violent Legacy of Eugenics." *Societies* 14 (5): 73. https://doi.org/10.3390/soc14050073.

Bai, Jennifer R., Montina Befus, Dhritiman V. Mukherjee, Franklin D. Lowy, and Elaine L. Larson. 2015. "Prevalence and Predictors of Chronic Health Conditions of Inmates Newly Admitted to Maximum Security Prisons." *Journal of Correctional Health Care : The Official Journal of the National Commission on Correctional Health Care* 21 (3): 255–64. https://doi.org/10.1177/1078345815587510.

Batbold, Sarah, Jennifer D. Duke, Kirsten A. Riggan, and Erin S. DeMartino. 2023. "Decision-Making for Hospitalized Incarcerated Patients Lacking Decisional Capacity." *JAMA Internal Medicine*, December. https://doi.org/10.1001/jamainternmed.2023.5794.

Beyer, Todd D., and Megan K. Applewhite. 2022. "Surgery on the Incarcerated Patient." In *Difficult Decisions in Surgical Ethics: An Evidence-Based Approach*, edited by Vassyl A. Lonchyna, Peggy Kelley, and Peter Angelos, 305–15. Difficult Decisions in Surgery: An Evidence-Based Approach. Cham: Springer International Publishing. https://doi.org/10.1007/978-3-030-84625-1_21.

Binswanger, I. A., P. M. Krueger, and J. F. Steiner. 2009. "Prevalence of Chronic Medical Conditions among Jail and Prison Inmates in the USA Compared with the General Population." *Journal of Epidemiology & Community Health* 63 (11): 912–19. https://doi.org/10.1136/jech.2009.090662.

Bradley, Catherine Megan. 2006. "Old Remedies Are New Again: Deliberate Indifference and the Receivership in Plata v. Schwarzenegger." *New York University Annual Survey of American Law* 62:703.

Braithwaite, Ronald L., Henrie M. Treadwell, and Kimberly R. J. Arriola. 2008. "Health Disparities and Incarcerated Women: A Population Ignored." *American Journal of Public Health* 98 (Suppl 1): S173–75.

Brinkley-Rubinstein, Lauren. 2013. "Incarceration as a Catalyst for Worsening Health." *Health & Justice* 1 (1): 3. https://doi.org/10.1186/2194-7899-1-3.

Brooks, Katherine C., Anil N. Makam, and Lawrence A. Haber. 2022. "Caring for Hospitalized Incarcerated Patients: Physician and Nurse Experience."

Journal of General Internal Medicine 37 (2): 485–87. https://doi.org/10.1007/ s11606-020-06510-w.

California Department of Corrections and Rehabilitation. 2019. "Offender Data Points Report." https://www.cdcr.ca.gov/research/offender-outcomes- -characteristics/offender-data-points/.

California State Auditor. 2014. "Sterilization of Female Inmates: Some Inmates Were Sterilized Unlawfully, and Safeguards Designed to Limit Occurren- ces of the Procedure Failed." 2013–120. https://auditor.ca.gov/reports/ summary/2013-120.

Courtney, Deborah, and Tina Maschi. 2013. "Trauma and Stress Among Older Adults in Prison: Breaking the Cycle of Silence." *Traumatology* 19 (1): 73– 81. https://doi.org/10.1177/1534765612437378.

Courtwright, Andrew, Theresa Raphael-Grimm, and Frances Collichio. 2008. "Shackled: The Challenge of Caring for an Incarcerated Patient." *American Journal of Hospice and Palliative Medicine®* 25 (4): 315–17. https://doi. org/10.1177/1049909108315912.

Davis, Angela Y., Gina Dent, Erica R. Meiners, and Beth E. Richie. 2022. *Abolition. Feminism. Now.* Haymarket Books.

Davis, Dána-Ain. 2019. "Obstetric Racism: The Racial Politics of Pregnancy, La- bor, and Birthing." *Medical Anthropology* 38 (7): 560–73. https://doi.org/10. 1080/01459740.2018.1549389.

Dehlendorf, C., Perry, J. C., Borrero, S., Callegari, L., Fuentes, L., & Perritt, J. (2024). Meeting people's pregnancy prevention needs: Let's not force people to state an "Intention." *Contraception, 135*, 110400. https://doi.or- g/10.1016/j.contraception.2024.110400

DiTomas, Michele, Joseph Bick, and Brie Williams. 2019. "Shackled at the End of Life: We Can Do Better." *The American Journal of Bioethics: AJOB* 19 (7): 61–63. https://doi.org/10.1080/15265161.2019.1618957.

Douglas, Anthony D., Mohammad Y. Zaidi, Thomas K. Maatman, Jennifer N. Choi, and Ashley D. Meagher. 2021. "Caring for Incarcerated Patients: Can It Ever Be Equal?" *Journal of Surgical Education* 78 (6): e154–60. ht- tps://doi.org/10.1016/j.jsurg.2021.06.009.

Elster, Aminah. 2021. "Reparations for CA Forced Sterilization Survivors: Support

AB 1007." *The Daily Californian*, April 2, 2021, sec. Op-Eds. https://www. dailycal.org/2021/04/02/reparations-for-ca-forced-sterilization-survivors--support-ab-1007/.

Enders, Sheila R., Debora A. Paterniti, and Frederick J. Meyers. 2005. "An Approach to Develop Effective Health Care Decision Making for Women in Prison." *Journal of Palliative Medicine* 8 (2): 432–39. https://doi.org/10.1089/jpm.2005.8.432.

Fearn, Noelle E., and Kelly Parker. 2005. "Health Care for Women Inmates:" *Californian Journal of Health Promotion* 3 (2): 1–22. https://doi.org/10.32398/cjhp.v3i2.1760.

Fedock, G., Cummings, C., Kubiak, S., Bybee, D., Campbell, R., & Darcy, K. (2019). Incarcerated Women's Experiences of Staff-Perpetrated Rape: Racial Disparities and Justice Gaps in Institutional Responses. *Journal of Interpersonal Violence*, 0886260519850531. https://doi.org/10.1177/0886260519850531

Fedock, G., Kubiak, S., Campbell, R., Darcy, K., & Cummings, C. (2016). Prison Rape Reform: Perspectives from Women with Life Sentences on the Impact of a Class Action Lawsuit. *Journal of Human Rights and Social Work*, *1*(3), 131–142. https://doi.org/10.1007/s41134-016-0017-9

Garcia-Grossman, Ilana R., Irena Cenzer, Michael A. Steinman, and Brie A. Williams. 2023. "History of Incarceration and Its Association With Geriatric and Chronic Health Outcomes in Older Adulthood." *JAMA Network Open* 6 (1): e2249785. https://doi.org/10.1001/jamanetworkopen.2022.49785.

Gilmore, Ruth Wilson. 2022. *Abolition Geography: Essays Towards Liberation*. Edited by Brenna Bhandar and Alberto Toscano. London New York: Verso.

Goldstein, Melissa M. 2014. "Health Information Privacy and Health Information Technology in the US Correctional Setting." *American Journal of Public Health* 104 (5): 803–9. https://doi.org/10.2105/AJPH.2013.301845.

Goshin, Lorie S., D. R. Gina Sissoko, Grace Neumann, Carolyn Sufrin, and Lorraine Byrnes. 2019. "Perinatal Nurses' Experiences With and Knowledge of the Care of Incarcerated Women During Pregnancy and the Postpartum Period." *Journal of Obstetric, Gynecologic & Neonatal Nursing* 48 (1): 27–36.

https://doi.org/10.1016/j.jogn.2018.11.002.

Grundy, Sara J., Meghan Peterson, and Lauren Brinkley-Rubinstein. 2022. "Comprehensive Reform Urgently Needed in Hospital Shackling Policy for Incarcerated Patients in the United States." *Journal of Correctional Health Care*, December. https://doi.org/10.1089/jchc.21.07.0070.

Haber, Lawrence A., Hans P. Erickson, Sumant R. Ranji, Gabriel M. Ortiz, and Lisa A. Pratt. 2019. "Acute Care for Patients Who Are Incarcerated: A Review." *JAMA Internal Medicine* 179 (11): 1561–67. https://doi.org/10.1001/jamainternmed.2019.3881.

Haber, Lawrence A., Lisa A. Pratt, Hans P. Erickson, and Brie A. Williams. 2022. "Shackling in the Hospital." *Journal of General Internal Medicine* 37 (5): 1258–60. https://doi.org/10.1007/s11606-021-07222-5.

Harada, Megan Y., Armando Lara-Millán, and Lauren E. Chalwell. 2021. "Policed Patients: How the Presence of Law Enforcement in the Emergency Department Impacts Medical Care." *Annals of Emergency Medicine* 78 (6): 738–48. https://doi.org/10.1016/j.annemergmed.2021.04.039.

Harner, Holly, and Ann W. Burgess. 2011. "Using a Trauma-Informed Framework to Care for Incarcerated Women." *Journal of Obstetric, Gynecologic & Neonatal Nursing* 40 (4): 469–76. https://doi.org/10.1111/j.1552-6909.2011.01259.x.

Hayes, C. M., Sufrin, C., & Perritt, J. B. (2020). Reproductive Justice Disrupted: Mass Incarceration as a Driver of Reproductive Oppression. *American Journal of Public Health*, *110*(S1), S21–S24. https://doi.org/10.2105/AJPH.2019.305407

Henderson, Garnet. 2023. "Few Survivors Have Been Paid as California Sterilization Reparation Program Winds Down." Rewire News Group. November 6, 2023. https://rewirenewsgroup.com/2023/11/06/few-survivors-have-been-paid-as-california-sterilization-reparation-program-winds-down/.

Hernandez, Joe. 2022. "More States Are Restricting the Shackling of Pregnant Inmates, but It Still Occurs." *NPR*, April 22, 2022, sec. National. https://www.npr.org/2022/04/22/1093836514/shackle-pregnant-inmates-tennessee.

Hogg, Robert S., Eric F. Druyts, Scott Burris, Ernest Drucker, and Steffanie A. Strathdee. 2008. "Years of Life Lost to Prison: Racial and Gender Gradients in the United States of America." *Harm Reduction Journal* 5 (January):4. https://doi.org/10.1186/1477-7517-5-4.

Jackson, Hannah Beth. 2014. *Inmates: Sterilization. Title 2 of Part 3 of the Penal Code.* https://leginfo.legislature.ca.gov/faces/billNavClient.xhtml?bill_id=201320140SB1135.

James, Jennifer E. 2021. "A Second Chance at Health." *IJFAB: International Journal of Feminist Approaches to Bioethics* 14 (2).

———. 2022. "Is It Ethical to Mandate Vaccination among Incarcerated Persons? Consider Enforcement and Ask People Living in Prisons and Jails." *The American Journal of Bioethics* 0 (0): 1–2. https://doi.org/10.1080/15265161. 2022.2089290.

———. 2023. "'We're Not Patients. We're Inmates': Older Black Women's Experience of Aging, Health, and Illness During and After Incarceration." *The Gerontologist*, August, gnad114. https://doi.org/10.1093/geront/gnad114.

James, Jennifer E., Leslie Riddle, and Giselle Perez-Aguilar. 2023. "'Prison Life Is Very Hard and It's Made Harder If You're Isolated': COVID-19 Risk Mitigation Strategies and the Mental Health of Incarcerated Women in California." *International Journal of Prisoner Health* 19 (1): 95–108. https://doi.org/10.1108/IJPH-09-2021-0093.

James, Jennifer Elyse. 2023. "The Problem Is Not (Merely) Mass Incarceration: Incarceration as a Bioethical Crisis and Abolition as a Moral Obligation." *Hastings Center Report* 53 (6): 35–37. https://doi.org/10.1002/hast.1542.

Jeske, Melanie, Jennifer James, and Kelly Joyce. 2023. "Diagnosis and the Practices of Patienthood: How Diagnostic Journeys Shape Illness Experiences." *Sociology of Health & Illness* n/a (n/a). https://doi.org/10.1111/1467-9566.13614.

Jewkes, Yvonne, Melanie Jordan, Serena Wright, and Gillian Bendelow. 2019. "Designing 'Healthy' Prisons for Women: Incorporating Trauma-Informed Care and Practice (TICP) into Prison Planning and Design." *International Journal of Environmental Research and Public Health* 16 (20): 3818. https://doi.org/10.3390/ijerph16203818.

Johnson, Corey. 2013. "Female Inmates Sterilized in California Prisons without

Approval." *Reveal*, 2013. https://www.revealnews.org/article/female-
-inmates-sterilized-in-california-prisons-without-approval/.

Joyce, K. A., James, J. E., & Jeske, M. (2020). Regimes of Patienthood: Developing an Intersectional Concept to Theorize Illness Experiences. *Engaging
Science, Technology, and Society*, 6(0), Article 0. https://doi.org/10.17351/
ests2020.389

Junewicz, Alexandra. 2014. "Shackled: Providing Health Care to Prisoners Outside
of Prison." *The American Journal of Bioethics* 14 (7): 13–14. https://doi.org/1
0.1080/15265161.2014.918210.

Kaiksow, Farah Acher, Deval Patel, and Norman Fost. 2023. "Q: What Are My
Obligations to My Incarcerated Patient?" *Cleveland Clinic Journal of Medicine*
90 (1): 18–21. https://doi.org/10.3949/ccjm.90a.22003.

Kaiksow, Farah Acher, Brie A. Williams, and Lawrence A. Haber. 2023. "Hospitalized While Incarcerated: Incarceration-Specific Care Practices." *Annals of
Internal Medicine* 176 (11): 1540–41. https://doi.org/10.7326/M23-1873.

Kramer, Camille, Karenna Thomas, Ankita Patil, Crystal M. Hayes, and Carolyn
B. Sufrin. 2023. "Shackling and Pregnancy Care Policies in US Prisons
and Jails." *Maternal and Child Health Journal* 27 (1): 186–96. https://doi.
org/10.1007/s10995-022-03526-y.

Law, Victoria. 2015. "Reproductive Health Care in Women's Prisons 'Painful' and
'Traumatic.'" Truthout. March 27, 2015. https://truthout.org/articles/
reproductive-health-care-in-women-s-prisons-painful-and-traumatic/.

Lehrer, Dana. 2021. "Trauma-Informed Care: The Importance of Understanding
the Incarcerated Women." *Journal of Correctional Health Care* 27 (2): 121–26.
https://doi.org/10.1089/jchc.20.07.0060.

LeMasters, Katherine, Lauren Brinkley-Rubinstein, Morgan Maner, Meghan Peterson, Kathryn Nowotny, and Zinzi Bailey. 2022. "Carceral Epidemiology:
Mass Incarceration and Structural Racism during the COVID-19 Pandemic." *The Lancet Public Health* 7 (3): e287–90. https://doi.org/10.1016/
S2468-2667(22)00005-6.

Levenson, Jill S., and Gwenda M. Willis. 2019. "Implementing Trauma-Informed
Care in Correctional Treatment and Supervision." *Journal of Aggression,
Maltreatment & Trauma* 28 (4): 481–501. https://doi.org/10.1080/1092677

1.2018.1531959.

Madrigal, Alexis. 2023. "California's Reparations Program for Survivors of Forced Sterilization Falls Short As Deadline Nears | KQED." November 1, 2023. https://www.kqed.org/forum/2010101894895/californias-reparations--program-for-survivors-of-forced-sterilization-falls-short-as-deadline-nears.

Maruschak, Laura, Jennifer Bronson, and Mariel Alper. 2021. "Medical Problems Reported by Prisoners: Survey of Prison Inmates, 2016 | Bureau of Justice Statistics." https://bjs.ojp.gov/library/publications/medical-problems-reported-prisoners-survey-prison-inmates-2016.

Massoglia, Michael. 2008. "Incarceration, Health, and Racial Disparities in Health." *Law & Society Review* 42 (2): 275–306. https://doi.org/10.1111/j.1540-5893.2008.00342.x.

McCauley, Heather L., Fallon Richie, Sara Hughes, Jennifer E. Johnson, Caron Zlotnick, Rochelle K. Rosen, Wendee M. Wechsberg, and Caroline C. Kuo. 2020. "Trauma, Power, and Intimate Relationships Among Women in Prison." *Violence Against Women* 26 (6–7): 659–74. https://doi.org/10.1177/1077801219842948.

McCormick, Erin. 2021. "Survivors of California's Forced Sterilizations: 'It's like My Life Wasn't Worth Anything.'" *The Guardian*, July 19, 2021, sec. US news. https://www.theguardian.com/us-news/2021/jul/19/california-forced-sterilization-prison-survivors-reparations.

Mendelson, Aaron, and Elly Yu. 2022. "Medical Parole Got Them Out Of State Prison. Now They're In A Decertified Nursing Home." LAist. May 3, 2022. https://laist.com/news/criminal-justice/medical-parole-state-prison-decertified-nursing-home.

Mitchell, Christine, and Akemi Amber Piatt. 2023. "From Crisis to Care: Ending the Health Harm of Women's Prisons." Oakland, CA: Human Impact Partners.

Moin, Emily E., and Dominic A. Sisti. 2019. "Jailers at the Bedside: Ethical Conflicts in Provision of Community Hospital Care for Incarcerated Individuals." *Journal of Correctional Health Care* 25 (4): 405–8. https://doi.org/10.1177/1078345819883012.

Neills, Ashley. 2021. "The Color of Justice: Racial and Ethnic Disparity in State

Prisons." The Sentencing Project. October 13, 2021. https://www.sentencingproject.org/reports/the-color-of-justice-racial-and-ethnic-disparity-in--state-prisons-the-sentencing-project/.

Nijhawan, Ank E., Rachel Salloway, Amy S. Nunn, Michael Poshkus, and Jennifer G. Clarke. 2010. "Preventive Healthcare for Underserved Women: Results of a Prison Survey." *Journal of Women's Health (2002)* 19 (1): 17–22. https://doi.org/10.1089/jwh.2009.1469.

Oser, Carrie B., Amanda M. Bunting, Erin Pullen, and Danelle Stevens-Watkins. 2016. "African American Female Offender's Use of Alternative and Traditional Health Services After Re-Entry: Examining the Behavioral Model for Vulnerable Populations." *Journal of Health Care for the Poor and Underserved* 27 (2A): 120–48. https://doi.org/10.1353/hpu.2016.0052.

Patterson, Evelyn J. 2013. "The Dose–Response of Time Served in Prison on Mortality: New York State, 1989–2003." *American Journal of Public Health* 103 (3): 523–28. https://doi.org/10.2105/AJPH.2012.301148.

Perry, David M. 2017. "Our Long, Troubling History of Sterilizing the Incarcerated." *The Marshall Project*, July 26, 2017. https://www.themarshallproject.org/2017/07/26/our-long-troubling-history-of-sterilizing-the-incarcerated.

Peteet, Tom, and Matt Tobey. 2017. "How Should a Health Care Professional Respond to an Incarcerated Patient's Request for a Particular Treatment?" *AMA Journal of Ethics* 19 (9): 894–902. https://doi.org/10.1001/journalofethics.2017.19.9.ecas3-1709.

Pettit, Becky, and Bruce Western. 2004. "Mass Imprisonment and the Life Course: Race and Class Inequality in U.S. Incarceration." *American Sociological Review* 69 (2): 151–69. https://doi.org/10.1177/000312240406900201.

Pierce, Ava. 2016. "Vulnerable Populations: The Homeless and Incarcerated." In *Diversity and Inclusion in Quality Patient Care*, edited by Marcus L. Martin, Sheryl L. Heron, Lisa Moreno-Walton, and Anna Walker Jones, 151–60. Cham: Springer International Publishing. https://doi.org/10.1007/978-3-319-22840-2_14.

Rayasam, Renuka. 2024. "Pregnancy Care Was Always Lacking in Jails. It Could Get Worse." *KFF Health News* (blog). February 23, 2024. https://kffhealthnews.org/news/article/pregnancy-care-jails-prisons-incarcerated-wo-men/.

Riddle, Leslie, Jennifer James, and Aminah Elster. 2022. "'You Were Pushed like Cattle through the Doors and Took Whatever You Got': Incarcerated Women's Health Care under the Shadow of California Eugenics Laws." In . APHA. https://apha.confex.com/apha/2022/meetingapp.cgi/Paper/514690.

Rold, William J. 2008. "Thirty Years After Estelle v. Gamble: A Legal Retrospective." *Journal of Correctional Health Care* 14 (1): 11–20. https://doi.org/10.1177/1078345807309616.

San Francisco Sheriff's Department. 2024. "Current Jail Data and Trends." https://www.sfsheriff.com/services/jail-services/current-and-historical-jail--data/current-jail-data-and-trends.

Sankaran, Sujatha. 2023. "Incarcerated Patients in the Hospital." In *Health Equity in Hospital Medicine : Foundations, Populations, and Action*, edited by Sujatha Sankaran, 83–86. Cham: Springer International Publishing. https://doi.org/10.1007/978-3-031-44999-4_15.

Scarlet, Sara, Erin S. DeMartino, and Mark Siegler. 2019. "Surrogate Decision Making for Incarcerated Patients." *JAMA Internal Medicine* 179 (7): 861–62. https://doi.org/10.1001/jamainternmed.2019.1386.

Scarlet, Sara, and Elizabeth Dreesen. 2017. "Surgery in Shackles: What Are Surgeons' Obligations to Incarcerated Patients in the Operating Room?" *AMA Journal of Ethics* 19 (9): 939–46. https://doi.org/10.1001/journalofethics.2017.19.9.pfor1-1709.

Scarlet, Sara, and Elizabeth B. Dreesen. 2019. "Delivering Hospital-Based Medical Care to Incarcerated Patients in North Carolina State Prisons: A Call for Communication and Collaboration." *North Carolina Medical Journal* 80 (6): 348–51. https://doi.org/10.18043/ncm.80.6.348.

———. 2021. "Surgical Care of Incarcerated Patients: Doing the Right Thing, Explicit Bias, and Ethics." *Surgery* 170 (3): 983–85. https://doi.org/10.1016/j.surg.2021.01.054.

Smith, Francis Duval. 2016. "Perioperative Care of Prisoners: Providing Safe Care." *AORN Journal* 103 (3): 282–88. https://doi.org/10.1016/j.

aorn.2016.01.004.

Stern, Alexandra Minna, and Alexandra Minna Stern. 2016. "Eugenics, Sterilization, and Historical Memory in the United States." *História, Ciências, Saú-
de-Manguinhos* 23 (December):195–212. https://doi.org/10.1590/s0104-
59702016000500011.

Sufrin, C. B., Devon-Williamston, A., Beal, L., Hayes, C. M., & Kramer, C. (2023).
"I mean, I didn't really have a choice of anything:" How incarceration
influences abortion decision-making and precludes access in the United
States. *Perspectives on Sexual and Reproductive Health*, *55*(3), 165–177. https://
doi.org/10.1363/psrh.12235

Sufrin, C., Kolbi-Molinas, A., & Roth, R. (2015). Reproductive Justice, Health Disparities And Incarcerated Women in the United States. *Perspectives on Sexual
and Reproductive Health*, *47*(4), 213–219. https://doi.org/10.1363/47e3115

Suh, Michelle Ihn, and Marc David Robinson. 2022. "Vulnerable yet Unprotected:
The Hidden Curriculum of the Care of the Incarcerated Patient." *Journal
of Graduate Medical Education* 14 (6): 655–58. https://doi.org/10.4300/JG-
ME-D-22-00228.1.

Tobey, Matthew, and Lisa Simon. 2019. "Who Should Make Decisions for Unre-
presented Patients Who Are Incarcerated?" *AMA Journal of Ethics* 21 (7):
617–24. https://doi.org/10.1001/amajethics.2019.617.

Treisman, Rachel. 2020. "Whistleblower Alleges 'Medical Neglect,' Questionable
Hysterectomies Of ICE Detainees." *NPR.Org*, September 16, 2020. https://www.npr.org/2020/09/16/913398383/whistleblower-alleges-medi-
cal-neglect-questionable-hysterectomies-of-ice-detaine.

Tuite, Helen, Katherine Browne, and Desmond O'Neill. 2006. "Prisoners in General Hospitals: Doctors' Attitudes and Practice." *BMJ* 332 (7540): 548–49.
https://doi.org/10.1136/bmj.332.7540.548-b.

Turnbull, Alison E., Diana C. Bouhassira, and Brendan Saloner. 2023. "Incapacitated and Incarcerated—Double Barriers to Care." *JAMA Internal Medicine*,
December. https://doi.org/10.1001/jamainternmed.2023.6067.

US Census Bureau. 2024. "U.S. Census Bureau QuickFacts: California." https://
www.census.gov/quickfacts/CA.

Valles, Sean A. 2023. "Fifty Years of U.S. Mass Incarceration and What It

Means for Bioethics." *Hastings Center Report* 53 (6): 25–35. https://doi.org/10.1002/hast.1541.

Wahidin, Azrini. 2006. "Time and the Prison Experience." *Sociological Research Online* 11 (1): 104–13. https://doi.org/10.5153/sro.1245.

Wang, Emily A., Nicole Redmond, Cheryl R. Dennison Himmelfarb, Becky Pettit, Marc Stern, Jue Chen, Susan Shero, Erin Iturriaga, Paul Sorlie, and Ana V. Diez Roux. 2017. "Cardiovascular Disease in Incarcerated Populations." *Journal of the American College of Cardiology* 69 (24): 2967–76. https://doi.org/10.1016/j.jacc.2017.04.040.

Wang, Emily A., Yongfei Wang, and Harlan M. Krumholz. 2013. "A High Risk of Hospitalization Following Release From Correctional Facilities in Medicare Beneficiaries." *JAMA Internal Medicine* 173 (17): 1621–28. https://doi.org/10.1001/jamainternmed.2013.9008.

Wildeman, Christopher, and Emily A Wang. 2017. "Mass Incarceration, Public Health, and Widening Inequality in the USA." *The Lancet* 389 (10077): 1464–74. https://doi.org/10.1016/S0140-6736(17)30259-3.

Wolff, N., Blitz, C. L., Shi, J., Bachman, R., & Siegel, J. A. (2006). Sexual Violence Inside Prisons: Rates of Victimization. *Journal of Urban Health*, *83*(5), 835–848. https://doi.org/10.1007/s11524-006-9065-2

Zust, Barbara Lois, Lydia Busiahn, and Kelly Janisch. 2013. "Nurses' Experiences Caring for Incarcerated Patients in a Perinatal Unit." *Issues in Mental Health Nursing* 34 (1): 25–29. https://doi.org/10.3109/01612840.2012.715234.

2

An Autopsy of Conceptualizing Health in Solitary Confinement: Diagnosing Knowledge Production in Solitary Confinement

Keramet Reiter, Dallas Augustine, Justin D. Strong, Melissa Barragan, Gabriela Gonzalez, & Natalie Pifer*

Abstract

In this chapter, we explore how health (and, more often, harm) have been conceptualized and measured for people in solitary confinement, analyze the tools (and their limitations) that have been deployed to measure health and harm, and ultimately argue that many measurements, and associated reform efforts, confuse harm mitigation for health. Importantly, two of the foundational studies attempting to document and measure harm in solitary confinement took place in the context of litigation, and many subsequent studies have been cited in litigation both in defense of and in opposition to solitary confinement practices. In other words, how harm in solitary confinement is conceptualized can determine whether courts deem the practice legal or illegal, constitutional or unconstitutional. Our central point of analysis is nearly a decade of work conducted by our research team in Washington state prisons analyzing both changing patterns in the state's use of solitary confinement and the lived experience of these conditions for both incarcerated people and staff.

* Author Affiliations: Keramet Reiter is a Professor in the Department of Criminology, Law & Society and at the School of Law at the University of California, Irvine; Dallas Augustine, Justin D. Strong, and Gabriela Gonzalez are Assistant Professors in the Department of Justice Studies at San Jose State University; Melissa Barragan is an Associate Professor in Sociology at Cal Poly Pomona; Natalie Pifer is an Associate Professor and Chair in the Department of Criminology and Criminal Justice at the University of Rhode Island.

In this chapter, we explore how health (and, more often, harm) have been conceptualized and measured for people in solitary confinement, analyze the tools (and their limitations) that have been deployed to measure health and harm, and ultimately argue that many measurements, and associated reform efforts, confuse harm mitigation for health. Importantly, two of the foundational studies attempting to document and measure harm in solitary confinement took place in the context of litigation (Grassian 1983; Haney 2003), and many subsequent studies have been cited in litigation both in defense of and in opposition to solitary confinement practices (e.g., O'Keefe et al. 2013 and Reiter et al. 2021 in *Harvard v. Dixon* (2019)). In other words, how harm in solitary confinement is conceptualized can determine whether courts deem the practice legal or illegal, constitutional or unconstitutional (*e.g.,* Lobel & Akil 2018; Reiter 2016).

Our central point of analysis is nearly a decade of work conducted by our research team in Washington state prisons analyzing both changing patterns in the state's use of solitary confinement and the lived experience of these conditions for both incarcerated people and staff. Our research team first started collecting data on experiences in solitary confinement in Washington state prisons in the spring of 2017, following more than two years of research planning and training to gain access and develop multi-method research protocols for data collection. We concluded our first phase of research in the state in 2020 and published a policy report on our initial work in 2021 (Reiter et al. 2021). In total, this project involved obtaining and analyzing 15 years of administrative data about solitary confinement use, administering 315 paper surveys to incarcerated people and staff, and conducting a total of 263 in-depth qualitative interviews with incarcerated people and staff. In 2022, we began a second phase of research evaluating the interventions of Amend, "a public health and human rights program that works in prisons to reduce their debilitating health effects on residents and staff," in Washington state prisons, with a particular focus on Amend's solitary confinement reform efforts ("About Amend at UCSF," ND). To date, we have administered 797 paper surveys to incarcerated people and staff and conducted 174 in-depth qualitative interviews with incarcerated people and staff; we expect to complete data collection on this second project in 2025. In sum, over eight years, we have conducted hundreds of interviews with people currently or formerly incarcerated in solitary confinement in Washington state, as well as with staff working in solitary confinement units, and thousands of surveys across these populations. We have also: conducted hundreds of hours of observations of daily life, structured activities, and procedural hearings in and around these units; reviewed hundreds of prisoner disciplinary and medical files; and analyzed administrative data about uses of solitary confinement in Washington state dating back to 2002. We draw on this work to provide concrete examples of how we have sought to conceptualize and measure both harm and health in solitary confinement, in conversation with a fast-evolving and exploding scholarship seeking to understand both the scale and impacts of solitary confinement use in the United States, and internationally.

The Colorado Study: Second Guessing the Harms of Solitary

Our team's studies of experiences working and living in solitary confinement in Washington state developed at least partially in response to a study of "administrative segregation" in Colorado state prisons published in 2013, just a few years before we began our work in Washington State (O'Keefe et al., 2013). The Colorado study, as it is commonly called, operationalized solitary confinement as segregation in cells for "23 hours per day," with "rigorous security procedures" and "restricted access to programs" (O'Keefe at 49) and asked whether people housed in these conditions would "show greater deterioration over time on psychological symptoms" than comparable non-segregated groups (O'Keefe at 49). To the surprise of researchers, corrections officials, and legal advocates (e.g., Haney 2018), the Colorado research team found no increase in psychological deterioration in segregated subjects relative to non-segregated subjects (O'Keefe at 49). In some ways, the very framing of this finding suggests how researchers are thinking not about the fundamental health and well-being of incarcerated subjects, but rather about the relative harms of different conditions of confinement, seeking to identify opportunities for mitigation, or what is often referred to as "harm reduction," rather than opportunities for supporting health and well-being.

More immediately, though, the main Colorado Study finding of "no increase in psychological deterioration" contradicted centuries of theorizing presuming solitary confinement to be harmful and decades of research documenting those harms. Charles Dickens dubbed American, Victorian-era solitary confinement "worse than any torture of the body" in the 1840s; the U.S. Supreme Court described the practice as, essentially, outdated and barbaric in 1890 (Reiter 2016: 4); and German psychiatrists documented hundreds of cases of psychoses associated with solitary confinement in the early twentieth century (Grassian 1983: 1451). Still, the practice persisted (Rubin & Reiter 2018). It faced renewed scrutiny with the birth of the supermax, designed for long-term and large-scale solitary confinement, in the late twentieth century; psychiatrist Stuart Grassian conducted clinical interviews with 14 people participating in a class action case to challenge their conditions of confinement in solitary confinement in 1983 and determined that their constellation of symptoms constituted a "major, clinically distinguishable psychiatric syndrome" (Grassian 1983: 1450). A decade later, psychologist Craig Haney made similar findings in clinical interviews with 100 people participating in another class action case to challenge their conditions of confinement in California's archetypal Pelican Bay Supermax; the idea of a "SHU syndrome," experienced by people in Security Housing Units and similar solitary confinement facilities, was born (Haney 2003; O'Keefe 2013). Medical and public health scholars, especially, have continued to produce a steady stream of evidence of both the psychological and physical harms of solitary confinement, from increased symptoms of anxiety, depression, paranoia, and post-traumatic stress disorder (Lovell 2008; Hagan et al. 2018; Reiter et al. 2020), to increased rates of self-harm, suicide, cardiovascular disease, skin irritation, and musculoskeletal pain (Kaba et al. 2014, Williams et al. 2019; Strong et al. 2020). These studies describe solitary confinement as fundamentally harmful – and unhealthy.

Nonetheless, second-guessing, or even denying outright the harms of solitary confinement was not and is not unprecedented. Grassian cites an "experimental" 1960s study by Walters that found "no mental or psychomotor deterioration" in 4 days in solitary confinement in 20 incarcerated men, as compared to 20 other incarcerated men not placed in solitary confinement (Grassian 1983; Walters et al. 1963). And O'Keefe et al. reference a series of studies by Gendreau and colleagues (see especially Gendreau & Bonta 1984, titled "Solitary confinement is not cruel and unusual punishment") that found "few negative impacts of segregation" (O'Keefe et al. 2013: 50). The debate only intensified after the publication of the O'Keefe study, with a series of meta-analyses, many heavily weighting the O'Keefe study, arguing that solitary confinement "may not produce any more of an iatrogenic effect than routine incarceration" (Morgan et al. 2016) and directly critiquing and questioning the credibility of the earlier clinical interview-based studies conducted by Grassian and Haney (Labrecque et al. 2020). Notably, the Colorado Study and subsequent meta-analyses building on it focus not on identifying specific markers of well-being or harm, but on relative harms between conditions and over time, again steering towards potential tools of harm mitigation, or exacerbation, rather than acknowledging individual experiences of health or harm. (This despite the strange use of the term "iatrogenic," which refers to harms arising incidentally from "medical examination or treatment" ("Oxford Languages" online), not harms arising for intentional state action.)

   Among scholars (from wide-ranging disciplines, from criminology to law to public health) grappling with the the Colorado Study's counterintuitive findings, much of the conversation revolved around the Study's methods (see, e.g., Haney 2018): were the comparison groups appropriate, were the conditions accurately described, was the BSI (Brief Symptom Inventory) survey properly administered, were participants followed over a long enough period of time? Haney raised a number of potential measurement problems, including the appropriateness of the Brief Symptom Inventory as a measurement tool and whether subjects were discouraged (either in individual interactions or by cultural norms) from accurately reporting the seriousness and severity of their mental health symptoms (Haney

2018: 395, 388, 390-94). But the majority of his and others' critiques of the Colorado Study have focused more on general methods rather than specific tools. In other words, the question of what tools – or combination of tools – from specific psychological and cognitive tests to specific interview questions – might be best deployed to measure harm has been less central to these debates. This question of tools, though, became central for our research team, when we had an opportunity to access data and design a research project to evaluate exactly this question of whether and what harm is associated with incarceration in solitary confinement.

The Colorado Study and its subsequent critiques influenced our work in Washington state prisons to understand the effects of solitary confinement in two central ways. First, the existence of the study galvanized many stakeholders to seek alternative evaluations of the harms of solitary confinement. So, while most prison research projects begin with researchers approaching prison systems to request access to data, or occasionally with prison systems hiring researchers to analyze data in order to defend or improve existing prison practices, our own research in Washington state had an unusual genesis. Washington State Department of Corrections officials and a private foundation invested in public health research and advocacy, encouraged by legal advocates challenging solitary confinement conditions, approached our project's principal investigator to express support for and encourage development of an independent evaluation of the uses and impacts of solitary confinement in Washington state prisons. In other words, correctional, policy, and legal stakeholders all sought an independent research evaluation (rather than one led by the prison system itself, as in the Colorado Study) that might re-conceptualize how to document the harms of solitary confinement, harms that each of these stakeholders had personally witnessed and sought to address. And we sought to design such a study. The second major influence of the Colorado Study was as a counterpoint: how could we identify tools and implement protocols that avoided the critiques the Colorado Study had faced? We turn to this question now, interrogating the available tools, with a particular focus on when and how tools prioritize facilitating harm mitigation in place of either establishing baseline standards for health and well-being or documenting the utter absence of such standards.

Measuring Health and Reducing Harm

When our team began developing a research protocol for understanding the impacts of solitary confinement on prisoners and staff in Washington state, we had two goals. First, we wanted to ensure that our data was robust and reliable. More specifically, we wanted to avoid at least some of the critiques that earlier research, conducted in the context of litigation (like the studies by Grassian and by Haney), or overseen by staff within departments of corrections (like the Colorado study), had faced. For instance, for our initial study, Washington state prison officials provided a list of all people housed in long-term solitary confinement across five Institutional Management Units (IMUs) in Washington state. We used this list to generate a random sample of more than 100 interview subjects (Reiter et al. 2020, Appendix A), seeking to avoid any claims of selection bias, like those faced by Grassian and Haney. As in the Colorado study, we planned to follow our interview subjects over one year. However, we focused primarily on comparing within individuals, looking at experiences over time, as compared to the Colorado study's primary focus comparing individuals in and out of solitary confinement. We also sought to gather a broader range of data than just standardized psychological assessments, as was the focus of the Colorado study.

Indeed, our second goal was to identify multiple tools and data sources for understanding people's experiences (and measuring their well-being) living and working in solitary confinement. Rather than choosing between clinical (or research) interviews, which Grassian and Haney used in their research, or psychological assessment tools, as the Colorado study researchers used, we opted for both. And we also reviewed medical and disciplinary records, analyzed administrative data about solitary confinement populations over time, and interviewed staff working in solitary confinement units. We have argued elsewhere that integrating multiple sources of data – especially quantitative measures from both administrative data and psychological assessment instruments with qualitative details from systematic coding of in-depth interviews – allowed us to not just measure health and well-being, but also to identify different constellations of health harms not measured in existing psychological and interview instruments, unique to solitary confinement (Reiter et al. 2020; Strong et al. 2021). Here we focus in on the strengths and limitations of each data source and tool we used, highlighting gaps in individual sources, and compliments across sources. We argue that individual tools, like a single psychological assessment, or even a structured interview, often generate a focus on specific harms, like discrete psychosis or incidents of suicidal ideation. Specific identifiable harms, in turn, are often presumed to be mitigable with associated targeted interventions, ultimately rendering solitary confinement legal or constitutional. By contrast, integrating a range of data sources and analytic tools generates a more comprehensive framework for understanding both well-being (or lack thereof) in solitary confinement, and the interrelationship of harms within the complex ecosystem of deprivations in solitary confinement.

In the following subsections we address four specific categories of data that have been used in studying the harms of solitary confinement: standardized psychological assessments, prison medical records, interviews with incarcerated people, and surveys and interviews with correctional staff. For each, we discuss the range of available tools for collecting and analyzing this data, the strengths and shortcomings of these tools, and the potential benefits of integrating data collected with carefully selected tools across these categories for better understanding experiences of solitary confinement.

Standardized Psychological Assessment Tools
    Drawing on traditional public health and medical research tools, one way researchers have sought to evaluate harm associated with solitary confinement is through the use of standardized psychological assessment tools, such as the Brief Psychiatric Rating Scale (BPRS), which was used in Washington State in the early 2000s (Cloyes et al., 2006) and used alongside the Brief Symptom Inventory (BSI) in the Colorado Study. Unlike the BSI,

which is a self-report measure that requires "less professional time" (Morlan & Tan 1998), the BPRS provides detailed information about up to 24 symptoms of psychopathy observed or self-reported during a set timeframe (i.e., the past two weeks). Typically, trained interviewers, whose ratings have been assessed for interrater reliability with other trained interviewers, administer the BPRS over the course of a streamlined interview (Overall & Gorham, 1962; Rhoades & Overall, 1988). The scale may be used either to create a point-in-time snapshot of an individual's psychological state or to track change in mental status over time.

Researchers have primarily used the scale in clinical settings such as hospitals and care facilities (Morlan & Tan 1998), though there is a growing body of research using the BPRS (either alone or alongside other assessment tools) in carceral settings. Carceral research utilizing the BPRS spans custody levels, including jail or pre-trial custody (Corrado et al. 2000; Hassan et al. 2011); medium-level or "general population" prison settings (Blaauw, et al. 2007; Senior et al. 2007; Senior et al. 2013; Walters 1987); and, more specifically, prison mental health units or programs (Lovell and Jemelka 1998; Lovell et al. 2001a; Lovell et al. 2001b). In comparison, relatively few studies have applied the BPRS in supermaximum security housing or restrictive housing settings (but see O'Keefe et al. 2013; Reiter et al. 2020).

Given the BPRS's status as "one of the very best rating scales" (Morlan & Tan 1998; Zanello et al. 2013), and the existence of a rigorous training protocol in administering the scale available to our team (Reiter et al. 2020, Appendix A), we opted to integrate this scale into our research protocol in our Washington study. One of the original creators of the scale (Ventura) trained our team in scale administration, and we embedded questions from the BPRS throughout our 96-question semi-structured qualitative interview instrument. In order to ensure maximally robust psychological assessment data in our sample, we supplemented our BPRS data with data from the Scale for the Assessment of Negative Symptoms (SANS) (Andreasen, 1989), a tool used for documenting symptoms of psychopathy through the relative absence of normal functions, such as affective flattening and anhedonia. In the second year of data collection, we also added several questions aimed at assessing the presence or absence of symptoms of Post-Traumatic Stress Disorder.

After we completed data collection and turned toward analysis, our team met to review both the BPRS scores of participants and our experiences in administering the scale. In discussing our experiences administering the scale, each team member independently noted examples of either gaps or contradictions between symptoms of psychological distress identified through the BPRS assessment and symptoms of psychological distress identified elsewhere – in medical file reviews or more open-ended questions about experiences in solitary confinement. For instance, we noted that our participants either exhibited or described experiences of mental health distress, or other adverse experiences of harm resulting from their time in solitary confinement, that were not captured in the BPRS scores.

As we discussed these gaps and inconsistencies that arose in our interview and rating experiences, we identified three key limitations of the BPRS, limitations that only became visible in relation to other, complimentary research tools we had deployed to gather sources of data beyond BPRS ratings. First, because the BPRS assesses symptoms during a specific time frame, it may miss experiences that occurred prior to the assessed period. Indeed, in our study, we noted that participants often described mental health crises or other forms of psychological distress that, while recent, fell outside the two-week cutoff the BPRS focuses on for assessing symptoms. The exclusion of these experiences meant that BPRS scores seemed to artificially underrate participants' psychological symptoms.

Second, we noted that participants frequently described experiences that were not "ratable" items on the BPRS.. Put differently, the unique qualities of restrictive housing produce distinct forms of psychological distress that a tool developed for clinical use can miss. Some of the psychological symptoms we identified that are not captured on the BPRS include: sensory deprivation, loss of social skills, adapting to an environment with little room for movement, and certain forms of hypersensitivity (Reiter et al. 2020; Strong et al. 2021). People held in long-term solitary confinement may also develop coping mechanisms in response to prolonged exposure, and these coping mechanisms may either mask ratable symptoms or generate new symptoms not specified on the scale (like hypersensitivity to light or noise) (see also Haney 2018). The BPRS, then, seemed unable to document subject experiences that indirectly indicated significant psychological impacts or that suggested cumulative trauma over time, particularly for those who had repeated exposures to solitary confinement.

Third, while some items on the BPRS are derived from researcher observation, many require the participant to self-report symptoms or emotions. We noted that, in some situations, our participants seemed to either lack the language necessary to articulate their symptoms, or were reticent to discuss emotions due to cultural or institutional dynamics. Importantly, the Brief Psychiatric Rating Scale, while useful and reliable as a tool, was designed by psychologists working with patients in a community-based treatment clinic, as opposed to incarcerated people whose institutional living conditions are drastically different, which may affect the experience and expression of ratable symptoms. The ways in which incarcerated people relate to and even talk about anxiety, depression, guilt, hypervigilance, delusions, and hallucinations may not necessarily match with standardized instruments.

As such, we question the extent to which the BPRS can fully translate across research settings, providing equal accuracy in clinical spaces, general population prison settings, and solitary confinement. Despite its demonstrated validity and reliability in clinical settings, the BPRS may not accurately capture serious mental illness and negative psychiatric indicators for people in prisons generally, and supermaximum facilities and restricted housing specifically.

Medical Records Reviews

One way we supplemented BPRS assessments (and identified gaps and inconsistencies in these assessments) was through reviewing the medical records of our interview participants. While a number of studies of prisons, and of solitary confinement more specifically, have used correctional databases of electronic medical records to understand the harms of solitary confinement (*e.g.*, Kaba et al. 2014), very few studies have involved actually physically reviewing tens of thousands of pages of paper records (*but see* Lovell 2008). In our study in Washington state, however we sought to replicate Lovell and team's earlier work and reviewed the paper medical files of our interview participants, taking notes, as Lovell and team did on "psychosocial histories, psychological evaluations, progress notes, and prescription records" (Lovell 2008: 987).

As with the selection of the BPRS as a psychological assessment tool, our team developed a systematized process for medical records review, integrated with and complimentary to other tools we deployed to evaluate experiences in solitary confinement. Per our interview protocol, interviewers would conclude each interview by asking participants if they provided their consent for a study team member to review their department of corrections-maintained medical records. From our sample of 106 participants, we were able to review 101 medical files; five participants either did not consent to file reviews or had files that were unavailable in the physical records office at the time of our review. Our review of these files was consistent with our team's semi-structured and mixed-methods approach to data collection in that we systematically looked for and logged several key variables from each set of participants' records and recorded additional items of interest in a "Qualitative Notes" section.

Our "File Review Notes" template armed each study team member with a single double-sided piece of paper organized into four main sections: 1) a 6x4 table to log specific, notable encounters with Health Services by encounter date, diagnosis code, and diagnosis description; 2) a 4x9 table to track prescribed psychotropic medications, with columns to track a prescription's start, fill, stop, and discontinued dates; the drug's name, class, and status; the attendant diagnosis code; and any other notable features about the medication; 3) free space for logging any other qualitative notes from the medical files; and 4) 2x5 table to log any substance abuse history with columns to track the American Society of Addiction Medicine (ASAM) Assessment Level, a primary and secondary drug of choices, a binary variable to log the presence or absence of any treatment notes in the medical files, and column for other notes identified by a study team member as of interest.

Our medical record review protocol also reminded reviewers to specifically document any evidence of changing or conflicting diagnoses, mentions of manipulation of healthcare providers, references to brain damage, physical ailments, and prescriptions for skin lotion and creams. These specific recommendations reflected findings from the earlier works of Lovell (2008) and Rhodes (2004) in Washington State, which noted the uneven quality of mental health care and the high prevalence of brain damage among those in solitary confinement, as well as findings from studies raising questions about the adequacy of light exposure and Vitamin D intake for incarcerated people generally (Nwosu et al. 2014), and especially those in solitary confinement (Reiter 2016). In sum, our attention to reviewing the medical records of our interview participants, using the review template we developed, was one of many tools we deployed, drawing on earlier literature, to try to capture multiple sources of complimentary data about experiences – especially of harm and well-being – in solitary confinement.

Ultimately, this medical file review process provided important context in our work to understand experiences of solitary confinement – especially through access to a much longer-term medical social history for people confined in solitary confinement than scales like the BPRS provide. For instance, as predicted, we found many indications of prior brain injury in the medical files we reviewed, as well as many records of prior involvement with foster care systems, revealing patterns of harm not just in solitary confinement, but also prior to placement in solitary confinement. And we found evidence of people attempting to access medical, dental, and mental health treatment, to varying degrees of success.

But we also found the process of distilling this evidence both challenging and revealing in unexpected ways. While we sought to systematize our medical record review process with a template outlining the information to be gathered from each file, the actual process of reviewing medical files was chaotic, at times, especially given the huge variety in the sizes of participants' medical files. In some cases, we could review a short medical file of a few dozen pages and note every encounter, prescription, and substance abuse diagnosis in the file. But, in other cases, medical files were thousands of pages long, and we could only skim for major themes or conflicts. But the very process of reviewing the records proved to be revealing, generating new information and contexts, beyond the factors we had identified in our initial medical file review template, for understanding the harms of solitary confinement.

First, the sheer volume of the medical files we reviewed constituted one form of evidence of the harm of solitary confinement. Reading, logging and analyzing these records was its own form of bleakness for our team as we waded through the unedited multiple, tiny snippets of pain and suffering contained in each set of records. In other words, the records provided multiple opportunities to stumble inadvertently into new examples of the harms of solitary confinement – and few if any examples of health or well-being.

Second, and relatedly, the massive scale of at least some participants' medical records revealed how information follows people at every step of their institutional life, shaping both their conditions of confinement and access to certain services. For instance, one record we reviewed described a "patient" complaining to a mental health provider that his treatment plan stated "high risk need is for sexual deviancy [treatment]". According to the providers' notes, the patient had only one sex crime at age 13 for indecent exposure. A series of subsequent notes in the file indicated that providers found the date of the sexual deviancy treatment plan recommendation but no attempt or plan to revise the recommendation. One provider recommended to the patient that he write to Department of Corrections headquarters about the plan, but the file contained no mention of any revision to the plan. (We noted that even the code-switching involved in our work, from interview "participant" to supermax "prisoner" to medical "patient": reveals the multiple conflicting identities – and associated potential varieties in conceptualizing harm – inherent in the work of understanding experiences of solitary confinement.) While we were not specifically looking for disagreements over treatment plans like this one, we stumbled upon it in reviewing the file and noted it in our qualitative notes section. In another example of a negotiation between a patient and a provider that we recorded in our qualitative notes section, a patient filed a medical "kite" (a prison form for requesting medical care) requesting an MRI for chronic hip pain. The patient explicitly sought to mobilize his legal rights in the kite, noting: "I'm pretty sure I have medical rights." The medical file included documentation that the patient did receive an x-ray, along with a blank physical therapy treatment plan. Again, the blank treatment plan suggests how problems are raised by but frequently only partially addressed for this population. These two examples of patient-provider engagement from the medical file reviews provide important narrative context, complimenting psychological rating scales and qualitative interviews, of how individuals experience accessing care (or not) from solitary confinement. In sum, unlike medical records data from electronic databases, which might provide specific dates of encounters or details of prescriptions, the paper medical files we reviewed included much more narrative content.

Third, the process of reviewing the medical records often allowed our team access to new spaces within the prison that we would not have otherwise seen. In some cases, this was just a breakroom in an administrative building, where other staff would stop in to get water or coffee, and we could chat more informally. In such breakrooms, reviewing medical records provided an important respite for team members from the grind of conducting multiple emotionally fraught interviews in the oppressive environment of solitary confinement units (where even bathroom access required being escorted through a series of centrally-controlled sliding steel doors). In other cases, the medical files were reviewed in prison medical units next to medical visiting rooms, or padded cells. On one notably horrifying occasion, we were reviewing medical files in a room that shared a wall with a holding cell where a prisoner was repeatedly banging his head against the cell wall.

In sum, while we conceptualized the medical file review step of our data collection as a systematized and straightforward process, we found the reviews challenging in surprising ways. But these challenges, too, were revealing. The substantive content of the medical files, as well as their scale and the context in which we reviewed them, together provided both important background information about the people who experience solitary confinement and specific details about the medical experiences associated with being in solitary confinement.

Surveys & Interviews with Incarcerated People

While we have focused in our first two sections on two examples of relatively concrete and self-contained data collection tools – the Brief Psychological Rating Scale and a Medical Records review protocol –we turn now to the use of more open-ended questions in surveys and interviews. More specifically, across multiple phases of our research in Washington State, we have conducted both paper surveys (distributed in person, at the beginning of a research day and collected, in person, a few hours later) and face-to-face interviews with people in solitary confinement. We often use the paper surveys as a foundational reference point for understanding basic details about our respondents' lives and self-reported health measures, and then use the results from these surveys to inform and refine qualitative interview instruments. In this section, we will focus in particular on how we developed specific face-to-face interview protocol questions designed to understand the breadth of experiences in, and especially the harms of, solitary confinement. In developing our interview protocols, we drew not only on responses to paper surveys, but also on interview instruments used in earlier studies of experiences of incarceration and, especially, solitary confinement (*see especially* Calavita and Jenness 2014; Lovell 2008; Rhodes 2004; Rudes 2022).

We highlight here two specific interview questions, along with the benefits of longitudinal interviews, for eliciting a broader understanding of the range of possible experiences and harms in solitary confinement. First, after reviewing multiple interview instruments from other projects probing experiences of incarceration, and discussing a range of experiences interviewing vulnerable and marginalized populations among members of the research team, we settled on an initial interview question for the first phase of our study. This question proved to be not just a good icebreaker but also to be surprisingly generative for understanding the range of possible harms people experience in solitary confinement, especially those not necessarily captured through more structured protocols like the BPRS or medical record reviews. The simple question: "What is a day like for you here?" This open-ended query often generated details about: conditions of confinement—including especially about lack of access to daylight and hygiene items; feelings of hopelessness regarding length of stay; as well as details about how people passed the time in solitary confinement day-to-day. Respondents' answers to our questions might have been particularly robust given the eagerness to talk with an empathetic listener; people we interviewed in solitary confinement had often gone weeks, if not months or years, without visits from family or friends, or the opportunity to have something approximating a normal face-to-face conversation with another human. Nonetheless, our opening interview questions gave respondents, very early on, the freedom to interpret our questions flexibly, generating responses that often revealed what was most pressing or challenging for them in the moment.

Second, even when we asked more pointed questions about health and well-being (outside of specific BPRS questions) we sought to make such questions maximally open-ended. Instead of asking standard self-rating questions about stress or health, we asked: "How has your health been while you've been in solitary?" While this question did not produce standardized, generalizable answers, it did produce a broader range of responses encompassing not just basic health but details about healthcare access, as well as descriptions of physical symptoms respondents tied to their experiences in solitary confinement, about which they had not been previously aware. Respondents described, for example, multiple specific examples about the challenges of accessing medical care in or outside of the facility: delays in being seen by a healthcare provider (because the process of leaving the solitary confinement cell requires at least two correctional officer escorts and handcuffs), trouble obtaining medical diagnoses, and difficulty in accessing medication or other treatments for diagnoses (especially because of restrictions on types of prescriptions allowed for prisoners in solitary confinement). These real-time findings then opened the door for researchers to probe on the spot about costs of seeing a healthcare provider, accessibility, and fears about repercussions of seeing health providers (like being labeled as needing mental healthcare). Ultimately, these types of questions allowed us to both verify evidence of mental health harms arising in and exacerbated by solitary confinement (as documented in both BPRS scores and medical file reviews) and to understand some of the mechanisms of harm exacerbation, like challenges in accessing healthcare. And these questions generated new insights about specific, understudied and under-acknowledged physical, as well as mental health, harms respondents experienced in solitary confinement (Strong et al. 2021; *see also* Williams et al 2019 on the cardiovascular health burdens of solitary).

In addition to the value of simple, open-ended questions, complimenting more systematized, generalizable questions like those in the BPRS, we also found longitudinal, follow-up interviews to be especially generative for better understanding the scope of the harms of solitary confinement. In the first phase of our study, we conducted one-year follow-up interviews with all participants who were still incarcerated. Among the subset of prisoners who had left solitary confinement in the second year (n=52 in our first study), we asked: "Please describe the day you left the IMU/your first day in this unit." The open-ended structure of this question allowed interviewers to focus not just on harm, but also on well-being. Respondents recalled feelings of excitement, as well as anxiety and nervousness, during the transition period from solitary confinement. This then allowed us to probe about other effects of transitioning out of solitary confinement, expanded opportunities to receive more frequent visits, leading to improving relationships with family and loved ones, and more opportunities for human engagement, activities, and classes. In all, responses to these sets of probes revealed improved well-being of prisoners after their release from solitary confinement. In those cases where the same research team member interviewed a respondent in both year one and year two, qualitative observations of changes in a participant's' appearance and demeanor – like better skin complexion as a result of having more access to natural light – became possible. Again, although we did not systematically track every participant's appearance, careful observation over time became yet one more tool in our multi-method toolbox for understanding experiences of solitary confinement. Ultimately, our methodological triangulation both allowed us to corroborate findings of mental health and allowed us to obtain new insights into other forms of health and well-being.

Still, interviews, much like the BPRS and medical file records, can also be constrained in their ability to reveal, document, or measure harm. For instance, an effect of isolation is that it can diminish a person's ability to make sense of their experiences (e.g., Guenther 2013). As social beings, we often understand ourselves and the world around us through relationships, linguistic exchanges, and the perspectives of others. If a participant's capacity for meaning-making has been diminished, or if the suffering they have experienced is beyond a linguistic register for them, then in-depth interviews, however good the questions and strong the rapport, will fail to access such harm, yet be no less besieged by it. To put the point differently, our inability to capture certain experiences in solitary confinement may itself be an outcome of the harm of such conditions.

Incorporating Staff in Studies of Experiences of Solitary Confinement

At the time we designed our initial study in Washington state, the majority of studies of solitary confinement focused on experiences of incarcerated people, not staff (*e.g.,* Grassian 1986; Haney 2003; O'Keefe et al. 2013). Indeed, just a few months before we launched the first phase of our research in Washington State, in a 2016 white paper for the National Institute of Justice, Sundt noted that few studies examine the experiences of correctional officers working in solitary confinement units (2016). Sundt and others have called for increasing attention to correctional staff working in solitary confinement units – and provided preliminary evidence that staff well-being might relate to incarcerated peoples' (Cloud et al. 2021; Rudes 2022). Our work to incorporate the perspective of staff in solitary confinement units developed in conversation with this literature.

Understanding that total institutions like prisons can have damaging effects on a wide range of people who live within, walk through, and also work behind prison walls, we sought to capture how working in solitary confinement units can impact several domains of workers' well-being: physical health, mental health, safety, and relationships. We did this through both paper surveys of staff working in solitary confinement units (usually distributed in person at the beginning of shifts and collected later in the shift, or the next day) and face-to-face, in-depth qualitative interviews. We will discuss here two specific groups of questions – one group on our surveys and one on our interview instrument – that have proved especially useful for understanding not only correctional officer well-being, but how this well-being relates to incarcerated people's well-being.

First, on our initial paper surveys of staff working in solitary confinement units in Washington State, conducted in 2017, we asked general questions about whether staff felt safe at work, and standardized questions about self-rating health, but we also asked a set of questions about whether they had ever experienced any of 11 specific violent interactions with incarcerated people while working in a solitary confinement unit. These 11 interactions included having feces or urine thrown at them, being spit on, attacked with a weapon, hit or punched, raped or sexually assaulted, pushed or shoved, taken hostage, bitten, had an object thrown at them, been injured while managing a disruptive prisoner, or while intervening in a fight between two incarcerated people. While two-thirds of staff (n=90) responded "no" to the question "do you ever feel unsafe working in [solitary confinement]?", a full one-third of staff (including some who *had* said they felt generally safe) reported having experienced anywhere from one to eight of the eleven violent interactions we asked about. Among sworn security staff (excluding healthcare providers, educators, and other non-security staff), the experience of violent interactions was even more prevalent. Nearly half (48% of the 60 sworn security staff) reported having had feces or urine thrown at them. These experiences suggest, perhaps unsurprisingly, that questions about specific interactions generated more nuance about the kinds of harms – and potentially harmful interactions with incarcerated people – staff experience working in solitary confinement.

Second, in our interviews with correctional staff, we focused in again on soliciting specific examples from staff, asking them to "describe a time when you felt at risk in [the solitary confinement unit]". Again, this question generated specific details that provide context for when and how staff feel unsafe – and how these feelings of (un)safety are intertwined with staff and incarcerated people's well-being. Responses to this question confirmed that hazards of the job are constant concerns, even while staff often described themselves as coping well with the challenges of working in a high-risk setting. One staff, for example, shared that they had developed respiratory problems after using "OC" (oleoresin capsicum, a chemical agent akin to pepper spray) while extracting a prisoner from their cell. This staff member feared bringing the case to their superior's attention, because they felt "if you disclose to someone you're struggling, it's going to put your job at risk." They also mentioned concerns with reaching out to the DOC-provided psychologist for help coping with the various PTSD triggers that the prison and IMU setting elicited, again for fear of being labeled as "unfit" by administrators: "You can lose your job over it. But the reality is, most of us face it...[yet] we're not even feeling safe to tell each other and get help." Another staff described symptoms of hypervigilance, particularly the feeling of being "alert and on all the time":

A guy could slip his cuff. A cuff could come undone. You can open a cuff port and get a bunch of crap thrown all over you...And when you get off work at the end of the day, or after a long week, you are tired... They say you're supposed to leave the prison up here when you get off work, but walk a mile in my shoe.

While staff do indeed get to go home at the end of day, unlike prisoners, these examples nonetheless point to a set of troubling dynamics for staff: the tools and strategies that are available to theoretically protect staff can also jeopardize their well-being. Importantly, these examples also suggest concrete ways that prisoner-staff interactions might be negatively affecting prisoners, too, who are experiencing OC spray, and engaging in behaviors suggestive of severe mental distress, like throwing feces.

In the second, more recent phase of our research in the Washington Department of Corrections, we have been evaluating the Department's work to address exactly these challenges. Washington state prison administrators have partnered with Amend, a public health initiative based at UCSF, which aims to address the harmful effects of incarceration on both prisoners and staff through systematic cultural change. One central strategy to Amend's approach is to send correctional staff to Norway to shadow and receive training on a radically different approach to corrections (Ahalt et al, 2019). While both American and Norwegian departments of corrections believe in the importance of rehabilitation, a key distinction with the latter is how staff are leveraged to promote this goal. In Norway, officers are trained in motivational interviewing to guide their engagement with the incarcerated; they engage prisoners in health-focused programming; they provide direct mentorship and advisement; and they intentionally socialize with the prisoners (e.g., share meals, play sports). Put simply, staff do much more than supervise, escort, and discipline prisoners; they are trained to develop positive relationships and play an active role in the rehabilitation of those they oversee. This dynamic, in turn, translates to better working conditions for staff, better living conditions for prisoners, and lower recidivism (Ahault et al., 2019). Following the initial trip, American correctional staff receive additional training from Norwegian corrections partners, and are tasked with designing strategies inspired by what they've learned – all with the goal of improving prisoner and staff well-being and behavioral change (Cloud et al., 2021). In North Dakota, reform efforts include the creation of Positive Behavior Reports to acknowledge the pro-social behaviors (e.g., empathy and kindness to others) and goals (e.g., education, clinical treatment) to track a person's progress while in solitary confinement. Rather than simply track the absence of a disciplinary infraction as positive behavior, staff are tasked with identifying other more affirming markers for growth or improvement (Cloud et al., 2021). The North Dakota DOC also created specialized units with enhanced care for those with serious mental health issues, including daily access to individualized mental health care, group counseling, and out-of-cell, group activities (e.g., art therapy, games).

Partnering with Amend, the Washington Department of Corrections is engaged in a similar battery of reforms, particularly within their solitary confinement units. As part of our work evaluating Amend's partnership with the Washington Department of Corrections, we are again surveying and interviewing staff about their health and well-being, and again using survey and interview questions that seek to identify specific moments of feeling unsafe and unhealthy in order to better understand how solitary confinement affects not just prisoners but also staff.

A Plurality of Uncategorized Harms

Conducting research in the state of Washington, our team has conceptualized harm in solitary confinement as a dynamic and open-ended phenomenon. Throughout our extensive fieldwork, we have been able to measure the prevalence of clinically significant symptoms of depression, anxiety, and guilt, examine medical histories, inquire about the constitutionality of basic living conditions, and document the realities of suffering, for prisoners and staff, that exceed both clinical and legal categories. For example, a participant may present with only moderate levels of anxiety, suffer from no known cognitive or behavioral health issue, and view their placement in solitary confinement as both legitimate and professionally managed, but they may nonetheless endure the existential pains of just *being*[1] in isolation.

On the other hand, even when harms within well-defined clinical and legal categories are documented and verified, those harms often need to be more robustly conceptualized, not just as potential effects or outcomes of harsh conditions of confinement but as reflections of larger institutional

---

1. Being as both one's present placement in inherently harmful conditions as well as being in the phenomenological sense. Through the deprivations of isolation, one's experience and capacity to make meaning of the world is reduced, the articulation and experience of desire dulled, the expression and formulation of identity restricted, and relationality of self and other alienated.

problems. For instance, according to a 2024 report by the Office of the Corrections Ombudsman in Washington, from 2014 to 2023 there were 176 suicide attempts and suicides of people held in solitary confinement. Fourteen people died by suicide in that ten-year period (Robertson & Kingsbury 2024). These numbers represent a straightforward measure of harm experienced in solitary confinement – acute indicators of psychological distress that require urgent and appropriate clinical intervention. But, in combination with our own interview experiences and data – in which participants discussed both self-harm and the general emotional turmoil experienced during periods of prolonged placement in solitary confinement – we must also consider desperate acts taken against the self as overdetermined by or, perhaps, symptomatic of, the degradation of existence imposed by solitary confinement in general.

In addition to attending to both clinical and legal categories of harm for incarcerated people and experiences of harm beyond those categories, we also attended to a kind of collateral harm experienced by people working in solitary confinement, through surveys and interviews with correctional staff. But, as we step back and reflect on the scope of this work, there is another category of collateral harm that surfaces and arguably deserves attention: the trauma of the research work itself. As a team, we have often discussed the painful side effects of conducting research within solitary confinement units. There is the vicarious trauma of conducting interviews where participants share particularly devastating and heart wrenching stories, or are actively experiencing emotional and psychological distress during the interview. Solitary confinement spaces are also incredibly dull and austere, which hastens and intensifies the fatigue of the work. You must constantly navigate the ever-so-subtle feelings of indignity, as you are dependent on others to let you access the bathroom, to retrieve the lunch and snacks you brought into the facility, or to just let you out of a locked room after completing an interview. Our experiences here echo a growing body of qualitative researchers' work reflecting on the challenges of research in extreme spaces (Barragan et al., 2023; Rhodes 2004), the emotional toll of "doing time" in carceral spaces (Moran 2012), and the importance of reflecting on the emotional content of prison research (Jewkes 2011).

At the same time, there is also a type of mania that sets in where you do all you can to collect the richest, most robust data possible. *Just one more interview, power through, who knows if we'll have access like this again.* Still, what have we actually inflicted upon ourselves to obtain this data? While the harm researchers experience is in no way comparable to the harm experienced by those forced to live in isolation, we should not discount experiences of harm in research, as these experiences are part of the conditions of possibility for the knowledge produced. Perhaps another way to evaluate studies on solitary confinement, then, is to ask researchers to write reflexively on how much they suffered in doing the work. It should give us pause if social scientists claim to have suffered very little, not at all, or are confused by the very question. How does one insulate themselves from the harms of solitary confinement without also compromising their understanding of the harms, however limited and incomplete?

Robustly conceptualizing a range of harms experienced in solitary from the legal to the clinical to the collateral also allows us to uncover the multiple mechanisms by which solitary confinement might cause harm. Some mechanisms of harm are obvious, like the harm stemming from sensory deprivation of bare concrete walls, lack of natural light and the ability to measure the passage of time (Reiter 2016; Haney 2018), and the harm stemming from social deprivation of physical contact and communication with the outside world through limitations on visits and phone calls (Gonzalez 2021). Other mechanisms of harm are more structural and less visible, like the more pervasive experience of social death in solitary confinement (Guenther 2013), or the violence of a necropolitical order using solitary confinement as a pretense of care during the COVID-19 pandemic (Lackey, Loblack, Foltz 2024).

In sum, through our seven years and counting as a research team, we have persistently thought about and strained to understand the plurality of harms inflicted by solitary confinement. Through this process of conceptualizing and operationalizing harm according to various epistemological presumptions, we have seen again and again how the variety of harms of solitary confinement implicate and compromise the research at every turn.

How the harms are conceptualized, operationalized, and then analyzed, in turn, has concrete legal and policy implications, which are too often only implicit in the debates about solitary confinement research and its harms. Making these legal and policy implications explicit is another aspect of studying solitary confinement and conceptualizing its harm that we argue should go hand-in-hand with multi-source and multi-method approaches to understanding experiences of solitary confinement.

Translating Evidence of Medical Harm into Law & Policy

To date, despite the work of social scientists – alongside community advocates, human rights organizations, and legal professionals – to document the harms of solitary confinement, the practice remains a common form of punishment. While litigation, and especially state-level legislation, have gained momentum in the movement to reduce reliance on solitary confinement, legal reform has been halting and uneven across the United States (ACLU 2013; Solitary Watch n.d.). Eighth Amendment jurisprudence evaluating whether solitary confinement is cruel and unusual seems to perpetually accept the practice as "hover[ing] on the edge of what is humanly tolerable" (*Madrid v. Gomez*, 1995, 1280). Still, recent litigation has established that, first, meaningful social contact is a human need covered by the Eighth Amendment and, second, social contact cannot be denied indefinitely, because doing so would expose incarcerated people to severe psychological harm (*Jensen v. Thornell* 2023). Litigation over nearly 30 years, though, has hardly constrained (or improved conditions in) solitary confinement. Likewise, even in states that have successfully passed legislation to ban or severely limit solitary confinement use, implementation has faced strong and successful resistance within corrections (*e.g.*, Sheridan 2024).

We as a society are still left to wade through the ethical dilemmas and institutional conundrums posed by solitary confinement – and the infliction of potentially humane forms of suffering. Within this context, the discourse of harm-reduction appears frequently in research and advocacy work on solitary confinement. Amend, out of the University of California, San Francisco, and their Scandinavian-inspired culture change work exemplify this discourse, asking: If the practice of solitary confinement remains with us, then how might we (researchers, advocates, policymakers, corrections professionals, and community organizers) best organize our capacities to understand and lessen the pain and suffering of those exposed to such extreme conditions of isolation? For instance, can staff be more humanizing in their interactions?

However, we remain critical of the context in which we find ourselves where the best possible option available is to somehow abate and make humane the administration of harm. What DiMario (2022) has termed palliative governance speaks to institutional measures by which life is barely maintained through the mitigation of harm and risk, while the structural conditions of suffering go unchanged. In this way, the issues and problematics of solitary confinement, as they relate to the provision of basic human need, the reduction of harm, and maintaining il/legal thresholds of suffering, are cast within broader governmental strategies of regulating vulnerability within minimalist terms of intervention and relief.

If the social and legal context in which we find ourselves is to palliate solitary confinement, then how do you reduce something that you cannot measure? Again, Eighth Amendment jurisprudence is only so helpful as the provision of minimal standards of humane treatment is to be calibrated with the inherent pains of solitary confinement. We might also reflect on the peculiarity of such circumstances in which experts, advocates, and other stakeholders assume the task of imagining, tinkering, and experimenting with the thresholds of human suffering. Whether it be through the law, social science, or the goodwill of advocacy, we risk engaging in dynamics by which we impose upon people—who possess little to no autonomy or agency—what we think is good for them, while acquiescing to the structural conditions of their suffering. To draw from the language of an incarcerated person we encountered during a recent field visit, do we wish to make *gilded cages* of the places in which existence is barely maintained?

As one concrete example of a gilded cage: Because of their limited exposure to sunlight, people held in solitary confinement may be given supplements to mitigate the adverse health consequences of vitamin D deficiency. But what is to be done to supplement one's capacity to make-meaning of their enjoyment of sunlight? Such is the difference between palliating harm and what we might call the instantiation of well-being. The abolitionist distinction between reformist reforms and non-reformist reforms aligns here. Whereas reformist reforms attempt to rationalize a system through gradual improvements that ultimately legitimize and perpetuate harm (Augustine et al., 2021), non-reformist reforms are efforts taken within a broader framework and movement for social transformation (Bell 2020). Save for another rallying cry to abolish prisons, how then do we move within such parameters where harm can so easily be reproduced–albeit potentially lessened in its frequency and severity–and well-being simultaneously degraded?

As we have discovered through the course of our research project, the complexity of suffering in solitary confinement is that it may at once be captured and evaded by common forms of quantitative and qualitative inquiry. Still, we think that both bearing witness to such complexity and holding ourselves open to the possibility of treating incarcerated people differently matters. To return to how we opened up this inquiry of ours - the scope and scale of the harms of solitary confinement exhaust the very tools and techniques we have available to speak about it and make sense of it. If we accept this premise, then the value of the dialogue between social science and the law is not in its capacity to measure suffering, determine the appropriate thresholds of suffering, and palliate harm. Instead, the value of the dialogue between social science and law is to generate an occasion for the plurality of suffering to irrupt within the legal and scientific scene.

In fact, if we begin with the assumption that the law and social science will inevitably fail in their efforts to address the structural conditions and realities of suffering, we might then orient ourselves by an entirely different set of questions, concerns, and expectations about harm. How do we hold ourselves open to be moved and overwhelmed by the suffering of solitary confinement? What are the different ways in which prisons attempt to ascertain a life and how does life exceed the very categories of knowing? What do we imagine to be the value of knowledge of harm, and how do our desires and disappointments of such knowledge factor into the research enterprise?

Works Cited

ACLU. 2013. "Stop Solitary – Recent State Reforms to Limit the Use of Solitary Confinement," *ACLU*, Jun. 16., available online at: https://www.aclu.org/documents/stop-solitary-recent-state-reforms-limit-use-solitary-confinement.

Ahalt, C., C. Haney, K. Ekhaugen, and B. Williams. 2020. Role of a US-Norway exchange in placing health and well-being at the center of US prison reform. *AJPH Perspectives* 110(S1), S27-S29.

"About Amend at UCSF." No date. Available online at: https://amend.us/.

Andreasen, N. C. 1989. The Scale for the Assessment of Negative Symptoms (SANS): conceptual and theoretical foundations. *The British journal of psychiatry*, 155(S7), 49-52.

Augustine, D., Barragan, M., Chesnut, K., Pifer, N.A., Reiter, K., & Strong, J.D. (2021). Window dressing: Possibilities and limitations of incremental changes in solitary confinement. *Health & Justice*, 9(21).

Barragan, M., Augustine, D., Gonzalez, G., & Reiter, K. (2023). Deconstructing the Power Dynamic of Prison Research. *The Prison Journal 103(6)*.

Blaauw, E., H.G., Roozen, and H.J.C. van Marle. 2007. "Saved by structure? The course of psychosis within a prison population." *International Journal of Prisoner Health* 3(4):248-256.

Calavita, K., V. Jenness. 2014. *Appealing to Justice: Prisoner Grievances, Rights, and Carceral Logic*. Berkeley, CA: University of California Press.

Cloud, D.H., D. Augustine, C. Ahalt, C. Haney, L. Peterson, C. Braun, and B. Williams. 2021. "We just needed to open the door:" A case study of the quest to end solitary confinement in North Dakota. *Health & Justice* 9(28).

Cloyes, K. G., Lovell, D., Allen, D. G., & Rhodes, L. A. (2006). Assessment of psychosocial impairment in a supermaximum security unit sample. *Criminal Justice and Behavior*, 33(6), 760-781.

Corrado, Raymond R., Irwin Cohen, Stephen Hart, and Ronald Roesch. 2000. "Comparative examination of the prevalence of mental disorders among jailed inmates in Canada and the United States." *International Journal of Law and Psychiatry*, 23(5): 633-647

Gendreau, P. and J. Bonta. 1984. "Solitary confinement is not cruel and unusual punishment: people sometimes are!" *Can J Criminol*, 26: 467-78.

Gonzalez, G. 2021. "Who has the power? Manipulating and reclaiming social support in solitary confinement." *Punishment & Society*. https://doi.org/10.1177/146247452110293.

Grassian, S. 1983. "Psychopathological effects of solitary confinement." *American Journal of Psychiatry*, 140(11): 1450-54.

Guenther, L. 2013. *Solitary Confinement: Social Death and Its Afterlives*. Minneapolis: University of Minnesota Press.

Hagan, B.O., E.A. Wang, J.A. Aminawung, C.E. Albizu-Garcia, N. Zaller, S. Nyamu, et al. 2018. "History of solitary confinement is associated with post-traumatic stress disorder symptoms among individuals recently released from prison." *J of Urban Health*, 95(2):141–48.

Haney, C. 2003. "Mental health issues in long-term solitary and "supermax" confinement." *Crime and Delinquency*, 49: 124-56.

__ 2018. "The Psychological Effects of Solitary Confinement: A Systematic Critique." *Crime and Justice*, 47: 365-416.

Harvard v. Dixon, Case No.: 4:19-cv-00212-MW-CAS (N.D. Fl., 2019).

Jensen v. Thornell, No. CV-12-00601-PHX-ROS (D. Ariz. Apr. 7, 2023).

Jewkes, Y. 2011. "Autoethnography and Emotion as Intellectual Resources: Doing Prison Research Differently." *Qualitative Inquiry*, 18(1): https://doi.org/10.1177/107780041142894.

Kaba F., A. Lewis, S. Glowa-Kollisch, J. Hadler, D. Lee, H. Alper, et al. 2014. "Solitary confinement and risk of self harm among jail inmates." *Am J Public Health*, 104(3):442–7.

Labrecque, R. M., P. Gendreau, R.D. Morgan, and M.M. King. 2020. "Revisiting the Walpole Prison Solitary Confinement Study (WPSCS): A content analysis of the studies citing Grassian (1983)." *Psychology, Public Policy, and Law*, 26(3), 378–391.

Lackey, D.J., A.C. Loblack, K.E. Foltz. 2024. "The COVID-19 Murders": Prison death-worlds and the fatal convenience of crisis." *Punishment & Society*, https://doi.org/10.1177/14624745241264299.

Lobel, J. & H. Akil. 2018. "Law & Neuroscience: The Case of Solitary Confinement." *Daedalus* 147(4): 61-75.

Lovell, D., D. Allen, C. Johnson, R. Jemelka. 2001. "Evaluating the effectiveness of residential treatment for prisoners with mental illness." *Criminal Justice and Behavior*, 28(1): 83-104.

Lovell D. 2008. Patterns of disturbed behavior in a supermax population. *Crim Justice Behav.*, 35(8): 985–1004.

Madrid v. Gomez, 889 F. Supp. 1146 (N.D. Cal. 1995).

Moran, D. 2012. "'Doing Time' in Carceral Space: Timespace and Carceral Geography." *Geografiska Annaler*, 94(4): 305-316.

Morgan, R. D., Gendreau, P., Smith, P., Gray, A. L., Labrecque, R. M., MacLean, N., Van Horn, S. A., Bolanos, A. D., Batastini, A. B., & Mills, J. F. 2016. "Quantitative syntheses of the effects of administrative segregation on inmates' well-being." *Psychology, Public Policy, and Law*, 22(4), 439–461.

Morlan, K.K., Tan, S. Y. 1998. "Comparison of the Brief Psychiatric Rating Scale and the Brief Symptom Inventory." *J Clin Psychol*, 54(7), 885-94.

Nwosu, B. U., L. Maranda, R. Berry, B. Colocino, C.D. Flores, K. Folkman, T. Groblewski, P. Ruze. 2014. "The Vitamin D Status of Prison Inmates." *PLoS One*, 9(3): e90623.

O'Keefe, M. L., K. J. Klebe, J. Metzner, J. Dvoskin, J. Fellner, A. Stucker. 2013. "A longitudinal study of administrative segregation." *J Am Acad Psychiatry Law*, 41(1):49-60.

Overall, John E., and Donald R. Gorham. "The brief psychiatric rating scale." Psychological reports 10, no. 3 (1962): 799-812.

Reiter, K. 2016. *23/7: Pelican Bay Prison and the Rise of Long-Term Solitary Confinement.* New Haven: Yale University Press.

Reiter, K., J. Ventura, D. Lovell, D. Augustine, M. Barragan*, T. Blair, K. Chesnut,

P. Dashtgard, G. Gonzalez, N. Pifer, and J. Strong. 2020. "Psychological Distress in Solitary Confinement: Symptoms, Severity, and Prevalence, United States, 2017-18," *American Journal of Public Health*, Vol. 110: S52-S56.

Reiter, K. with K. Chesnut, G. Gonzalez, J. Strong, R. Tublitz, D. Augustine, M. Barragan, P. Dashtgard, and N. Pifer. "Reducing Restrictive Housing Use in Washington State: Results from the 2016-2020 Study 'Understanding and Replicating Washington State's Segregation Reduction Programs,' Contract No. K11273," available online at https://www.doc.wa.gov/corrections/incarceration/docs/restrictive-housing-university-california-irvine-report.pdf.

Rhoades, H. M., and J. E. Overall. "The semistructured BPRS interview and rating guide." *Psychopharmacology bulletin* 24, no. 1 (1988): 101.

Rhodes, L.A. 2004. *Total Confinement: Madness and Reason in the Maximum Security Prison*. Berkeley, CA: University of California Press.

Robertson, C. & E. Kingsbury. 2024. *Solitary Confinement: Part I*. Olympia, WA: Office of the Corrections Ombudsman. Available online at: https://oco.wa.gov/sites/default/files/OCO_SolitaryConfinementReport_Part1_June2024.pdf.

Rubin, A.T. and K. Reiter, 2018. "Continuity in the Face of Penal Innovation: Revisiting the History of American Solitary Confinement," *Law & Social Inquiry*, Vol. 43.4: 1604-32.

Rudes, D. With S. Magnusson, A. Hattery. 2022. *Surviving Solitary: Living and Working in Restricted Housing Units*. Palo Alto, CA: Stanford University Press.

Sheridan, J. 2024. "Department of Corrections violated solitary confinement law, judge rules." *News10*, Jun. 21, available online at: https://www.news10.com/news/ny-news/department-of-corrections-violated-solitary-confinement-law-judge-rules/.

Senior, J., L. Birmingham, M. A. Harty, L. Hassan, A. J. Hayes, K. Kendall, C. King et. al. 2013. "Identification and management of prisoners with severe psychiatric illness by specialist mental health services." *Psychological medicine*, 43(7): 1511.

Solitary Watch. N.D. "Resources for Action," available online at:

https://solitarywatch.org/resources-for-action/.

Strong, J., K. Reiter, D. Augustine, M. Barragan, K. Chesnut, P. Dashtgard, G. Gonzalez, N. Pifer, and R. Tublitz. 2020. "The Body in Isolation: The Physical Health Impacts of Incarceration in Solitary Confinement," *PLOS ONE*, Vol. 15(10): e0238510.

Sundt, J. 2016. "Chapter 8: The Effect of Administrative Segregation on Prison Order and Organizational Culture." In *Restrictive Housing in the U.S.*, Washington, D.C.: National Institute of Justice, 297-330.

Walters, R. H., J.E. Callagan, and A. F. Newman. 1963. "Effect of solitary confinement on prisoners, *American Journal of Psychiatry*, 119(8), 771–773.

Williams, B.A., A. Li, C. Ahalt, P. Coxson, J.G. Kahn, K. Bibbins-Domingo. 2019. "The cardiovascular health burdens of solitary confinement." *J Gen Intern Med.*, 34(10):1977–80.

Zanello, A, L. Berthoud, J. Ventura, M.C.G. Merlod. 2013. "The Brief Psychiatric Rating Scale (version 4.0) factorial structure and its sensitivity in the treatment of outpatients with unipolar depression." *Psychiatry Res.*, 210(2): 626-33.

3

Deportations, Detentions, and Incarcerations as Social Determinants of Health: The Impact of Family Separation on Men and Women in Vulnerable Houston Communities

Yajaira Ceciliano-Navarro*

Abstract
In this exploratory study, we apply the Legal Determinants of Health (LDH) framework to examine how deportations, detentions, and incarcerations affect the health outcomes of men and women in vulnerable communities. Drawing on survey data collected in Houston (2022–2024) from 356 participants who had a relative removed through deportation, detention, or incarceration, we find that both men and women—across different family structures, generations, and legal statuses—experienced significant emotional and financial burdens associated with family separation. Participants' health is shaped not only by the existing financial and social limitations of living in vulnerable communities, but these events also increase their vulnerabilities, impacting them in both the short and long term. Therefore, we argue that deportations, detentions, and incarcerations function as legal determinants of health, as legal institutions in these cases are not only causing emotional and mental health harm, but also preventing families from building and sustaining wealth in both the short and long term—factors that have a direct impact on their overall health and well-being across legal statuses and generations.

Introduction

Law is a critical determinant of health, impacting it through statutes, regulations, and public institutions that shape factors like education, food, housing, and healthcare (Burris 2011; Thomson 2022). Effective laws can enhance health and equity by establishing standards, building strong health systems, and ensuring accountability (Stronks et al. 2016; Genn 2019).

* Assistant Professor, Sociology. University of Houston-Downtown, 1 Main St, Houston, TX 77002, USA

However, harmful or discriminatory laws can restrict access to care, limit rights, and exacerbate inequalities, ultimately undermining health for individuals and populations (Genn 2019). As Braveman et al. (2011) and Castaneda et al. (2015) argue, the social determinant of health framework shows how structural factors beyond medical care, shaped by social and economic policies and inequalities, profoundly impact health outcomes. In this context, institutions such as the judicial system have also been recognized as significant determinants of health, particularly within vulnerable communities. In this regard, cases of deportations, detentions and incarcerations serve as key examples of how individuals from communities of color are impacted by the judicial system (Hinton, Henderson, and Reed 2018; Harris et al. 2009; Pettit and Gutierrez 2018). Studies on deportations have discovered various impacts on individuals, including the effects of the deportation process, the detention experience, and their subsequent exile to unfamiliar locations on the deported person (Hamilton, Orraca-Romano, and Vargas Valle 2023; Saadi et al. 2020). These deported individuals often face challenges related to criminalization, safety, and economic conditions in their new environments, which significantly affect both them and their families (Golash-Boza and Navarro 2018; Brotherton and Barrios 2011; Brabeck, Lykes, and Hershberg 2011).

Studies on incarceration have also emphasized the impacts of detention and incarceration on individuals. While some aspects of healthcare may be more available during incarceration, the overall effect of incarceration on health is complex and often detrimental in the long term (Addison et al. 2022, Semenza & Link 2019, and Wang & Wildeman 2011). Particularly after individuals are released, studies indicate that factors such as discrimination, stigma, negative interactions with law enforcement, solitary confinement, and difficulties in finding employment are strongly linked to poor health outcomes for formerly incarcerated individuals (Shaw 2023; Hatzenbuehler, Phelan, and Link 2013). These challenges also extend to their families and communities (Addison et al. 2022). While extensive research has examined the impacts on the individual deported, detained, or incarcerated, there is a lack of to assess the compounded health consequences for men and women from mixed-status families when they have a relative deported, detained, or incarcerated. These families often encounter unique challenges that can exacerbate health disparities. Therefore, the research questions of this study are:

1. What are the main emotional and financial impacts for women and men experiencing deportations, detentions, and incarceration?
2. How do these experiences can shape health outcomes for men and women?

2. Literature Review

The concept of legal determinants of health focuses on the profound influence of laws and judicial decisions on public health outcomes (Thomson 2022; Gostin et al. 2019). As stated by Thomson (2022), "law has an essential and important role in constituting and enabling these institutions and regulating health services and interventions" (3). Judicial rulings on environmental regulations, workplace safety, and healthcare access shape community well-being. In this regard, an extensive body of social epidemiological research establishes that social, economic, and environmental factors impact individual and population health more than individual biology or clinical care. Considering this, Genn (2019) states that the influence of social and environmental determinants on health status can be between 45% and 60% (Genn 2019).

Considering the criminal justice system, policies related to incarceration, drug enforcement, and healthcare provision impact the health of individuals involved and their communities (Nowotny and Kuptsevych-Timmer 2018; Parmet 2019; Nosrati et al. 2021; Schnittker and John 2007). For scholars, deportations, detentions, and incarcerations function as health determinants since these events perpetuate social conditions that limit access to health services, decrease income, and increase housing stability, among others (Cabral and Cuevas 2020; Nowotny and Kuptsevych-Timmer 2018; Williams and Mohammed 2009). Second, they act as mechanisms through which the stress associated with these events translates into health outcomes such as insomnia, anxiety, stigma, and fear that directly impact individuals' educational and job opportunities (Moran 2012; Yamanis et al. 2021). For Genn (2019), repeated or long-term exposure to stressful living and working conditions can lead to high blood pressure, diabetes, and ischemic heart disease. In other words, being consistently stressed, also known as 'allostatic overload', can make people ill (Genn 2019). Stress does not just directly impact health, but it can also indirectly impact individuals' ability to pursue educational and job opportunities, limiting their access to resources and opportunities.

2.1 Deportations and Detentions as Determinants of Health

The literature on immigration as a social determinant of health explores how policies and experiences related to immigration significantly impact health outcomes, particularly among vulnerable communities (Parmet 2019; Wallace et al. 2019; Asad and Clair 2018; Cabral and Cuevas 2020; Castañeda et al. 2015; Hacker et al. 2015). Immigrants' health is affected by several factors, such as limited financial resources that often restrict their access to adequate healthcare services (Akresh 2009). The nature of their jobs can be more hazardous, contributing to worse health outcomes (Schenker 2008). Legal status additionally complicates access to healthcare and other services (Hacker et al. 2015), while fear of immigration enforcement exacerbates these issues, leading to significant negative impacts (Vargas, Sanchez, and Juárez 2017). Moreover, there has been increased immigration enforcement and unprecedented levels of deportation, which have negatively impacted the health of individuals and their families in these communities (Hacker et al., 2012 (Pinedo et al. 2021).

For scholars such as Harrigan et al. (2017), the threat of deportation is a critical social determinant of mental illness, surpassing traditional socioeconomic factors due to substantial disruptions and fear within these families. The fear of deportation leads to widespread anxiety and stress, impacting both the mental and physical health of individuals (Yamanis et al. 2021; Goodman 2020). Beyond the fear, and as a result of deportations, families often face severe disruptions, including financial instability and emotional distress, as they grapple with the sudden loss of a family member who may be a primary caregiver or financial provider (García 2018; Artiga and Lyons 2018). The impacts of deportations on families are extensive. Initially, the shock of experiencing the detention and removal of a loved one can be profoundly distressing (García 2018). This emotional chaos is combined with the immediate loss of income, which can destabilize the family's financial situation (Artiga and Lyons 2018; Ceciliano-Navarro and Golash-Boza 2021). Subsequently, families must suffer significant restructuring, including relocating homes, assuming new roles, and adapting to altered daily routines (Lovato and Abrams 2021). Additionally, families may need to send remittances to support the deported individual, adding financial strain (Weber and Massey 2023). These cumulative effects disrupt family stability and lead to severe health impacts.

Families not only deal with their own problems but they worry for the individual who is deported (Pedroza 2022), since deportees are often forced to return to places where they may not have lived in for years (Golash-Boza and Navarro 2018; Brotherton and Barrios 2011). In many cases, deportees face criminalization or other challenges due to local conditions such as insecurity or violence, which complicate their reintegration process (Ceciliano-Navarro and Golash-Boza 2021; Kretsedemas and Brotherton 2018). Their inability to secure employment and generate income makes reintegration even more difficult, impacting their families since families have to provide for them (Golash-Boza and Navarro 2020; Hamilton, Orraca-Romano, and Vargas Valle 2023).

Detention, in the US and in the context of immigration, can be understood as a place to hold individuals awaiting immigration proceedings or deportation (Gilman and Romero 2018). In this regard, the literature has shown that immigration detention can have severe negative impacts on individuals and families (Dirkzwager et al. 2021; Sidamon-Eristoff et al. 2022; Filges et al. 2015). Literature has shown how the mental health of immigrants, immigrants' children, and asylum seekers has been impacted due to the detention (Sidamon-Eristoff et al. 2022; Filges et al. 2015; Dirkzwager et al. 2021). Other scholars, such as Patler and Branic (2017), have studied the impacts of immigration detention on families. Patler and Branic (2017) show that despite individuals being incarcerated for immigration offenses or minor violations and awaiting deportation, detention often replicates the experience of criminal incarceration. Not only are these individuals treated like criminals, but their families also go through a similar process when trying to maintain contact since their families are also compelled to undergo a similar process when attempting to visit their relatives (Saadi et al. 2020). For Patler and Branic (2017), demographic background, the type of detention facility, and children's legal status shape these visitation experiences. In addition to the logistical challenges, Patler (2015) also demonstrates that, although detention is intended to be short-term, it is increasingly common for individuals to be detained for extended periods. Unlike in the criminal court system, immigration bonds must be paid in full for a respondent to be released. As a result, detainees and their families, whose economic situations are often strained by lost wages due to detention, may face additional hardship due to the high bond amounts affecting families' ability to cover essential needs such as utility bills, medical care, and food (Patler 2015).

2.2 Incarcerations as Determinants of Health

Research consistently shows that incarceration is a significant social determinant of health, particularly for minority communities such as Latinos and Black men, as well as their families (Nowotny & Kuptsevych-Timmer, 2018; Rodriguez & Turanovic, 2018). Due to preexisting social disadvantages, these communities already experience higher rates of health issues, and incarceration often exacerbates these problems (Wang & Wildeman, 2011). Mass incarceration perpetuates health inequities by disrupting social networks, increasing exposure to violence, and limiting access to healthcare (Massoglia & Pridemore, 2015).

The health consequences for incarcerated and formerly incarcerated individuals have been extensively studied (Addison et al., 2022; Williams & Bergeson, 2019). These studies reveal that incarceration can severely disrupt an individual's life, leading to mental and physical health deterioration (Henry, 2020). For individuals incarcerated, research shows that incarceration is linked to a high prevalence of chronic health conditions, with the experience of being incarcerated often having a greater impact on health than the duration of imprisonment. In addition to general health issues like physical functioning, research in this area has also examined specific conditions such as infectious diseases, cardiovascular problems, weight gain, hypertension, and cancer (Massoglia and Pridemore 2015). For formerly incarcerated individuals, one major concern is their social reintegration, which involves significant challenges such as finding stable employment, securing affordable housing, and accessing mental health or substance abuse treatment (Visher & Travis, 2011; Harding et al., 2014; Keene et al., 2018; Ricciardelli & Peters, 2017; (Golash-Boza, Aquino, and Ceciliano-Navarro 2024). The stigma and discrimination they face can limit their reintegration efforts and contribute to higher rates of recidivism (Maruna, 2012; Moran, 2012). These factors collectively lead to the deterioration of physical and mental health, often resulting in mental health disorders, substance abuse, and homelessness (McNiel et al., 2005).

For families, the incarceration of relatives has profound emotional and financial impacts (Rodriguez and Turanovic 2018). Emotionally, family members often endure anxiety, depression, and stigma due to their relative's incarceration (Arditti, 2012; Western et al., 2015). Financial hardship is a common issue, as the loss of income causes economic instability, making it difficult to meet basic needs (Arditti, 2018; Shaw, 2023; Watts & Nightingale, 1996). Family dynamics are disrupted, with remaining members assuming additional responsibilities, and the separation from a parent can negatively affect children's emotional well-being, academic performance, behavior, and health (Wildeman, Goldman, and Turney 2018). Families may also experience social stigma and isolation, amplifying their emotional and psychological distress (Hood & Gaston, 2022; Shaw, 2023).

Health outcomes in Black and Latino communities

According to a report from The Commonwealth Fund (2024), racial and ethnic disparities in health have long existed in the United States, with Black and American Indian/Alaska Native (AIAN) populations being particularly affected. On average, they live fewer years than white and Hispanic individuals and face higher risks of dying from treatable conditions, pregnancy-related complications, and infant mortality. Additionally, they are more susceptible to chronic conditions like diabetes and hypertension. The COVID-19 pandemic worsened these disparities, leading to a sharper decline in life expectancy for Black, Hispanic, and AIAN people compared to white individuals since 2020 (Dolan and Rutherford 2020; Lopez, Hart, and Katz 2021). This is relevant to consider since the communities we are studying are already socially and financially vulnerable (Colen et al. 2024). Individuals in these communities often face pre-existing health issues, and the added burden of these practices such as deportations, detentions, or incarcerations, only worsens their health outcomes.

Resilience and other positive aspects of deportations, detentions, or incarcerations
The literature on deportations and incarcerations has shown how, in some instances, the removal of a violent family member is potentially beneficial for the remaining family unit. While this is not the norm, it is important to acknowledge these exceptions, as the absence of a violent or disruptive relative may bring a sense of relief and safety (Dreby 2012; McKay et al. 2018). Additionally, emerging research on resilience in the context of deportations and incarcerations shows how individuals and families develop coping strategies as a form of resilience when facing events such as detention, deportation, or incarceration. These findings demonstrate their capacity to overcome adversity (Bomysoad and Francis 2022; Garcini et al. 2022; Coifman, Flynn, and Pinto 2016).

The Houston context
The experiences of men and women with the criminal and immigration systems are highly relevant in the Houston area. Texas is one of the states with the highest number of prisons, and therefore has high rates of incarceration, as well as a growing number of immigration detention centers. Immigration detention and deportation are highly active in the Houston area, reflecting both state and federal priorities. Texas detains more immigrants than any other state, with facilities near Houston—such

as the Montgomery County and Joe Corley Processing Centers—holding over 2,000 individuals daily (Axios, 2025). Harris County alone is home to approximately 481,000 undocumented residents (Houston Chronicle, 2025), and as of August 2023, the Houston immigration courts had over 40,000 pending asylum cases, mostly from Latin American countries (Migration Policy Institute, 2023). Additionally, the use of solitary confinement in detention facilities has raised human rights concerns, with 542 people placed in isolation between 2018 and 2023 at one Houston-area center (Houston Landing, 2023). On the other hand, incarceration remains a critical issue in Houston, particularly in Harris County, where the jail system frequently exceeds its capacity of 9,575 inmates, with daily populations surpassing 10,000 as of 2022 (Davis 2025). A striking 80.5% of those incarcerated are held in pretrial detention, among the highest rates in Texas. Racial disparities are also pronounced: although Black residents make up about 20% of the county's population, they represent a disproportionately higher share of the jail population (Safety and Justice Challenge, 2023). Moreover, individuals from marginalized communities—especially Black and Latino men—are overrepresented among those with frequent jail contact(Baillargeon et al. 2000). These patterns raise significant concerns about systemic inequities and the broader social and health impacts of mass incarceration in this area.

Therefore, understanding the emotional and financial impacts of the criminal and immigration systems on men and women—and how these translate into health outcomes—is especially relevant in the Houston area, a diverse urban hub that often overlooks the daily challenges faced by immigrants and mixed-status families.

2.3 Theoretical contribution

After reviewing the literature on deportations, detentions, and incarcerations, we can state that these events serve as social determinants of health due to the loss of resources from the removal of a breadwinner, increased family instability, and limited access to healthcare (Pedroza 2022; Pettit and Gutierrez 2018; Pettit and Western 2004). The literature also shows impacts on families, particularly on women, children, and youth. However, the impacts on men, and women, from mixed-status families have not been sufficiently addressed. Therefore, this study aims to demonstrate how the health of adults, men and women from mixed-status families is also affected by deportations, detentions, and incarcerations. This is particularly relevant in Houston, a large city with systematic issues of segregation, a significant influx of immigrants, and a lack of community connections between families and neighborhoods that can exacerbate health issues for both men and women. Therefore, the research questions of this study are:

1. What are the main emotional and financial impacts for women and men experiencing deportations, detentions, and incarceration?
2. How do these experiences can shape health outcomes for men and women?

3. Methods

In this research, I aimed to explore the experiences of individuals who have or had a relative deported, detained, or incarcerated and how these events emotionally impact men and women in Houston. Additionally, I examined the potential effects of these experiences on their overall health. Participants were randomly selected based on the criteria for having a family member who has been deported, detained, or incarcerated. Using the snowfall method, a survey with closed- and open-ended questions was created and distributed through Google Forms during Fall 2023 and Spring and Summer 2024.

The recruitment process of people completing the surveys began with the lead researcher utilizing close contacts and expanding using snowball sampling and advertising. To be eligible for this study, participants must have been 18 or older and have a relative who is or has been deported, detained or incarcerated. Additionally, students in the special project class collected data for their papers and surveyed individuals in different communities, neighborhoods, and across the Houston area. The survey was completely anonymous, and participants were not asked to provide personal information or any data that could identify them.

The survey included open-ended questions in which participants described the emotional, financial, and health impacts they experienced. This qualitative information was coded by the most salient topics and used to organize this paper.

3.1 Profile participant in the survey

A total of 343 people participated in the survey. Fifty-five individuals reported having a relative detained, 143 were deported, and 140 were incarcerated. Data indicates that more men than women are removed due to detentions, deportations, or incarcerations (Table 1). However, it is important to note that in this sample, some women have also been deported. The survey included participants from diverse racial and ethnic backgrounds, with a significant representation of individuals who identified themselves Black and Latino individuals. Regarding immigration status, most participants reported it to be citizens, though other legal statuses were also present in the study. As seen in Table 2, beyond parents, other individuals from both nuclear and extended families have also been removed.

Relative removed from the household

Table 2 shows that more men than women are removed from households, consistent with previous research on the gendered aspects of deportations, detentions, and incarcerations (Golash-Boza & Hondagneu-Sotelo, 2013; Ropes Berry et al., 2020). However, this study indicates that, beyond parents, many other relatives within the family system are also removed, including uncles, brothers, and sons, as well as women in the case of deportations. In summary, deportations, detentions, and incarcerations impact individuals across genders, ages, generations, and immigration statuses.

4. Findings

Considering our research questions—*what are the main emotional and financial impacts for women and men experiencing deportations, detentions, and incarceration,* and *how do these experiences shape health outcomes for both?*

It is important to emphasize that the experiences of detention and

Table 1: Participant Demographics by Type of Removal of Relative (Deportation, Detention, or Incarceration) N=343

Category	Detentions	Deportations	Incarcerations	Total
Participants by Type of Removal of Relative (Deportation, Detention, or Incarceration)	55	143	140	343
Gender of Participants				
• Female	31	96	93	223
• Male	18	43	46	111
• Other	6	4	1	9
Total Gender	55	143	140	343
Legal Status				
• Citizen		99	81	162
• DACA Recipient	2	8	1	11
• Resident	6	14	4	25
• Undocumented	4	9	1	14
• Under Visa	0	3	1	4
• Other	0	2	1	3
• NR (Not Reported)	3	8	51	62
Total Legal Status	55	143	140	343
Race/Ethnicity				
• White / Caucasian	30	65	49	146
• Black or African American	4	9	62	75
• Latino	7	32	18	59
• Asian / Pacific Islander	5	14	5	24
• American Indian or Alaskan Native	5	7	5	18
• NR (Not Reported)	4	13	0	18
• Other	0	3	1	3
Total Race/Ethnicity	55	143	140	343

Source: Data collected in the Houston Area, 2023-2024

Table 2: Type of Relative Removed (Nuclear or Extended Family), Reported by Participants

Category	Family Members	Number of Mentions
Nuclear Family	Father	66
	Mother	19
	Brother	53
	Sister	7
	Husband	4
	Myself	3
	Son	1
	Mother-in-law	1
	Total (Nuclear)	154
Extended Family	Uncle	64
	Cousin	29
	Aunt	9
	Grandfather	4
	Nephew	1
	Total (Extended)	107
	Other/Non-specific	82
	Total (Other)	82
Total		343

Source: Data collected in the Houston Area, 2023-2024

deportation are like those of incarceration in terms of emotional and financial burdens (Tosh, Berg, and León 2021; Patler and Golash-Boza 2017). Due to the high criminalization of immigrants, they are often marginalized and treated as criminals, along with their families, who undergo similar hardships as those affected by incarceration. These challenges intensify mental health issues in mixed-status families.

Considering the experiences of both men and women, they may express emotions differently. However, despite these differences, both experience similar stress and anxiety. Considering the specific experiences of men, it is important to recognize that those left behind after the removal of relatives often take on emotional roles for which they may not be prepared, in addition to facing increased financial responsibilities. However, in general, both men and women take on new emotional and material responsibilities that affects them in the short and long term, making them more likely to lack the necessary resources for their medical care. These events also lead to disruptions in education and employment, affecting individuals' ability to aspire to social mobility and maintain a stable income (Potochnick and Perreira 2010). Consequently, this impacts their earnings and limits their access to better financial opportunities and health resources. Therefore, practices such as deportations, detentions, and incarcerations can definitely act as a social determinant of health (Saadi et al. 2020; Rotter and Compton 2022).

4.1. Deportations, detentions, and incarcerations as social determinants of health for women

The removal of a loved one, whether through deportation, detention or incarceration, significantly impacts families' emotionally and financially (Arditti 2012; Artiga and Lyons 2018; Pettit and Western 2004). Since most individuals removed are men, women are often left behind to bear the burden of new financial and emotional responsibilities (Christian and Thomas 2009; Golash-Boza and Hondagneu-Sotelo 2013). Women must work more to compensate for the lost income, and other household members may also contribute (Bruns 2019). The lack of income often leads to housing instability and increased emotional stress, which occurs whether the removal is due to deportation, detention, or incarceration (Pedroza 2022; Lipsitz 2011)

4.1.1 Incarcerations

In this section, we examine how a range of emotions—such as sadness, anger, devastation, disappointment, and loneliness—can impact women's health. When these emotions are compounded by financial burdens, they can lead to extreme stress and anxiety, significantly affecting both mental and physical well-being (Genn 2019). This heightened stress can contribute to conditions such as high blood pressure, heart disease, and diabetes, while also disrupting sleep and appetite, compromising overall health (Feldman et al. 1999; Genn 2019).

Feelings of devastation, along with financial burdens and educational responsibilities, can be challenging for women. For some women, the experience of familial incarceration can be devastating, as this participant, who is 22 years old, expressed regarding the incarceration of her brother 2 years ago: *'It was devastating when I was told about my brother's incarceration.'* For this young woman, who identifies as African American and is currently a student, her brother's incarceration also brought financial challenges. She explained, *'It was difficult at first to manage with a tighter income after the incarceration.'* Despite these challenges, she has been trying to remain focused on her studies: *'I kept focusing on finishing my education despite financial restraints.'* As described by this participant, we can observe the spillover effects of his brother's incarceration. She not only deals with the emotional burden but also faces significant financial impacts, all while striving to continue her education despite the significant financial constraints placed on her and her family.

Emotions of guilt, along with new caregiving roles and financial burdens, can be quite challenging for women. For this participant, a female who is 22 years old, who identifies as white, and whose uncle has been incarcerated for over 10 years, shares the reactions emerging due to these events: *'Feeling guilty that life doesn't stop, heartbroken knowing time passes, the world changes, people grow up, and they're missing it all due to the incarceration.'* For this participant, her uncle's incarceration brought additional burdens: *'We became responsible for his well-being, covering expenses like food, phone bills for communication, and supporting his children. It can strain personal finances while trying to balance one's own life.'* In this case, despite the incarcerated individual being an extended family member, the impacts are direct. She not only has to support herself and her cousins but also her incarcerated uncle. Additionally, it is important to consider the long-lasting financial impacts that have accumulated over the 10 years of his incarceration.

Emotional and financial hardships extending across generations are mentioned by some participants. This 20-year-old female participant, who identifies as white, shared regarding her uncle's detention. Despite the removal of her uncle was 8 years ago, she remembers how family dynamics were affected and how, as a child, she could not understand what happened: *'The feeling I remember most was confusion. I didn't understand why they were in jail and not at my grandparents' house when I visited.'* She also shared how her grandparents, the primary ones affected, were deeply impacted: *'My grandma was saddened by the news, and my grandpa appeared angry.'* Additionally, she explained how her grandparents and other relatives were financially impacted as they worked to raise bail money: *'My grandparents and family members worked harder to gather the bail money.'* This testimony reveals how the incarceration of a relative, even an extended family member, can have profound and far-reaching effects on the emotional and financial stability of the entire family, particularly across generations.

As a result of these events, individuals may experience deep depression, which can lead to isolation and avoidant behaviors, such as not seeking help or discussing these painful experiences. For some individuals experiencing incarcerations family members can have suicidal thoughts, as expressed by a female participant, 49 years old, who identifies as American Indian and refers to her father's incarceration: *'I really don't like to talk about it because of the emotional and physical toll it took on my family. Some were in deep depression, and some even contemplated suicide. Thank God things turned around,' (Female, 49 years old, father incarcerated).* Dealing with a relative's suicidal ideation places an additional severe emotional burden on the family, which is already struggling to cope with the challenges of having an incarcerated relative. Therefore, families may be reluctant to discuss the experience due to the intense emotional stress it caused within the family. From a health perspective, avoiding talking about these events or seeking emotional support due to these unresolved emotions can worsen over time, leading to isolation and, therefore, to deeper mental health issues such as anxiety and depression (Feldman et al. 1999).

Stress and anxiety are the most frequently reported outcomes by participants, and they are the result of intense emotions, financial burdens, and new responsibilities associated with incarceration. One female participant, 25 years old, expressed feelings of *"depression and anxiety"* when discussing her brother's incarceration five years ago. Another participant, 24 years old, noted, *"It stresses out the entire family,"* referring to the ongoing incarceration of her uncles and cousins. As explained earlier, individuals with incarcerated relatives experience a range of emotions, from anger to sadness. However, the predominant outcome is a pervasive and constant stress that extends to the entire family system.

Findings show the emotional and financial burdens women face when a relative is incarcerated. These burdens are experienced regardless of whether the incarcerated individual is part of the immediate or extended family. Furthermore, the impact extends across generations, causing estrangement and strained relationships. Emotional and financial burdens are deeply intertwined; long-term financial pressures can cause emotional strain, while emotional distress can exacerbate financial difficulties. This cycle of intergenerational financial vulnerability increases health disparities as families face a lack of financial resources and prolonged exposure to emotional stressors.

4.1.2 Deportations and detentions

Studies have consistently shown the severe emotional impacts that the removal of a father due to deportations and detentions has on the women and children left behind (Harrigan, Koh, and Amirrudin 2017; Artiga and

Lyons 2018). In this study, women experiencing the deportation or detention of relatives describe how they experienced sadness, worry, uncertainty,
fear, and desperation, among others. Like incarceration, these emotions
compound with new emotional and financial family responsibilities, leading
to extreme stress, anxiety, and depression.

Feelings of being overwhelmed and sad, along with financial burdens, are
expressed by the participants. As this female participant, 29 years old, who
identifies as Latina and whose uncle was deported 12 years ago, expressed:
*'Sadness that we are apart, helplessness that I cannot change the situation, I feel over-
whelmed.'* For this participant, an additional burden beyond being separated
is the responsibility of sending him money, as she noted, *'Financially helping
my uncle'* has become a new responsibility for her family. In this case, and
despite the deportation that occurred 12 years ago, the emotional toll
remains as they continue to support her uncle, a situation that cannot be
changed. The testimony not only describes the emotional and financial toll
deportation has on her family, but also stresses its intergenerational impacts,
as her niece is directly affected by the financial burden caused by her uncle's
deportation.

Desperation and the urgent need for family reunification are additional
emotions expressed by these participants, along with the emotional weight
of supporting individuals who are detained or living abroad, as this female
participant, 26 years old, who identified as undocumented, described *'I am
currently on depression medication because, after many years of living in the USA on my
own, I saved enough money to afford a "coyote" to bring my two younger brothers with
me, but the outcome was not what we expected. One of my brothers is detained, and the
other was deported. I miss my family, and I cannot do anything about it at this time.'*
Moreover, the failure of her efforts to reunite her family has had a profound
psychological impact, contributing to her depression and other mental
health issues such as anxiety and feelings of helplessness. For this participant, experiencing both detention and deportation within her family, along
with the need to support her relatives in Mexico, is deeply overwhelming,
as she stated, *"I have to fight to get my brother out of the detention center as soon as
possible and continue supporting my parents in my country.'* For this female partici-

pant, the situation is even more complicated since she cannot travel abroad due to her undocumented status.

Fear is another emotion that shapes individuals lives and health outcomes (Matthew and Brodersen 2018). One participant, a 38-year-old woman who identifies as American Indian, expressed that the detention and eventual deportation of her cousin eight years ago had a tremendous effect on her. She explained that these events made it difficult for her to focus on school, as she was constantly *'worried about deportation or harassment.'* She added, *'When you are so heavily preoccupied mentally, worrying about other people, you do not have the mental capacity to study to your best ability.'* As scholars have noted, the fear of deportation extends beyond the individual directly affected, translating to other relatives and making daily life activities more challenging (Vargas, Sanchez, and Juárez 2017).

Stress, depression, and anxiety are also reported outcomes by participants experiencing deportations and detentions arising from fear, uncertainty, and significant financial and emotional responsibilities. One female participant, 34 years old, stated, *'As a mother of a 4-year-old son with autism and with my husband not being present, it has been very stressful emotionally and financially.'* Another participant, 22 years old, shared the overwhelming emotions she experiences due to her father's and uncles' deportations: *There are a lot of issues—financial troubles, emotional stress, early signs of anxiety in the toddlers in the family, and a lack of belonging.'* As previously noted, it can be challenging to separate the complex interplay of emotions, responsibilities, and health outcomes such as stress, depression, and anxiety. However, it is essential to recognize that these emotions often emerge in contexts where families are already vulnerable, and the additional burdens significantly intensify their health experiences.

As described, events such as incarcerations, deportations, and detentions exacerbate women's mental health issues, leading to an overwhelming emotional toll also impacting their ability to manage daily life. In some cases, we observe extreme outcomes, such as familial suicidal ideation or the need for depression medication, which emphasize the severity of these emotions and their profound impact on women's health. Moreover, the relocation of financial resources—such as diverting money to support incarcerated, detained, or deported family members—can have negative impacts since it can limit their ability to afford food, healthcare, and housing, directly affecting their physical and mental health.

Summary

Deportations, detentions, and incarcerations act as significant social determinants of health, particularly for women in vulnerable and financially unstable communities. These women often live in environments marked by fear and stigma, where stress is already a constant factor (Genn, 2019). Growing up and living in these stressful conditions increases their susceptibility to illness (Genn, 2019). In addition to these challenges, after deportations, detentions, or incarcerations, women experience overwhelming stress and anxiety, compounded by severe financial burdens, all of which contribute to negative physical and mental health.

4.2 Deportations, detentions, and incarcerations as social determinants of health for men

The literature has consistently shown that more men than women are removed from their households due to deportations, detentions and incarcerations (Golash-Boza and Hondagneu-Sotelo 2013; Christian and Thomas 2009), with women often being the ones left behind, suffering both emotionally and financially. However, in this study, we found that many men can also experience familial deportation, detention, or incarceration. Therefore, it is important to try to understand what are some emotional and financial burdens that men experience, and how these emotional and financial burdens could potentially affect their health. In this regard, findings indicate that men who experience familial detention, deportation, or incarceration face a range of emotions that affect their mental and physical health. In addition to financial burdens, many men must assume caregiver roles, mature more quickly, and become the heads of their households. These emotional and financial pressures can ultimately lead to negative health outcomes for men.

4.2.1 Incarcerations

The incarceration of a relative leads to significant emotional and financial burdens (Arditti, 2012; Ceciliano-Navarro & Golash-Boza, 2021). In this study, male participants recount how their families were impacted both emotionally and financially, explaining how the incarceration led to increased responsibilities, shifts in family dynamics, and financial strain.

For example, one participant, a 29-year-old man whose uncle was incarcerated eight years ago, stated, *'There was less help, therefore more responsibilities, like looking after extended family.'* Another participant, a 35-year-old man whose brother was incarcerated two years ago, said, *'More was added to my plate,'* and later explained that even after his brother's release, they struggled to return to normal life as his brother faced challenges in finding a job.

The financial dimension was also emphasized by a 21-year-old participant whose father was incarcerated for 15 years: *'Only having one income is just always hard,'* he shared, adding that his father still struggles to find stable, suitable employment: *'Definitely him getting a GOOD job—one free of so much labor—but it's all they'll accept.'* These testimonies illustrate how incarceration profoundly impacts families on both emotional and financial levels, often with long-lasting effects.

Financial burdens as the one mentioned before, can have very negative impacts on families, being one of them housing instability (Blankenship et al. 2023). For scholars' housing vulnerability after incarceration can also lead to different health outcomes such as elevated stress, anxiety, and depression, which may exacerbate preexisting health conditions or contribute to the development of new ones (Wildeman 2014, Blankenship et al. 2023). Furthermore, unstable housing makes it difficult to maintain consistent access to healthcare, adhere to medical treatments, or manage chronic conditions (Blankenship et al., 2023). Housing vulnerability also brings emotional and financial burdens, such as being forced to relocate or remain in a smaller space with extended family, which increases family stress. This environment can disconnect young individuals from a sense of home, potentially driving them toward activities that may be harmful or unsafe, therefore, affecting their overall health. As described by one participant, now 21 years old, the impact of his father's incarceration was profound. He recalls, *'It cut off the main source of income, so we were forced to sell our house and move away,'* additionally, he remember how the event of detention of his father occurred, when he was only 5 years old *'The hardest part was seeing the police drag my father away from the house and take him to jail. I had to witness that entire scene.'* Another participant, a 20-year-old male whose mother was incarcerated, explained how the tense home environment made him more prone to engaging in escapist behaviors: *'It just created a stressful environment, making me more likely to escape through other activities.'* Similarly, a 45-year-old male participant reflected on how his father's incarceration, combined with a loss of income, resulted in housing instability: *'We couldn't afford a good place to live.'* These testimonies show the emotional and behavioral impacts of incarceration on men, particularly how housing instability can create a sense of disconnection or a lack of belonging. This sense of displacement may lead individuals to engage in harmful activities, either because of the unfamiliar environments they are forced to move into or due to the need to seek out communities or groups where they feel they can belong.

Stigma related to incarceration has been extensively reported in the literature (Shaw 2023; Schnittker and John 2007; Moran 2012). This stigma is not only experienced by the person incarcerated, but it also extends to their families and communities (Moran 2012). In this regard, when men describe how they feel regarding the removal of a relative due to incarcerations, they describe emotions such as sadness, sorrow, fear, disappointment, or even shame. Recognizing all these different emotions is vital since they allow us to understand health related outcomes. For example, when individuals experience shame, it can lead to several negative health outcomes. Shame is also closely related to stigma, and both stigma and shame can lead to social isolation, and social isolation is greatly related to health outcomes (Holt-Lunstad and Steptoe 2022). For this participant, 25 years old, who identifies as Hispanic expressed feeling deep shame regarding his father's incarceration, which occurred a couple of years ago. He shared, *'The main emotional impact is the fear and shame that comes with having to admit that a family member was in jail.'* In addition to these emotions, he also recalled the financial burden he faced: *'As the eldest, I had to contribute more of my earnings to help support the family.'* The emotional and financial burdens described by this participant can have several significant impacts on his health, particularly as he struggles to cope with societal stigma and the pressure to support his family financially. Emotions such as shame and isolation are crucial in discussions of health, as these feelings can lead to social withdrawal, increased stress, and anxiety. This, in turn, may result in unhealthy coping mechanisms, such as substance use or avoidance behaviors (Schnittker & John, 2007).

Men experiencing the incarceration of relatives face a variety of emotional and financial burdens, all of which can lead to stress, anxiety, and isolation. This is especially significant as these men often belong to already stigmatized communities. As some have expressed, the incarcerations only add more stress to their already complex circumstances.

4.2.2 Deportations and detentions

Most of the literature focuses on the negative emotional impacts of deportations on children and teenagers experiencing the removal of a relative (Ceciliano-Navarro and Golash-Boza 2021; Artiga and Lyons 2018). However, in this study, we rely on accounts from adults who have experienced the removal of a family member due to deportation or detention. As we will describe, emotional and financial burdens intertwined to create intense stress or anxiety. The narratives of these events are relevant, considering the early age at which they occurred and the long-lasting impact they have on many individuals.

Uncertainty and the need to grow up quickly are common themes in the testimonies shared by participants in this study. For example, a 20-year-old participant, who is a citizen and whose father was deported three years ago, shared, *'Missing him. Not knowing if he's okay. Not sure what to do next'.* This young man's primary concern is his father's well-being and the possibility of reuniting with him: *'I'm stressed about whether I'll see him again.'* On top of these emotions, he also faces new responsibilities, stating, *'I have to be the man of the house.'* As we can observe, young men experience many burdens after deportation. The uncertainty about the future, fear, and new responsibilities compounds and negatively affects his health.

The suppression of emotions, along with new roles and financial responsibilities, compounds the impacts of deportations on the participants in this study. For example, as this participant, a 21-year-old U.S. citizen who experienced his father's deportation 10 years ago *"I had to struggle to become independent at such a young age. To stand up and become the "man of the house" and be strong for the others. To not cry, even though I wanted to'* (Male, 21 years old, father deported). He also described how his mother had to find a job to support the family: *"My mom had to find a job and support us. It was not the same but we had to find ways to support each other."* This participant later reflected on how he missed his childhood due to his father's deportation: *'Instead of enjoying our childhood and having fun, we were selling anything we could just to make a dime. Saturdays weren't free days for us. We had to grow up, while other kids our age were going on trips and having fun.'* His testimony illustrates how he had to become independent at an early age, supporting his household while suppressing his emotions. These accounts reflect that, despite the events occurring years ago, many emotions—such as resentment—persist. As mentioned earlier, it is crucial to recognize these feelings and, more importantly, to understand how they impact individuals' health in both the short and long term.

Severe financial strain is commonly reported by participants, particularly when family members are detained, whether due to bail payments or the need to support female relatives left behind. Understanding how young men use their savings to support relatives can lead to feelings of guilt and obligation, resulting in emotional distress and anxiety about future financial stability. As one participant expressed, *"It was difficult to pay bail and then legal fees for my brother, I helped pay bail with the money I had saved up"* (Male, 23 years old, brother detained 4 years ago). Another participant said, *"I used some of my savings to help my aunt financially"* (Male, 22 years old, uncle detained one year ago). Both testimonies help to comprehend the intergenerational financial impacts and how the future of young individuals can be compromised by allocating their own resources. This is particularly significant during youth because it can shape their long-term financial stability and opportunities. Additionally, it seems that all these situations are often normalized, but they can have severe emotional and financial impacts. While it may seem routine to make these financial efforts, they can create strain, obligation, and anger, potentially leading to other negative behavioral consequences.

Stress, depression and feeling drained are among the most prominent emotions reported by participants, as this 19-year-old male whose father was detained and later deported, expressed *'It was very difficult seeing my father be deported; it resulted in me falling into depression and anxiety'* (Male, 19 years old. Father detained and later deported). A third participant, who is 26 years old, and who states that is a DACA recipient, emphasized the emotional challenges, stating that *'The most difficult part for me is the emotional struggle. I miss her very much, and sometimes I feel emotionally drained because of that'* (Male, 26 years old. Mother deported). These testimonies show both physical and mental health are profoundly affected by the stress, trauma, and emotional weight of family separation and the burdens that follow. Finally, another participant, a 35-year-old whose uncle was deported, stated, *"Stress and depression were some of the emotional impacts I had to endure during this difficult time."* For him, even though the deportation occurred five years ago, the situation remains troubling. He explained, *"The hardest experience is knowing that if they decide to come back, they could face federal jail time. It is a dangerous situation, whether staying or returning."* The emotional impacts manifest as constant worry and stress following deportations, as families are concerned about the safety of their relatives abroad and the potential negative consequences if those relatives attempt to return (Brotherton and Barrios 2011; Golash-Boza 2017).

As noted, events such as deportations and detentions significantly increase the mental and physical health challenges faced by men. The added responsibilities of managing a household, along with the need to provide financial support and access substantial savings, can create considerable anxiety and stress, leaving them feeling that their financial future is at risk.

Summary

Deportations, detentions, and incarcerations function as critical social determinants of health, particularly for men in economically unstable and at-risk communities. Living in environments marked by fear and stigma, these individuals often endure chronic stress, making them more vulnerable to health issues (Genn 2019). The removal of a loved one amplifies their stress and anxiety, increasing the risk of illness and negative health outcomes. Additionally, men often face greater challenges in accessing mental and physical health resources (Lynch, Long, and Moorhead 2018).

Discussion

Deportations, detentions, and incarcerations as social determinants of health

Entangled Systems. Deportations, detentions, and incarcerations functions as social determinants of health and vulnerable communities and impacting particularly mixed status families. Due to the mixed composition of many families—including both U.S. citizens and undocumented immigrants—vulnerable communities are often simultaneously exposed to the immigration and criminal justice systems. In these contexts, undocumented individuals may encounter the criminal legal system through their citizen relatives, while U.S. citizens can be questioned or impacted by immigration enforcement due to the undocumented status of family members. As a result, entire families and communities face overlapping forms of surveillance, scrutiny, and vulnerability.

Compounded impacts. First, individuals in these communities who experience the removal of a relative due to deportations, detentions or incarcerations often have less disposable income to allocate to their health needs since a significant portion of their financial resources is redirected toward supporting not only their immediate families but also extended family members and those who have been deported, detained, or incarcerated, straining their ability to prioritize healthcare. *Second*, the emotional burden of having someone removed from the household, combined with the overload of new emotional and financial responsibilities, places individuals in a prolonged state of stress and anxiety. This chronic stress has significant health impacts, often leading to isolation, depression, reliance on

medication, and in some cases, suicidal ideation within the families. *Third,*
disruptions due to detentions, deportations and incarcerations go beyond
emotional and financial hardships, also affecting education and employment
prospects (Potochnick and Perreira 2010). As a result, individuals impacted
by these circumstances face difficulties in pursuing social mobility and
securing a stable income, which in turn restricts their financial stability and
access to essential healthcare services.

**Men versus women experiencing deportations, detentions,
and incarcerations.** The emotions experienced by men and women
when having a relative deported, detained, or incarcerated can be similar
with some nuances related to the nature of the event. However, the
health-related outcomes are similar, with stress and anxiety being present
in men and women. Gender influences the nature of emotions experienced
by men and women; however, the key difference that needs exploration is
the behavioral responses of men and women under extreme stress, anxiety,
or isolation. In the case of incarceration, men may express a tendency to
engage in certain behaviors related to their housing or home environment.
In contrast, when faced with deportations, men often feel compelled to
take on the role of provider and being the head of the household. In this
context, both men and women experiencing deportations and detentions
demonstrate a significant element of resilience that deserves attention.

Persistent financial and emotional burdens. Men and women
testimonies reveal that the emotional and financial burdens for these families
are long-lasting. Not only do families have to support themselves, but they
are also responsible for caring for extended family members left behind, as
well as providing for the incarcerated, detained, or deported relative. Even
if the relative returns after deportation, families continue to support them
as they live in the shadows and struggle to find employment. Similarly,
formerly incarcerated individuals face difficulties securing good-paying jobs,
requiring ongoing family assistance. As a result, the emotional and financial
burdens are permanent and persist over time.

Broad social and economic impacts. Due to intense stress and
anxiety, both men and women may struggle to maintain employment or

achieve career advancement, resulting in reduced lifetime earnings. Mental health challenges can also lead to indirect costs related to lost productivity, including decreased workplace performance, absenteeism, and long-term disability.

Conclusions

Deportations, detentions, and incarcerations function as social determinants of health by impoverishing already vulnerable families and communities. Men and women from vulnerable communities and mixed status families live under extreme stress and anxiety, which hinders their ability to succeed both professionally and academically, therefore increasing poverty and contributing to negative health outcomes.

Future research should explore deeper into access to healthcare, particularly for men experiencing mental health challenges and isolation. In a city like Houston, accessing healthcare can present significant challenges. Moreover, it is crucial to explore the impacts of severe stress on young individuals, especially those in education, as it can limit their ability to stay in school and therefore affect their prospects, such as career opportunities and income. Similarly, the effects of stress on working individuals deserve attention, as extreme stress, anxiety, or fear can limit their ability to work effectively.

Some limitations of this study relate to the sensitive nature of the topics addressed. Individuals experiencing deportations, detentions, and incarcerations often face stigma and fear, which may explain why some participants omitted information regarding their legal status, even though the survey was anonymous. Additionally, since the survey was designed to be completed via a link on a phone, iPad, or laptop, it may have excluded individuals from certain socioeconomic backgrounds who lack access to these devices. However, it is important to recognize that those with access to technology or specific socioeconomic and immigration statuses have also been impacted by these events.

Policy recommendations

At the Federal-Level Interventions it is important to expand access to trauma-informed care by funding community clinics, schools, and reentry programs that serve immigrant and formerly incarcerated populations, as well as develop and support reintegration programs that help individuals and families reconnect with social institutions such as schools, workplaces, and faith communities to rebuild trust and promote long-term well-being.

At the State and Local-Level Interventions, it is vital to support and implement city- and state-level policies (e.g., sanctuary policies, non-cooperation ordinances) that reduce collaboration between local law enforcement and immigration authorities. These efforts can help lower fear and increase public trust in social services. Finally, it is relevant to fund and expand local community-based organizations that provide services—legal aid, employment support, housing referrals, and language access—especially in neighborhoods with high rates of detention, deportation, and incarceration.

Acknowledgment

I would like to thank the Organized Research and Creative Activities (ORCA) Program at the University of Houston–Downtown for awarding a course release that enabled the completion of this research and manuscript.

Works Cited

Addison, Helena A, Therese S Richmond, Lisa M Lewis, and Sara Jacoby. 2022. "Mental health outcomes in formerly incarcerated Black men: A systematic mixed studies review." *Journal of advanced nursing* 78 (7): 1851-1869.

Akresh, Ilana Redstone. 2009. "Health service utilization among immigrants to the United States." *Population Research and Policy Review* 28: 795-815.

Arditti, Joyce A. 2012. "Child trauma within the context of parental incarceration: A family process perspective." *Journal of Family Theory & Review* 4 (3): 181-219.

Artiga, Samantha, and Barbara Lyons. 2018. "Family consequences of detention/deportation: effects on finances, health, and well-being." *San Francisco, CA:*

Henry J. Kaiser Family Foundation.

Asad, Asad L, and Matthew Clair. 2018. "Racialized legal status as a social determinant of health." *Social science & medicine* 199: 19-28.

Axios. "Texas Holds Most Immigration Detainees in the U.S." *Axios Houston*, March 11, 2025. https://www.axios.com/local/houston/2025/03/11/texas-immigration-detainees-houston

Baillargeon, Jacques, Sandra A Black, John Pulvino, and Kim Dunn. 2000. "The disease profile of Texas prison inmates." *Annals of epidemiology* 10 (2): 74-80.

Blankenship, Kim M, Alana Rosenberg, Penelope Schlesinger, Allison K Groves, and Danya E Keene. 2023. "Structural racism, the social determination of health, and health inequities: The intersecting impacts of housing and mass incarceration." *American journal of public health* 113 (S1): S58-S64.

Bomysoad, Rachel N, and Lori A Francis. 2022. "Associations between parental incarceration and youth mental health conditions: The mitigating effects of adolescent resilience and positive coping strategies." *Current Psychology* 41 (12): 8746-8757.

Brabeck, Kalina M, M Brinton Lykes, and Rachel Hershberg. 2011. "Framing immigration to and deportation from the United States: Guatemalan and Salvadoran families make meaning of their experiences." *Community, Work & Family* 14 (3): 275-296.

Brotherton, David, and Luis Barrios. 2011. *Banished to the homeland: Dominican deportees and their stories of exile.* Columbia University Press.

Bruns, Angela. 2019. "The third shift: Multiple job holding and the incarceration of women's partners." *Social Science Research* 80: 202-215.

Burris, Scott. 2011. "Law in a social determinants strategy: a public health law research perspective." *Public health reports* 126 (3_suppl): 22-27.

Cabral, Jacqueline, and Adolfo G Cuevas. 2020. "Health inequities among Latinos/Hispanics: Documentation status as a determinant of health." *Journal of racial and ethnic health disparities* 7 (5): 874-879.

Castañeda, Heide, Seth M Holmes, Daniel S Madrigal, Maria-Elena DeTrinidad Young, Naomi Beyeler, and James Quesada. 2015. "Immigration as a social determinant of health." *Annual review of public health* 36 (1): 375-392.

Ceciliano-Navarro, Yajaira, and Tanya Maria Golash-Boza. 2021. "'Trauma makes you grow up quicker': The financial & emotional burdens of deportation & incarceration." *Daedalus* 150 (2): 165-179.

Ceciliano-Navarro, Yajaira, and Tanya Golash-Boza. 2021. "Social, Human and Positive Psychological Capital in the Labour Market Re-integration of People Deported to the Dominican Republic." *International Migration* 59 (2): 221-238.

Christian, Johnna, and Shenique S Thomas. 2009. "Examining the intersections of race, gender, and mass imprisonment." *Journal of Ethnicity in Criminal Justice* 7 (1): 69-84.

Coifman, Karin G, Jessica J Flynn, and Lavinia A Pinto. 2016. "When context matters: Negative emotions predict psychological health and adjustment." *Motivation and Emotion* 40: 602-624.

Colen, Cynthia G, Kelsey J Drotning, Liana C Sayer, and Bruce Link. 2024. "A matter of time: Racialized time and the production of health disparities." *Journal of Health and Social Behavior* 65 (1): 126-140.

Davis, Cierria. 2025. "Recidivism, Reentry, and Integration in the Texas Criminal Justice System." Walden University.

Dirkzwager, Anja JE, Robert Verheij, Paul Nieuwbeerta, and Peter Groenewegen. 2021. "Mental and physical health problems before and after detention: a matched cohort study." *The Lancet Regional Health–Europe* 8.

Dolan, Brian, and George Rutherford. 2020. "How history of medicine helps us understand COVID-19 challenges." *Public Health Reports* 135 (6): 717-720.

Dreby, Joanna. 2012. "The burden of deportation on children in Mexican immigrant families." *Journal of Marriage and Family* 74 (4): 829-845.

Feldman, Pamela J, Sheldon Cohen, Stephen J Lepore, Karen A Matthews, Thomas W Kamarck, and Anna L Marsland. 1999. "Negative emotions and acute physiological responses to stress." *Annals of Behavioral Medicine* 21: 216-222.

Filges, Trine, Edith Montgomery, Marianne Kastrup, and Anne-Marie Klint Jørgensen. 2015. "The impact of detention on the health of asylum seekers: a systematic review." *Campbell Systematic Reviews* 11 (1): 1-104.

García, San Juanita. 2018. "Living a deportation threat: Anticipatory stressors confronted by undocumented Mexican immigrant women." *Race and Social*

Problems 10: 221-234.

Garcini, Luz M, German Cadenas, Melanie M Domenech Rodríguez, Alfonso
    Mercado, Liliana Campos, Cristina Abraham, Michelle Silva, and Manuel
    Paris. 2022. "Lessons learned from undocumented Latinx immigrants:
    How to build resilience and overcome distress in the face of adversity."
    Psychological services 19 (S1): 62.

Genn, Hazel. 2019. "When law is good for your health: mitigating the social deter-
    minants of health through access to justice." *Current Legal Problems* 72 (1):
    159-202.

Gilman, Denise, and Luis A Romero. 2018. "Immigration Detention, Inc." *Journal
    on Migration and Human Security* 6 (2): 145-160.

Golash-Boza, Tanya. 2017. "Structural racism, criminalization, and pathways to
    deportation for Dominican and Jamaican men in the United States." *Social
    Justice* 44 (2-3 (148): 137-162.

Golash-Boza, Tanya, Michael_David Aquino, and Yajaira Ceciliano-Navarro.
    2024. "Returning from Prison to a Changed City: How Does Gentrifi-
    cation Shape the Employment and Housing Opportunities of Returning
    Citizens?" *Social Currents*.

Golash-Boza, Tanya, and Pierrette Hondagneu-Sotelo. 2013. "Latino immigrant
    men and the deportation crisis: A gendered racial removal program." *Lati-
    no Studies* 11: 271-292.

Golash-Boza, Tanya, and Yajaira Ceciliano Navarro. 2018. *"My Whole Life is in
    the USA:" Dominican Deportees' Experiences of Isolation, Precarity, and Resilience.*
    Springer.

——. 2020. "Reintegration nach Abschiebung. Erfahrungen von aus den USA abges-
    chobenen Dominikanern und Brasilianern." *PERIPHERIE–Politik• Ökono-
    mie• Kultur* 39 (156): 7-8.

Goodman, Adam. 2020. *The deportation machine: America's long history of expelling immi-
    grants.* Princeton University Press.

Gostin, Lawrence O, John T Monahan, Jenny Kaldor, Mary DeBartolo, Eric A
    Friedman, Katie Gottschalk, Susan C Kim, Ala Alwan, Agnes Binagwaho,
    and Gian Luca Burci. 2019. "The legal determinants of health: harnessing
    the power of law for global health and sustainable development." *The lancet*

393 (10183): 1857-1910.

Hacker, Karen, Maria Anies, Barbara L Folb, and Leah Zallman. 2015. "Barriers to health care for undocumented immigrants: a literature review." *Risk management and healthcare policy*: 175-183.

Hamilton, Erin R, Pedro P Orraca-Romano, and Eunice Vargas Valle. 2023. "Legal status, deportation, and the health of returned migrants from the USA to Mexico." *Population Research and Policy Review* 42 (2): 16.

Harrigan, Nicholas M, Chiu Yee Koh, and Amirah Amirrudin. 2017. "Threat of deportation as proximal social determinant of mental health amongst migrant workers." *Journal of immigrant and minority health* 19: 511-522.

Harris, Casey T, Darrell Steffensmeier, Jeffrey T Ulmer, and Noah Painter-Davis. 2009. "Are Blacks and Hispanics disproportionately incarcerated relative to their arrests? Racial and ethnic disproportionality between arrest and incarceration." *Race and social problems* 1: 187-199.

Hatzenbuehler, Mark L, Jo C Phelan, and Bruce G Link. 2013. "Stigma as a fundamental cause of population health inequalities." *American journal of public health* 103 (5): 813-821.

Hinton, Elizabeth, LaShae Henderson, and Cindy Reed. 2018. "An unjust burden: The disparate treatment of Black Americans in the criminal justice system." *Vera Institute of Justice* 1 (1): 1-20.

Holt-Lunstad, Julianne, and Andrew Steptoe. 2022. "Social isolation: An underappreciated determinant of physical health." *Current opinion in psychology* 43: 232-237.

Houston Chronicle. "Texas Has the Most Unauthorized Immigrants in the U.S. Here's Where They Live." *Houston Chronicle Projects*, 2025. https://www.houstonchronicle.com/projects/2025/texas-illegal-unauthorized-immigrant-counts/

Houston Landing. "'Worst Nightmare of My Life': Solitary Confinement Rises at Houston-Area ICE Detention Center." *Houston Landing*, October 3, 2023. https://houstonlanding.org/worst-nightmare-of-my-life-solitary-confinement-rises-at-houston-area-ice-detention-center/

Kretsedemas, Philip, and David C Brotherton. 2018. *Immigration policy in the age of punishment: detention, deportation, and border control.* Columbia University Press.

Lipsitz, George. 2011. "In an avalanche every snowflake pleads not guilty: The collateral consequences of mass incarceration and impediments to women's fair housing rights." *Ucla L. Rev.* 59: 1746.

Lopez, Leo, Louis H Hart, and Mitchell H Katz. 2021. "Racial and ethnic health disparities related to COVID-19." *Jama* 325 (8): 719-720.

Lovato, Kristina, and Laura S Abrams. 2021. "Enforced separations: A qualitative examination of how Latinx families cope with family disruption following the deportation of a parent." *Families in society* 102 (1): 33-49.

Massoglia, Michael, and William Alex Pridemore. 2015. "Incarceration and health." *Annual review of sociology* 41 (1): 291-310.

Matthew, Pravin, and Donka Mirtcheva Brodersen. 2018. "Income inequality and health outcomes in the United States: An empirical analysis." *The Social Science Journal* 55 (4): 432-442.

McKay, Tasseli, Justin Landwehr, Christine Lindquist, Rose Feinberg, Megan Comfort, Julia Cohen, and Anupa Bir. 2018. "Intimate partner violence in couples navigating incarceration and reentry." *Journal of Offender Rehabilitation* 57 (5): 273-293.

Migration Policy Institute. *Houston's Changing Immigration Landscape: A Report on Local Trends and Asylum Backlogs.* August 2023. https://www.migrationpolicy.org/sites/default/files/publications/mpi_houston-report-2023_final.pdf

Moran, Dominique. 2012. "Prisoner reintegration and the stigma of prison time inscribed on the body." *Punishment & Society* 14 (5): 564-583.

Nosrati, Elias, Jacob Kang-Brown, Michael Ash, Martin McKee, Michael Marmot, and Lawrence P King. 2021. "Incarceration and mortality in the United States." *SSM-Population Health* 15: 100827.

Nowotny, Kathryn M, and Anastasiia Kuptsevych-Timmer. 2018. "Health and justice: framing incarceration as a social determinant of health for Black men in the United States." *Sociology Compass* 12 (3): e12566.

Parmet, Wendy E. 2019. "Immigration law as a social determinant of health." *Temp. L. Rev.* 92: 931.

Patler, Caitlin, and Tanya Maria Golash-Boza. 2017. "The fiscal and human costs of immigrant detention and deportation in the United States." *Sociology Compass* 11 (11): e12536.

Pedroza, Juan Manuel. 2022. "Housing Instability in an Era of Mass Deportations." *Population Research and Policy Review* 41 (6): 2645-2681.

Pettit, Becky, and Carmen Gutierrez. 2018. "Mass incarceration and racial inequality." *American journal of economics and sociology* 77 (3-4): 1153-1182.

Pettit, Becky, and Bruce Western. 2004. "Mass imprisonment and the life course: Race and class inequality in US incarceration." *American sociological review* 69 (2): 151-169.

Pinedo, M, J Beltrán-Girón, Z Correa, and C Valdez. 2021. "A qualitative view of migration-related stressors on the mental health of Latinx Americans in the current sociopolitical climate of hostility towards migrants." *Journal of immigrant and minority health* 23 (5): 1053-1064.

Potochnick, Stephanie R, and Krista M Perreira. 2010. "Depression and anxiety among first-generation immigrant Latino youth: key correlates and implications for future research." *The Journal of nervous and mental disease* 198 (7): 470-477.

Rodriguez, Nancy, and Jillian J Turanovic. 2018. "Impact of incarceration on families and communities." *The Oxford Handbook of Prisons and Imprisonment*: 189-201.

Rotter, Merrill, and Michael Compton. 2022. "Criminal legal involvement: A cause and consequence of social determinants of health." *Psychiatric services* 73 (1): 108-111.

Saadi, Altaf, Maria-Elena De Trinidad Young, Caitlin Patler, Jeremias Leonel Estrada, and Homer Venters. 2020. "Understanding US immigration detention: reaffirming rights and addressing social-structural determinants of health." *Health and Human Rights* 22 (1): 187.

Safety and Justice Challenge. (2023). *Harris County Jail Fact Sheet*. Retrieved from https://safetyandjusticechallenge.org

Schenker, Marc. 2008. Work-related injuries among immigrants: a growing global health disparity. BMJ Publishing Group Ltd.

Schnittker, Jason, and Andrea John. 2007. "Enduring stigma: The long-term effects of incarceration on health." *Journal of health and social behavior* 48 (2): 115-130.

Shaw, Marcus. 2023. "Financial strain, the transference of stigma, and residential instability: A qualitative analysis of the long-term effects of parental incarceration." *Family Relations* 72 (4): 1773-1789.

Sidamon-Eristoff, Anne Elizabeth, Emily M Cohodes, Dylan G Gee, and Catherine Jensen Peña. 2022. "Trauma exposure and mental health outcomes among Central American and Mexican children held in immigration detention at the United States–Mexico border." *Developmental Psychobiology* 64 (1): e22227.

Stronks, Karien, Brigit Toebes, Aart Hendriks, Umar Ikram, and Sridhar Venkatapuram. 2016. "Social justice and human rights as a framework for addressing social determinants of health." *World Health Organization.*

Thomson, Michael. 2022. "Legal determinants of health." *Medical Law Review* 30 (4): 610-634. https://www.ncbi.nlm.nih.gov/pmc/articles/PMC9384623/pdf/fwac025.pdf.

Tosh, Sarah R, Ulla D Berg, and Kenneth Sebastian León. 2021. "Migrant detention and COVID-19: pandemic responses in four New Jersey detention centers." *Journal on Migration and Human Security* 9 (1): 44-62.

U.S. Immigration and Customs Enforcement (ICE). "ICE Houston Deports 174 Criminal Aliens to Mexico in 2 Weeks, Who Account for 610 Criminal Convictions." *ICE News Releases*, March 28, 2025. https://www.ice.gov/news/releases/ice-houston-deports-174-criminal-aliens-mexico-2-weeks--who-account-610-criminal

Vargas, Edward D, Gabriel R Sanchez, and Melina Juárez. 2017. "Fear by association: perceptions of anti-immigrant policy and health outcomes." *Journal of health politics, policy and law* 42 (3): 459-483.

Wallace, Steven P, Maria-Elena De Trinidad Young, Michael A Rodríguez, and Claire D Brindis. 2019. "A social determinants framework identifying state-level immigrant policies and their influence on health." *SSM-population health* 7: 100316.

Weber, Rosa, and Douglas S Massey. 2023. "Assessing the Effect of Increased Deportations on Mexican Migrants' Remittances and Savings Brought Home." *Population Research and Policy Review* 42 (2): 24.

Wildeman, Christopher, Alyssa W Goldman, and Kristin Turney. 2018. "Parental incarceration and child health in the United States." *Epidemiologic reviews* 40

(1): 146-156.

Williams, David R, and Selina A Mohammed. 2009. "Discrimination and racial disparities in health: evidence and needed research." *Journal of behavioral medicine* 32: 20-47.

Yamanis, Thespina J, Ana María del Río-González, Laura Rapoport, Christopher Norton, Cristiana Little, Suyanna Linhales Barker, and India J Ornelas. 2021. "Understanding fear of deportation and its impact on healthcare access among immigrant Latinx men who have sex with men." In *Sexual and gender minority health*, 103-131. Emerald Publishing Limited.

4

Investigational New Drugs and IRB Liability: How a University Committee on Human Experimentation Navigated the Laws and Regulations Around Prison Research in the Early 1970s

Brian Dolan, PhD*

Abstract

Several policies and regulations were established in the 1960s to help protect human subjects in biomedical research. One major development was the requirement of institutional review boards (or equivalent committees) to review research protocols that received federal funding. Often celebrated as an advance in the development of bioethics, it proved easier to establish a review committee than to agree on what exactly its authority was to disapprove or otherwise intervene with a study design. The declaration of principles, guidelines, and regulations, pointed in the direction of protecting research participants' rights, but the lack of definition of terms and apparent legal loopholes often caused confusion on behalf of ethics committee members. This became a critical matter in the 1970s when research participants who claimed their rights were violated sued university review committees for negligence, in particular when investigational new drugs (INDs) were used in experiments. This article focuses on how one institutional review board – established at the University of California, San Francisco (UCSF) in 1971 – handled the task of defining "informed" in the assessment of offering consent, and also struggled to assess the risk put to human subjects when the investigators themselves did not know the risks, and even argued that the ingredients of the drugs they were working with were protected trade secrets.

* Department of Humanities and Social Sciences, University of California, San Francisco

Prelude: Two Cases to Consider

Case 1: At the second meeting of the newly established UCSF Committee on Human Experimentation (CHE) on October 21, 1971, Committee Chair Leslie Bennett read a letter he had received from John Bowers (dated August 17, 1971). Bowers was a Los Angeles attorney who worked with the National Legal Program on Health Problems of the Poor (est. 1969, now called National Health Law Program), an organization focused on "protecting the interests of inmates at California correctional institutions who volunteer to be subjects in investigations of new or experimental drugs." Bowers explained that he was representing a group "composed of fifteen Black, Chicano, and Caucasian former inmates, relatives of current inmates, and other persons concerned with the welfare of correctional populations."[1]

Bowers had learned about medical experiments conducted at the California Medical Facility (CMF), a prison hospital in Vacaville, about an hour north of San Francisco. He had sent inquiries about this research to Dr. John E. Gorman, Medical Director of California Department of Corrections, to Dr. R. Curtis Morris, Jr., a physician at UCSF and chair of the previous *ad hoc* committee on human experimentation, and eventually to Dr. Leslie Bennett, as Chair of the reformed UCSF Senate Committee on Human Experimentation.[2]

In his correspondence, Bowers included lists of experiments that were conducted by UCSF faculty at CMF. The UCSF archive does not have the list that Bowers shared, but the archive does have a list of studies that was subsequently provided to the committee by Dr. Henry Elliott, a physician at UC Irvine and Chair of the Board of Directors of the Solano Institute for Medical and Psychiatric Research (SIMPR), an organization established within the prison hospital to oversee non-therapeutic human experimentation at CMF.

Bowers asked CHE chair Leslie Bennett what the standards of ethics review were at UCSF that would have been used to evaluate medical research projects involving human subjects. In a letter of reply dated

November 23, 1971, Bennett stated that, "The standards distributed by
Vice Chancellor Harper in September, 1966, to the best of my knowledge
still represent the official policy of this campus."[3] In addition, Bowers
wanted "copies of full protocols of all currently active experiments at
institutions administered by either the Department of Corrections or the
Department of Mental Hygiene in which UCSF Medical Center personnel
are involved." Bennett replied that because he was unaware of any "master
list" that would enable him to identify such protocols, it was an impractical
request but that, in compliance with the California Public Records Act,
Bowers was welcome to visit the campus and search through the records
himself.[4]

In a follow-up letter, Bowers sought to know whether the UCSF
committee had reviewed and approved the research conducted by UCSF
faculty at CMF. So memorable was this request that eight years after this
correspondence, Leslie Bennett, in a plenary address to a conference
on Institutional Review Boards (IRBs), reflected on this moment. He
remembered that Bowers "challenged the University of California, San
Francisco's alleged participation in the research carried out upon inmates in
the medical correctional facility at Vacaville." He said that Bowers "made
many demands. I might add that the exchange with Mr. Bowers and my
consultations with Mr. Arnold Leong and Mr. Dorinson of the General
Counsel's Office furthered very rapidly my education in certain aspects of
the law."[5] We will return to this case below.

Case 2: In 1968 Otis Clay, who was incarcerated at a federal prison in
Atlanta serving a ten-year sentence on narcotics charges, was transferred to
the Addiction Research Center – a laboratory of the National Institute of
Mental Health – in Lexington, Kentucky. He was told that by enrolling in a
drug research study at that facility he would have superior living conditions,
that he would receive payment for his participation, and that he would be
credited with "meritorious good time." He claimed also to have "heard"
that he would have access to narcotics.[6] As a subject of experimental
research, he was administered morphine, pentazocine, chlorpromazine,

and naltrexone. A week after being injected twice with naltrexone, in doses that he was assured were too small to cause harm, he suffered a severe heart attack and was hospitalized.

In 1971, he sued three doctors employed by the Public Health Service, the U.S. Surgeon General, the U.S. Attorney General, the Director of the Bureau of Prisons, and the U.S. Government, alleging "inhumane treatment" and also alleged improper experimental research protocol review owing to a conflict of interest because the principal investigator was also the director of the Addiction Research Center and a member of the institutional review board that approved the study. His case was heard before the Southern District Court of New York and was dismissed by the judge, who stated that "he believed that prisoners in general were capable of giving informed consent and that Mr. Clay in particular had been sufficiently informed about the risks of the research and gave his informed consent to the research."[7] However, the court later granted a motion to restore the case to the civil docket, and in 1974 an amended suit was filed by the American Civil Liberties Union under the aegis of their National Prison Project (established in 1972) on behalf of nine inmates at the Maryland House of Correction. At that facility, the individuals had been involved in a research program conducted by the Division of Infectious Diseases at the University of Maryland School of Medicine. This lawsuit included members of the University of Maryland's IRB, the president of the university, and the principal investigators of the study. Eventually, in 1979, Clay's complaint was dismissed by a court that disagreed that the experiments which allegedly harmed him were conducted in a "negligent and reckless" manner.[8] While other defendants continued to pursue damages for injuries to them caused by the principal investigators, "all aspects of the case involving the IRB and its chairman were dismissed."[9]

An Ethical Duty

In the time between the requests for institutional review records on behalf of the National Legal Program on Health Problems of the Poor in 1971 and the lawsuit filed by the ACLU's National Prison Project against the IRB members linked to prison research in 1974 (the two cases above), several legal cases had scrutinized the conduct of university ethics review committees. During these formative years of IRB history, it was becoming apparent that alleged disregard for the safety of human subjects in medical experimentation referred not only to the conduct of the researchers, but that members of the IRBs (or equivalent committees) could potentially be found negligent for allowing such abuses to occur.[10]

The increased concerns about the legal obligations of ethics review raised several questions among committee members about what exactly their responsibilities were in assessing proposed research projects. Moreover, there was lingering uncertainty about what authority committees had to ensure that the research complied with written proposals, or what authority they had to discontinue any research project that they disagreed with.[11]

The strong objection by researchers in the medical profession against what they saw as legislative encroachment on "the routine and accepted practice of medicine" and the application of skilled clinical judgment swayed ethics review toward the experimental research realm and away from therapeutic trials.[12] Yet, reviewing research projects in the experimental realm (where non-therapeutic interventions could be tested for commercial or other purposes) begged the question of how to assess the scientific merit, social benefit, or unforeseen risks involved in order to offer adequate protection of human subjects. As Alexander Capron, a University of Pennsylvania Professor of Law, opined in testimony to congress in 1973: "Researchers defend their work by pointing to the benefits they may turn up 'for society,' but it is doubtful that even with review by professional colleagues, they would have the proper capability or authority to weigh all the societal benefits against the costs or consequences involved in their research."[13]

Lofty assessments of what qualifies as research of value to society left much room for debate in institutional review committee meetings, but certain other matters for review, such as assuring informed consent, appeared to be more programmatic. That is, until the meaning of the terms "informed" and "consent" were deliberated.

It was long recognized that a fundamental tenet of ethical conduct in research was to obtain informed consent, an obligation enforced by law as established in Salgo[14] in 1957 with a revision of its scope in Natanson[15] in 1960. In 1966, William H. Stewart, Surgeon General of the U.S. Public Health Service, issued a memorandum which required securing informed consent for all extramural research supported by the Public Health Service, thus necessitating institutions to establish some form of mandatory ethics review committee.[16] In 1974, the National Research Act established the National Commission for the Protection of Human Subjects of Biomedical and Behavioral Research in part in response to testimony about experimental surgery, prison research, university-centered research abuses, the Tuskegee Syphilis Study, and genetic manipulation. Of particular concern to the drafters was that a research participant's consent be based on full disclosure, free of any form of coercion. Regarding subjects who were considered vulnerable to coercion, the Commission was asked to "identify the requirements for informed consent to participation in biomedical and behavioral research by children, prisoners, and the institutionalized mentally infirm."[17]

But until those "requirements" were submitted in a report by the Commission in 1978, institutional review committees remained uncertain about how to assess the appropriateness of research protocols involving vulnerable populations. The arrival of lawsuits against IRBs on behalf of prisoners claiming they had been coerced into research participation only heighten tensions among review members about their legal responsibilities.[18] Apprehension grew when, in 1978, the Commission's report [known as the Belmont Report] went as far as to say that, "IRB members may be personally liable to subjects and investigators for 'malpractice' or negligence in discharging their IRB functions."[19]

According to an evolving legal principle in this context, when one undertook to protect others by serving on an IRB, they must exercise reasonable care in carrying out their review. If a subject was injured during an experiment, that person could allege negligence by IRB members who assessed the risks of the proposed research. IRBs have faced multiple

high-profile lawsuits since the early 1970s, but these cases typically ended
with confidential settlements or without rulings on substantive issues. In
Robertson v. McGee, an Oklahoma court ultimately dismissed the case for
lack of subject-matter jurisdiction. However, before dismissal, the Office
for Human Research Protections criticized the IRB for inadequate ongoing
supervision during the clinical trial.[20] Nevertheless, legal commentators have
concluded that, "If IRBs are found legally negligent and IRB members are
named as individuals in the suit, they may possibly have to pay out of their
own pockets if ordered by the court or as part of a settlement. The IRB
may be joined as part of a hospital or university, in which case, the larger
entity would pay."[21]

Yet for a decade preceding the Belmont report – stemming at least from
the 1966 Public Health Service mandate of institutional review – IRBs
struggled with uncertainties about what competencies review members
should have in order to execute their duties. Consideration over the role of
IRB also extended to the legal obligation they had to perform their duties to
a "reasonable standard."[22]

A particularly prickly part of institutional reviews was determining
how to assess risk to the subject, and whether such risks were going to be
explained to the prospective participant adequately enough for them to be
informed in their consent. This became more complicated when investigational new drugs (INDs) were being tested, where the risks might not yet be
known, even by the investigator. As we will explore below, various loopholes
in the procedures for obtaining "investigational new drug" status placed a
barrier between what an investigator was legally bound to disclose and the
ability of an IRB to perform its duty to a "reasonable standard."

All too often, review committees looked to see if a form certifying
informed consent was present in a proposed protocol where the participant's
signature would indicate written consent. However, there was disagreement
about how detailed such a form should be. As critics noted, just looking
to see if a form existed might not be a reasonable standard of review.
The highly variable circumstances of each research project created mixed
sentiments about how informed consent could be obtained. In 1967, a legal

writer on informed consent practices declared that most researchers agreed "that highly legalistic or idealistic images of what 'ought to be' – i.e., of freely given and informed consent – can probably be satisfied through the routinization of consent forms but that the outcome of the medical-research situation itself, as a result of personality factors and subtle pressures that may operate as restrictions on free choice, may often disappoint ideals."[23] So where in the space between idealism and real-life situations did review committees operate?

As Laura Stark has shown in her study of early IRBs at the NIH Clinical Center, review boards in the 1970s often developed authority and precedent through localized deliberation and interpersonal dynamics more than through formal regulations.[24] In the case study presented here, we see that the UCSF Committee on Human Experimentation mirrored this pattern as it navigated uncertain jurisdiction over prison research, resisted deference to faculty authority, and struggled to define what counted as sufficient disclosure in contexts where even the investigators lacked key toxicological knowledge. Unlike Stark's NIH case, however, the UCSF committee sometimes faced the added barrier of regulatory opacity surrounding investigational new drugs, a feature that severely constrained the committee's ability to judge risk—especially in nontherapeutic prison-based trials.

What follows is a detailed examination of an institutional review committee who grappled with these issues. Specifically, the concerns were: whether risks were adequately explained to prospective participants; whether the consent was swayed by coercion; and whether there was any benefit to society or if the research was frivolous. We see in this case study that part of the challenge was getting investigators themselves to clarify matters of concern about the experiments they were proposing to conduct.

A Question of Assessing Risk

In August 1972 Dr. Julien Hoffman, UCSF Professor of Pediatrics and new chairman of the Committee on Human Experimentation, relayed to the committee a conversation he had with an author and investigative journalist named Jessica Mitford. Mitford had gained notoriety following the publication of her 1963 best-selling book *The American Way of Death*, an exposé of the funeral home industry which stimulated congressional hearings on unethical business practices involving the manipulation of grieving families. Mitford explained to Hoffman that she was now researching a new book "which will concern medical experimentation conducted on prisoners." She had collected information about experiments at California Medical Facility being conducted by UCSF faculty members that she wanted to share with the committee. Therefore, she accepted an invitation to attend the committee's meeting the following week.

From notes recorded in the minutes of that meeting, Mitford sought information from the committee about research being conducted at the prison by UCSF faculty; about any experiments being performed that had not been reviewed or approved by the CHE; and about compensation made to prisoners that was used as incentive for subjects to participate.[25] While there is no record of the committee's immediate response to her queries, notes from a committee meeting the following month indicate that they had consulted UCSF legal counsel "about the liability of the university in the case of investigators using their faculty title" in research conducted at another institution.[26]

A suggestive reason why the chair of the Committee on Human Experimentation would consult legal counsel was because Mitford was also soon to publish an article in *The Atlantic* that would allege harm done to inmates who were used as experimental subjects at California Medical Facility. In particular, this article referenced experiments being conducted by UCSF faculty, who I will refer to as Dr. X and Dr. Y. Writing a piece about the forthcoming Mitford article, a reporter from the *Los Angeles Times* talked to Julien Hoffman in December 1972 who, in the words of the reporter, "verified that studies have been done at Vacaville without his committee's approval."[27] The Committee was soon to discover that this research would become a matter of national attention.

Between the January 1973 publication of Mitford's article in *The Atlantic*, titled "Experiments Behind Bars," and the publication of her book published later that year titled *Kind and Usual Punishment: The Prison Business*, the revelations of medical experiments on inmates would not only highlight the weaknesses of institutional ethics review, but would generate human rights concerns that would ultimately result in a number of state and federal legislative reforms for how prisoners were treated in biomedical research.[28]

Of particular concern to the UCSF Committee on Human Experimentation was an account that Mitford provided of a lawsuit filed on behalf of a prisoner against Dr. William Keating, superintendent of the Vacaville prison, and two university physicians who performed harmful "pain tolerance studies," Dr. X and Dr. Y.[29] Legal documents reviewed by Mitford described the adverse effects of intramuscular injections of an anti-inflammatory agent called Varidase in experiments funded by the drug's manufacturer, Lederle Laboratories. Besides reporting the pain and discomfort experienced by the subjects, the article also revealed that the experiments were conducted without knowing what risks to health the drug may pose, "because I never heard of this thing," Dr. Y declared during an interview at that time.[30]

As a result of not knowing about "this thing," the individual who received injections of Varidase had sued for harm done, alleging he "suffered an agonizing, near-fatal disease of the muscles, in the course of which his weight dropped from 140 to 75 pounds. He subsequently developed chronic stomach ulcers as a result of being treated for his conditions with steroids ...."[31]

If the physician, Dr. Y, who oversaw the administration of an experimental drug to human subjects, lacked knowledge of the drug or risks involved with its use, then who could provide information to the participants about risks? As we will see, the experimental drugs being used were sometimes developed in private labs, and investigators relied on the fact that the company provided information to the U.S. Food and Drug Administration to obtain Investigational New Drug (IND) approval. This means that before a manufacturer of a novel drug could test whether it is reasonably safe to give to humans, the manufacturer submits to the FDA an IND application with data that shows it "screened the new molecule for pharmacological activity and acute toxicity potential in animals, [and] wants to test its diagnostic or therapeutic potential in humans."[32] IND approval by the FDA restricts the use of the drug to certain testing conditions.

However, the information that a drug company provides to the FDA is in large measure protected by the Defend Trade Secrets Act (DTSA, 18 U.S.C. Section 1839), meaning that the formulas and engineering information are held secret.[33] This means that even physicians who are commissioned by the companies to conduct experiments might be ignorant of the formulas they are working with. Yet once a drug company or manufacturer receives regulatory approval by obtaining the designation of Investigational New Drug, the company would then rely on the physicians performing the trial to conduct the experiments in a safe manner.[34]

A representative from Lederle, the lab that manufactured Varidase (the drug that allegedly caused a near-death experience and resulted in the lawsuit against Dr. X and Dr. Y referred to above[35]), acknowledged that companies who commissioned experiments took a hands-off approach to study design because the physician-investigators "knew what's best." The Lederle representative said:

It's the responsibility of the investigator to follow the guidelines and obtain a proper consent form. We don't dictate to the clinician how he runs these things. I'm sure you're aware that the more prestigious the clinician is, the more convinced he is that he knows what he's doing. If you use him, you have little choice but to trust what he says he does.[36]

Performing a medical experiment on a human without any reasonable judgment about what harm it may cause was (and remains) a fundamental breach of ethical research protocols. In fact, the lack of articulation or explication of risks involved when seeking to obtain informed consent was the most common reason for the Committee on Human Experimentation to deny approval of a research protocol.

One example such a denial occurred in November 1971, when the CHE reviewed a protocol submitted by Dr. Y titled "Topical Absorption

Studies with Pyridinethione Disulfide." This refers to a chemical formula that is derived from a major compound called pyrithione, which was known to function as a fungicide and bactericide and adapted in a formula later used in medicated shampoos.[37] In the 1960s and 1970s, the U.S. Army took an interest in its potential use as a prophylactic against ringworm infection, which led to a series of studies using derivative chemical formulas.[38]

The committee voted to reject the protocol citing a lack of information, seeking to know "what the animal studies are on this project and if there are none, why is this being done on humans"; "why is this being done [at all] – what are the benefits to be received from the study that are not otherwise obtainable"; and "what are the specifics of the synthesis and characteristics of the drug being used."[39] In particular, the committee sought information about the toxicity of the drug that was to be administered to humans.[40]

In this case, even though studies involving pyrithiones would later yield anti-dandruff shampoos, in its questions to Dr. Y the committee seemed more concerned with the *toxicity* of the drug than whether the experiments were *trivial*. For the ethics review committee, "toxicity" was important not merely because of the inherent risk to health if a substance was toxic, but because many of these non-therapeutic investigations were designed to test *when a toxic effect manifests* in humans who are administered different doses of a new chemical or drug.[41] Neither the immediate nor long-term effects of such exposure were known. Such experiments have been subject to major criticism because such studies often serve commercial ends, rather than provide medical benefits to society.[42] (This uneasy juxtaposition between significant physiological risk and trivial commercial outcome echoes the work of dermatologist Dr. Albert Kligman at Holmesburg Prison, where, as detailed in Allen Hornblum's book, *Acres of Skin*, prisoners were routinely exposed to potentially harmful substances in experiments that ultimately served cosmetic or dermatological product development.[43])

On November 10, 1971, Dr. Y replied to the committee, saying that an Investigational New Drug (IND) application for Pyridinethione Disulfide had been filed with the FDA by the manufacturer but it was confidential, adding that "the FDA is in a better position than the Committee to ascertain 'the safety, stability, and lack of toxicity of drug substances'." (A note that Leslie Bennett scribbled on the margin of the letter reads "Committee has obligation to know toxicity.") It is probable that Dr. Y and his colleagues were unable to answer the question about the toxicity of the drug, since there is no historical evidence that this chemical compound had yet been adequately investigated.[44]

But was the FDA in a better position than the Committee to ascertain the drug's safety as Dr. Y alleged? In the 1960s, the pharmaceutical industry, touting its scientific "know-how" and expertise (citing a high number of PhDs in research and development), had established a dominant position over the FDA. According to a report by Dr. Barbara Mouton, a former medical officer with the New Drug Division of the FDA, the agency had become "merely a service bureau for the drug industry."[45]

The FDA had a history of being more reactive to drug disasters than proactive in preventing them.[46] Its cautious approach to regulating the development or testing of new drugs was governed by an implicit understanding that companies should be able to benefit from being the first to discover, develop, and market a drug. The secrecy of the New Drug Application (NDA) allowed for the practical equivalent of patent protection, giving companies a firm grip on the market. The FDA was bound by statutes that protected trade secrets. Section 301(j) of the Federal Food, Drug, and Cosmetic Act prohibited the disclosure of any "method or process" that is a "trade secret."[47] The U.S. Criminal Code also forbade unauthorized disclosure by officials of "trade secrets, processes," and "confidential statistical data."[48] While the FDA relied on data provided by drug sponsors in their IND applications, trade secret protections limited transparency and made it difficult for the FDA and researchers to fully assess the risks associated with investigational new drugs.[49] The lack of transparency also made it more difficult to obtain truly informed consent from research participants, and demonstrates the challenges faced by review boards who lacked complete information due to these protections.

Returning to the example referred to above where the UCSF committee disapproved a protocol because of its lack of knowledge about a drug's toxicity, the physician who submitted the material for institutional review raised his own counter-objection. "Every new drug may have some toxicity that is not immediately recognized," Dr. Y said. "The consent form is written in such a way that this exigency is taken into account. However, it is not possible to indicate what toxicity, if any, might occur."[50] Again the committee rejected the notion of FDA confidentiality, saying that members of the ethics committee "have the authority to request such information and the duty to judge the use of the drug," and since Dr. Y failed to provide information concerning toxicity, the protocol remained unapproved.[51]

So infuriated was Dr. Y for the committee's rejection of his protocol that on November 10, 1971, he wrote to them to say, "We had hoped that the new Committee would act with more wisdom and dispatch than its predecessor. If not, the type of research that I have outlined will either stop completely or gravitate underground from whence it came."[52]

A Question of Informed Consent

University ethics review committees across the country were contemplating the ethical challenges of human experimentation and the meaning of informed consent practices. Indeed, a seminal article by the ethicist Jay Katz published in 1976 still critiqued the medical community's apprehension toward fully embracing informed consent, especially in research contexts, exposing the ethical tensions between therapeutic obligations and the imperatives of experimental research.[53] As Faden and Beauchamp have shown in their classic 1986 book *A History and Theory of Informed Consent*, during this formative period the concept of informed consent was still undergoing significant conceptual clarification, with early review committees often conflating the act of signing a consent form with the deeper ethical obligation of ensuring that subjects truly understood the nature, risks, and voluntariness of their participation.[54]

The UCSF Committee on Human Experimentation itself struggled with several issues when reviewing proposed research protocols that was to be conducted at California Medical Facility. They debated and searched for institutional guidance on the use of prisoners as human subjects. In part, their concerns related to principles that bore upon questions of coercion and the vulnerability of subjects, many of whom were under psychiatric treatment. (Indeed, the name of the medical facility's coordinating office, the Solano Institute for Medical and Psychiatric Research (SIMPR), signals that mental health issues were themselves a focus of experimental research.[55])

The committee also struggled to have faculty comply with standards of informed written consent. The forms that were submitted for review often lacked details about experimental procedures, the risks involved to the subjects, the toxicity and dosage of novel drugs being used, or the purpose of the experiments themselves. If the committee was not being provided with this information, then what assurance was there that prisoners would be duly informed about all these matters?

In attempt to assure the CHE that appropriate protocols of informed consent were being followed, in 1971 a copy of the template consent form that was developed by SIMPR was given to the committee. The form consisted of three paragraphs and two signature lines where the only space to add new information was where the participant's name would be inserted and signatures added. The form declared that "all possible inconveniences and hazards, to be reasonably expected, have been explained to me," though nowhere was there a place to write down specific "hazards." Also, the second paragraph of the form provided an exculpatory clause preventing a participant from holding any authority liable should something go wrong, a phrase (according to Mitford) that was added by SIMPR to avoid a repeat lawsuit such as the Varidase case.[56] However, such a clause was in direct violation of guidelines for consent forms.

The standard phrase on the consent form asking subjects to acknowledge that the experiments and any risks involved "have been explained to me" was not adequate to ensure that such communications were made. The UCSF human experimentation committee, therefore, requested that investigators provide on the consent form a "complete description of the procedure(s), the risks and the possibilities which were 'fully explained to me' must be spelled out in the consent form. In addition, any waiver of responsibility on the part of the investigator must be deleted."[57]

When reviewing CHE discussions of protocols and their decisions whether to approve them or not, it is clear that an accurate description of the experiments and associated risks must be provided. Yet writing down these details remained challenging for those conducting the experiments. When appealing the committee's disapproval of a protocol based on inadequate information, investigators working at the California Medical Facility resorted to offering a reassurance that Dr. X and Dr. Y were better at verbal communication than with writing out statements. For example, writing to the ad hoc committee on human experimentation in 1968, Sidney Riegelman, Chair of the UCSF Department of Pharmacy (and later member of the CHE when it was established in 1971), explained:

[Dr. Y] and the medical staff [at California Medical Facility] are experts in communicating with these prisoners and explaining procedures to them. It is our belief that the prisoners can be made completely aware of the aspects and background of the tests by these conversations. It is our contention that no amount of written words will ever substitute for these oral discussions. I hope that the Committee will agree with this and not insist upon a revision of the form to the degree that it would be necessary to make it unambiguously 'intelligible' to a grade school mind.[58]

Those who conducted human research at the CMF most frequently, including Dr. X and Dr. Y, took the "trust me" approach to convincing an ethics review committee that they were following federal and institutional policies in the rigor of information provided when seeking informed consent. This was acknowledged by the committee itself when one reviewer noted that, following a conversation with Dr. X, "They assure us that the project will be thoroughly and honestly discussed to the subjects before asking them to sign the consent form."[59]

Such practices of deferring to investigators with institutional prestige was common among early ethics review committees elsewhere in the country, as Laura Stark discussed in her book *Behind Closed Doors*. Stark shows how IRBs created a tension in the assessment of expert knowledge, where reviewers display an expertise in *rules*, but investigators were steadfast in claiming expertise in their *knowledge domain*, sometimes describing those involved in the research as "world famous."[60] However, in this case, the UCSF committee decided not to accept such implicit assurances, and would repeatedly reject protocols that did not provide adequate written explanation of the procedures.[61] The fundamental reason for enforcing this was that it was the accepted standard for ethics review that information be written and not merely presented orally. Whatever challenges investigators faced in writing down information that could be intelligible "to a grade school mind," they were not grounds for waiving the right of individuals to be given intelligible information, or for investigators to prove that they provided such information in writing.

However, such adherence to standards of providing *informed* and *written* consent was more importantly to ensure that no experiments were conducted that were considered unnecessarily dangerous.[62] To this end, the committee paid particular attention to assessments of risk, and especially to what was known about the toxicity of new drugs. As the following examples illustrate, such concerns provided legitimate grounds for seeking more information about experimental procedures.

What Information Did an Ethics Review Committee Have?

What follows is a close reading of the ethics committee's deliberations about the use of incarcerated individuals in research, where they debate whether to consider the scientific merit of the study, where they seek clarity about their own authority, and where they consider matters of potential coercion to enroll participants.

Philip Thomas Brylke, Jr., served seven years in prison in the 1960s, including time at the California Medical Facility in Vacaville.[63] After his release, from 1969 to 1971 he was enrolled as a student at UC Berkeley studying criminology. In 1972, he described himself as co-director of the California Prisoners' Union.[64]

Brylke was connected to John Bowers, the attorney who represented the incarcerated individuals and their families who sought to reform California's correctional facilities and obtain justice for unethical human medical experimentation within the system. In Bowers' correspondence with Leslie Bennett, Chair of UCSF Committee on Human Experimentation (CHE), he recommended that Mr. Brylke be invited to review proposals for research at CMF, to which Bennett replied, "When a protocol indicates that a prisoner will be a subject, I am sure the Committee [CHE] will be happy to consider consulting Mr. Brilke [sic] or others who have been former inmates or those who are now inmates."[65]

Committee minutes reflect that Mr. Brylke attended a meeting on January 13, 1972, a week after the committee had received, and began discussion of, a research protocol submitted by UCSF faculty member Dr. X titled, "Percutaneous Penetration of Pesticides in Man," with the experiments to be conducted on inmates at California Medical Facility.[66] The minutes indicate that Brylke spoke to the committee from first-hand knowledge about a range of medical experiments that occur at the facility by UC faculty, including the allegations that brain surgery (lobotomies) were proposed on Vacaville inmates taken to UCSF's Moffitt hospital. (On this, Brylke is recorded as saying that, "officially the application had been shelved but that diagnostic procedures are continuing in the prison with the help of several people with appointments at UC."[67])

Recognizing that UCSF faculty had been engaged with medical experimentation at CMF which, to the committee's knowledge, had not been reviewed or approved, they considered this, and other, protocols submitted that involved incarcerated individuals. One question that was raised was about what role the university had in relation to research performed at another institution, in this case, the Solano Institute for Medical and Psychiatric Research (SIMPR), located at the California Medical Facility (CMF) at Vacaville. The matter for deliberation was whether another institution's review board(s) satisfy the university's requirements for internal review of human experimentation that was conducted by UCSF faculty. As we will see, the answer to this was no, which was in line with the policy of the NIH that required review no matter where the research took place.

However, another matter of concern was the relationship UCSF had with SIMPR. The committee would soon discuss whether a financial relationship (where UCSF transferred funds to another institution) and UCSF being named in collaborative research projects implicate UCSF in any legal or liability issues that may emerge. The committee also questioned whether full FTE (full-time equivalent) faculty employed by UCSF can hold any position outside the university – performing medical duties or research that align with their primary university appointment – but have that work be considered non-UCSF work. As we will see, the answer to this by Academic Affairs was no, that all professional work, in whatever location it is conducted, must be considered part of UCSF duties, and reviewed and approved accordingly.

This point about the relationship between UCSF and SIMPR is important because, as further explained below, Dr. Henry Elliott (director of SIMPR) would argue that their own review practices were sufficient, rendering the need for UCSF to perform a separate review unnecessary and excessively bureaucratic. However, an audit by the State of California of the SIMPR's research activities between 1973-1976 would later conclude that "deficiencies" in its review structure created a conflict of interest between those who approve research and those (same people) who perform the experiments.[68] Such conflicts of interest contradicted established national and UCSF policies governing peer review and protocols for obtaining informed consent.

At a January 1972 meeting, the committee discussed the use of prisoners in any experiments as a matter of principle, but especially as subjects in an experiment with potential high risk and no possible benefit to the subject. The topic of fees paid prisoners (or any subjects) was also discussed and it was decided to request information concerning a reimbursement or compensation on every protocol from that point on. Finally, it was decided to simply ask Dr. X "why this particular population of normal subjects will be used," instead of any other population outside the prison system.[69] While the ethical problems surrounding the use of prisoners for medical research was well known and considered at the national level by the U.S. Department of Health, Education, and Welfare, the issue of payment appears to have added a new dimension to the committee's deliberations.

As we will see, the question was one of coercion in gaining consent and what had elsewhere been characterized as "psychologically harmful" practices to enroll participants in medical research. It is worth underscoring here that the issue of payment to research participants was recognized as particularly problematic when the participants were incarcerated individuals, who sought to earn money by any means available. Interestingly, this fact was later used as a defense of the practice of payment, with some prisoners themselves articulating the benefit of earning money.

The minutes of the Committee on Human Experimentation at UCSF do not reflect whether, or to what extent, the members discussed the risks to the study participants who were subject to having pesticides applied to their skin or intravenously injected. In fact, questioning the scientific merit of the study itself was unstable ground for the committee. At the committee meeting on November 29, 1971, a statement was read from UCSF anesthesiologist H. Barrie Fairley, who was a member of the committee, where he opined on the scope of the committee:

My attitude is that it is the responsibility of a Human Experimentation Committee to assess the balance of benefit and risk, to ensure that the patient will be appropriately informed, and to ensure that the proposed form of consent will provide the appropriate protection for both the subject, the investigator and the latter's employers. The Human Experimentation Committee is not in the peer review business, and should only criticize protocols where the proposed approach would sufficiently invalidate the data as to reduce the benefit to risk ratio. Thinking along these lines, criticism as to scientific merit, will not be indicated when the risks are negligible …[70]

In apparent agreement with this line of reasoning, the committee seemed more focused on whether a prison population could objectively *consent* to participation. Fundamentally, the committee wanted to know why *this* population, and no other, was subject to this sort of research, regardless of its perceived scientific merit.

To seek elucidation on this, committee chair Leslie Bennett sent a letter to Dr. X articulating further concerns over his pesticide research as expressed by the review committee. Bennett wrote, "Specifically, the committee wishes precise information as to the dosage of the pesticides to be used, and the nature of the toxicity of these compounds. In particular, it wishes information regarding whether any of these procedures might increase absorption, and thus increase the hazard from toxicity of the compounds. In addition, the committee would like to know what the compensation to the subject would be, and some individuals have questioned the use of the word 'volunteer' when individuals are, in fact, paid to serve at subjects."[71]

It is clear from these questions, raised by the CHE upon review of Dr. X's application for protocol approval, that the material submitted for review lacked crucial detail about the experiments to be conducted. If the Committee on Human Experimentation was not privilege to this information, what guarantee was there that human subjects would be informed of toxicity and risks? For the institution to perform its function to a "reasonable standard" and ensure ethical conduct in human research, all material relating to research design, protocols, and information relayed to potential participants needed to be submitted and reviewed.

There was a dissenting view by at least one member of the committee regarding the objection to the use of prisoners as subjects for medical experimentation, as the next meeting of the committee demonstrated.

On February 3, 1972, Dr. Sidney Riegelman, Chair of the Department of Pharmacy and committee member, wrote to his colleagues on the committee that, "I believe that prison inmates should have an equal right to participate in these studies as other people. We are, in effect, establishing a set of double standards by preventing them from expressing their willingness to participate. I agree that there may be some special limitations and considerations placed upon the types of studies and characteristics of the selection of subjects, as well as the payment that may be offered to the subjects. These are details which need to be worked out. As I expressed earlier to the committee, the prison inmates offer a unique group of subjects who have extensive free time on their hands and can be available for continuous monitoring. It should be their privilege to participate in studies as long as their welfare is being protected."[72]

This statement articulates three points that would continue to be debated by the committee over the next few months: first, that the controlled environment (fixed schedule, constant surveillance, etc.) rendered these human subjects easily manageable, but also subject to manipulation; second, that this environment was beneficial to the medical researcher who considered such a controlled environment ideal for monitoring, but this could unfairly determine selection criteria (no randomization, a preference for those willing to do anything); third, that payment to participants could be coercive, yet a "standard fee structure" was established policy at California Medical Facility.

Dr. X expressed his own interests to the committee during his attendance on February 10. However, he appears not to have presented any evidence that the prison population was in any way *medically essential* to his investigation but rather that it was beneficial to him to continue a long-standing research project on a population "he found it desirable" to work with.[73]

It appears that for the sake of convenience, and with an unresolved position on the principles governing the use of incarcerated individuals for medical experimentation, the CHE agreed to change their position and approve his research to continue for one year.[74]

Deliberations on the Protection of Vulnerable Populations

In 1978, two agencies – the National Commission for the Protection of Human Subjects in Biomedical and Behavioral Research and the Food and Drug Administration – provided independent recommendations to establish new standards for IRBs. The revised language distinguished between *informed consent* and the *consent form*. "Informed consent is designed to serve the interests of the research subject. … Researchers provide [subjects] with an opportunity to protect themselves by deciding whether the benefits are worth the risks."[75] But what if there are no benefits? The *consent form*, by contrast, is to protect the investigator and institution from legal liability. However, critics of the written consent form were to argue that the signed consent forms might actually put the subject at risk by betraying the confidentiality and privacy of the individual.[76]

One aspect of the consent process is ensuring that the act of participation is voluntary. Yet, in the context of prison research, the very concept of free will was problematic. As Ratnoff and Smith recognized in 1968 in the *Fordham Law Review*, "Although prisoners are repeatedly told that volunteering for medical experiments will in no way influence their privileges, how are we to say that there still does not exist the hope that a parole board might conclude that the volunteer has paid his debt to society?"[77]

Context matters. The conditions of life while incarcerated at California Medical Facility are important to examine. CMF was opened in 1955 to provide psychiatric diagnosis, treatment, and care for inmates suffering from serious emotional and psychiatric disorders. Because many notorious inmates were institutionalized at CMF, including serial killers Juan Corona and Charles Manson, the facility was often covered by the press, with newspaper articles offering glimpses of incarcerated life through inmate interviews. Common sentiments expressed among inmates were loneliness, despondency, boredom, and suicidal thoughts.[78]

Where the medical investigators saw a controlled environment for them to study the effects of experimental chemicals on humans, the human subjects saw a restricted space designed as punishment. The lack of self-concern, or the overwhelming desire to break daily routines, or the need to have canteen money, or having the aim to garner favors from those in power, were all reasons why prisoners were identified as human subjects in need of special consideration in ethics review. Concerns such as this are precisely why an ethics panel faced a challenging task when reviewing incentives for prisoners to volunteer their bodies for medical experimentation. If the inmates "lacked motivation" (in the words of the chief psychiatrist) for their own wellbeing, the question they needed to consider was who would step in to protect inmates' health?

Would an inmate who is recognized as lacking motivation for wellness participate in research for the purpose of performing a social good? When asking "What sort of volunteer is acceptable?" when contemplating the use of prison inmates, the Law-Medicine Research Institute at Boston University advised that: "Serving as a subject in a medical experiment is obviously an act of good conduct, is frequently unpleasant and occasionally hazardous and demonstrates a type of social consciousness of high order when performed primarily as a service to society."[79] What assessment was made of a "social consciousness" among the selection of inmates at CMF who were used in experiments?

Interestingly, in 1979 UCLA hosted a National Conference of Christians and Jews where participants were to discuss questions concerning prison research and whether prisoners could provide informed consent. In preparation, a questionnaire was sent to Robert Bradwell, chairman of the California Medical Facility, seeking to know whether prisoners agreed or disagreed with statements related to coercion, financial rewards, and comprehension of risks when participating in medical research. In reply, Bradwell forwarded responses from five incarcerated individuals, a limited number ostensibly because, in his words, "We do not wish to burden you with a large amount of reading." Each of the five inmates registered their uniform disagreement with the survey's statements that implied that their incarcerated position somehow compromised their judgment when deciding to participate.[80] While the document may provide insight into the perspectives of a small group of incarcerated research participants, its credibility as a representative account is limited by the absence of methodological transparency, the remarkable uniformity of views, and the fact that these particular respondents were selected by an institutional authority. Given the broader historical context of public controversy over coercion and consent in prison research during the 1970s, the selective inclusion of only supportive testimonies suggests a potential bias toward legitimizing ongoing research programs.

The entire context of understanding the mental status of incarcerated individuals and the complicated principle of compensation for becoming a human subject for experimentation was what the UCSF CHE waded through in the first year of its policy making. The more the committee learned about the extent and scope of experiments being conducted at CMF, the more cautious they became in approving any protocols for research among prisoners.

To be sure, going back to Mr. Brylke's attendance at the CHE meeting in January 1972, the committee sought his feedback on information that was provided by Dr. X who had apparently described his methods of obtaining informed consent. The committee minutes for the January 6, 1972 meeting refer to chair Leslie Bennett citing a letter from Dr. X dated July 6, 1971, and to the motion of "getting information from Thomas Brylke who read Dr. X's letter … and he questioned three points from that letter: subjects selected on voluntary basis, required to sign a consent form, and [Dr. X's statement that] 'the benefits of the procedures involved are unknown; however no hazards are involved and the volunteers are informed of the procedures employed before they are admitted to the project.'"[81] By "questioning" these three points, Brylke appears to have challenged the thoroughness of the protocol described, which would explain why the committee would later ask Dr. X to appear in person to elaborate his procedures.

This prompted the committee to revisit over a few meetings the vexing questions about what exactly was "beneficial to the inmates" about these experiments and whether compensation was appropriate. In the minutes for the meeting on February 15, 1973, the committee noted "a possible conflict of interest with prisoners not wishing to report problems because of the possibility of losing compensation." Second, the committee asked, "Why will this be done on prisoners? Could this be done on any other population?"[82]

The committee identified the salient ethical concern about coercive recruitment practices. Whatever the convenience to the researchers of having a population confined to a setting that provided constant surveillance, the dependency on the funds offered for participation could easily lead to decisions that act against self-interest. The question as to why any other population was not being used reinforces this point: if no one else would agree to participate because their perception of risk outweighed benefit, then it could demonstrate how desperate the prison population was to gain financial reward at any cost to their wellbeing.

Conclusion

The UCSF Committee on Human Experimentation faced numerous challenges as it navigated emerging laws and regulations related to medical research involving human subjects in the early 1970s. These challenges stemmed from several sources, including unclear ethical guidelines, conflicting legal principles, and the complexities of assessing risk and obtaining informed consent, especially within vulnerable populations like prisoners.

One of the central issues confronting the committee in its early years was defining and ensuring informed consent. While the concept of informed consent was a fundamental tenet of ethical research conduct, its practical application proved difficult. The committee struggled to determine how to enforce the disclosure of information that should be provided to potential participants, particularly regarding the risks involved. This challenge was compounded by the fact that investigators themselves may not have been fully aware of the potential hazards, especially when working with investigational new drugs (INDs)].

The laws protecting trade secrets meant that researchers were sometimes ignorant of the formulas of the drugs involved in the experiments. This put the review committee in a difficult position, as they were tasked with assessing the risks to human subjects without having all the necessary information. Even when the FDA had granted a drug IND status and approved its use in medical experiments, the manufacturer was still protected by trade secret laws, limiting the information available to researchers and review boards. This directly impacted the ability of the review committee to perform its duties to a "reasonable standard" to ensure ethical conduct in human research.

The committee also grappled with the question of coercion, particularly in the context of prison research. Given the inherent power imbalances and the potential for incarcerated individuals to seek benefits such as better living conditions or early release, it was difficult to ensure that their consent was truly voluntary. The committee debated whether payment to prisoners for participating in research was ethical, as it could be seen as coercive. The committee considered the concerns that prison life might unduly influence them to participate in medical research.

The committee's struggles were further complicated by the lack of clear institutional guidance and the threat of legal liability. As lawsuits were filed against IRBs for alleged negligence, committee members became increasingly concerned about their legal responsibilities. This apprehension led to greater scrutiny of research protocols and a more cautious approach to approving research involving vulnerable populations.

Ultimately, the UCSF Committee on Human Experimentation faced a complex and evolving landscape as it sought to navigate the ethical and legal challenges of medical research involving human subjects. The committee's experiences reflect a broader struggle within the scientific and medical communities to balance the pursuit of knowledge with the protection of human rights. It is worth noting that in 1979, UCSF established the "Experimental Subject's Bill of Rights" that was intended to be given to every person asked to be in a research study.[83]

The work of the UCSF Committee on Human Experimentation highlights the critical importance of ongoing dialogue and reflection on the ethical implications of medical research. As scientific knowledge continues to advance, it is essential that review boards and policymakers remain vigilant in protecting the rights and welfare of human subjects.

Endnotes

1   John Bowers to John Gorman, MD, Medical Director, California Department
of Corrections, August 17, 1971, in UCSF Archives, AR86-23, Box 001, Folder
009, f. 113. See also John Bowers, "Prisoners' rights in prison medical experimentation programs. *Clearing House Review* 6 (1972), 319-333. Here he exami-
nes the ethical, legal, and human rights issues surrounding medical experimentation on incarcerated individuals, delving into the complexities of conducting
medical research within prison settings, focusing on the balance between
scientific advancement and the protection of prisoners' rights. He emphasizes
the challenges in obtaining genuine informed consent from prisoners, given the
inherent power dynamics and potential for coercion within correctional facilities. He argues that the confined environment may compromise the voluntariness of prisoners' participation in research studies.

2   John Bowers to John Gorman, MD, Medical Director, California Department
of Corrections, August 17, 1971, in UCSF Archives, AR86-23, Box 001, Folder
009, ff. 113-118.

3   Leslie Bennett to John Bowers, November 23, 1971, in UCSF archives, AR86-
23, 001, 003, f. 180.

4   Ibid.

5   Leslie Bennett, typescript speech, "UC 1979 Systemwide IRB Conference"
(September 16-18, 1979, at Asilomar), in folder "Proceedings," in Box 12, IRB
Office Archive.

6   Clay v. Martin, 509 F.20 109 (2nd Cir. 1975). Quotations are from the case
summary provided by IRB 1979.

7   Quotation from IRB 1979. Additional comments about the lawsuit and defendants from the University of Maryland were provided by another defendant,
William Woodward,

8   The course of the lawsuit is discussed by Nancy Campbell, *Discovering Addiction: The Science and Politics of Substance Abuse Research* (Ann Arbor: University of
Michigan Press, 2019): "A government motion to dismiss Clay's 1975 appeal
was granted in June 1977. On September 8, 1978, the U.S. government filed
a motion for summary judgment, which is considered a harsh remedy that is

granted only where material issues of fact no longer remain to be tried. The Court partly granted this motion after determining that Clay's heart attack was not caused by drugs administered at the ARC. However, the Court viewed as unsettled the issue of whether Clay's consent was voluntary and informed, and thus it allowed an investigation to determine whether the naltrexone experiment was conducted in a "negligent and reckless" manner. Three days after these matters were tried on March 12, 1979, the Court dismissed Clay's complaint in its entirety with prejudice." (p. 152, and p. 254 footnote 19).

9   Quote from William Woodward, "An Investigator/Defendant Corrects the Record," *IRB: Ethics & Human Research* 5:1 (1979), p. 10. Woodward was one of the physician PIs being sued.

10   L. Edward Bryant, Jr., The Burgeoning Law of Medical Experimentation Involving Human Subjects, 8 *J.*

Marshall J. Prac. & Proc. 19 (1974). https://repository.law.uic.edu/lawreview/vol8/iss1/2; David Cavers, "The Legal Control of the Clinical Investigation of Drugs: Some Political, Economic, and Social Questions," *Daedalus* 98: 2 (1969), 427-448.

11   Even more recent conversations about reforming IRBs exposes a system inherent with conflicts of interest, lack of resources, and insufficient expertise of review members. See for example E.J. Emanuel, A. Wood, A. Fleischman, et al., "Oversight of human participants research: identifying problems to evaluate reform proposals," *Ann Intern Med* 141: 4 (2004), 282-291.

12   For discussion of change of emphasis between therapeutic versus experimental settings for informed consent, see Jay Katz, Alexander Morgan Capron, Eleanor Swift Glass, *Experimentation with Human Beings: The Authority of the Investigator, Subject, Professions, and State in the Human Experimentation Process* (Russell Sage Foundation, 1972).

13   Alexander Capron, "Medical research in prisons. Should a moratorium be called?" *The Hastings Center Report* 3: 3 (1973), pp. 4-6.

14   *Salgo v. Leland Stanford Jr.* University Board of Trustees, 317 P.2d 170 (1957).

15   *Natanson v. Kline* 350 P.2d 1093 (1960) and 354 P.2d 670 (1960).

16   "Memorandum of Surgeon General William H. Stewart to the Heads of Institutions Conducting Research with Public Health Grants (February 8, 1966). In:

Jay Katz, *Experimentation with Human Beings* (New York: Russell Sage Foundation, 1972), 855.

17   Public Law 93-348, p. 349.

18   The Commission's report, known as the Belmont Report, was printed in *Federal Register* 43 (No. 231): 56174-56198, November 30,1978. It cites the 1974 lawsuit against the University of Maryland on p. 56195, footnote 18. The case was cited in the Federal Register as Baily v. Mandel, Civil Action No. K-71-110 (DC, Md, 1974) and is further discussed in Holder 1979, p. 7, where the author relays information provided by a defendant named in the lawsuit. Additional details were provided by another defendant in Woodward 1979.

19   Report printed in *Federal Register* 43 (No. 231): 56174-56198, November 30,1978, on p. 56193. The report cited the 1974 civil suit against the University of Maryland (including the chair of the IRB and other officials, referred to above) alleging that research involving incarcerated individuals did not provide adequate informed consent. See p. 56195, footnote 18.

20   *Nielson v Regents of the University of California.* Civil No. 655-049 (SF Super Ct 1973); *Bailey v Mandel.* No. 74-110 (D Md 1974); *Robertson v McGee.* WL 535045 (ND Okla 2002).

21   Micah Onixt and Robyn Sterling, "Institutional Review Board Liability for Adverse Outcomes," *Virtual Mentor.* 2009;11(4):306-310. doi: 10.1001/virtualmentor.2009.11.4.hlaw1-0904.

22   This is a concern that has lasted for decades. See D.L. Icenogle, "IRBs, conflict and liability: will we see IRBs in court? Or is it when?" *Clin Med Res* Jan;1:1 (2003), 63-68. doi: 10.3121/cmr.1.1.63. PMID: 15931289; PMCID: PMC1069025; Sharona Hoffman and Jessica Wilen Berg. "The suitability of IRB liability." *U. Pitt. L. Rev.* 67 (2005): 365.

23   John Fletcher, "Human Experimentation: Ethics in the Consent Situation," *Law and Contemporary Problems* 32 (1967), 620-649, p. 635.

24   Laura Stark, *Behind Closed Doors: IRBs and the Making of Ethical Research* (Chicago: University of Chicago Press, 2011).

25   "Selected Excerpts from the CHR Minutes," March 1983. Typescript in Box 12, IRB Office Archive. Entry August 24, 1972. [N.B., the typescript mistakenly dates this August 24, 1982]

26   "Selected Excerpts from the CHR Minutes," March 1983. Typescript in Box
       12, IRB Office Archive. Entry September 24, 1972.

27   Harry Nelson, "Unauthorized Medical Tests on Inmates Told," *Los Angeles Ti-
       mes*, December 20, 1972, p. 3. This is substantiated by a letter from CHE Chair
       Leslie Bennett to Henry Elliott, Chair of SIMPR and Professor of Medical
       Pharmacology at UC Irvine, November 29, 1971, citing CMF studies for which
       "we could find no evidence of review on the San Francisco campus." UCSF
       Archives, AR86-23, Box 1, Folder 3, folio 174; see also Leslie Bennett to Dean
       Julius Krevans, November 23, 1971, AR86-23, Box 1, Folder 3, folio 179, citing
       15 studies for which they could not find any CHR review.

28   The National Commission for the Protection of Human Subjects in Biomedi-
       cal and Behavioral Research, "Research Involving Prisoners." DHEW Publica-
       tion NO. (OS) 76-131. (1976).

29   Jessica Mitford, "Experiments Behind Bars: Doctors, drug companies, and
       prisoners," *The Atlantic* (January 1973), 64-73, on pp. 70-71.

30   Ibid.

31   Jessica Mitford, *Kind and Usual Punishment: The Prison Business* (New York: Knopf,
       1973), in Chapter 9, "Cheaper than Chimpanzees," p. 159.

32   Information from FDA "Investigational New Drug (IND) Application" websi-
       te. Accessed May 2, 2023.

33   U.S. Food and Drug Administration, Code of Federal Regulations, Title 21
       [21CFR601], accessed here on May 2, 2023.

34   See the 1972 article by William Pendergast which addresses the tension be-
       tween the public's right to know and the necessity to protect confidential busi-
       ness information. It highlights the challenges the FDA faces in balancing these
       interests, especially when public health considerations are at stake: William
       Pendergast, "The Responsibility of the FDA to Protect Trade Secrets and Con-
       fidential Data," *Food, Drug, and Cosmetic Law Journal* (27 Food Drug Cosm. L.J.
       366).

35   I recognize that "Dr. X" has subsequently denied being involved in the expe-
       riments with Varidase. Here I am quoting the material published by Mitford (a
       source "Dr. X" has attempted to discredit as inaccurate) because the claims she
       made in her published work were read and discussed by the ethics review com-

mittee who saw the issue – regardless of the accuracy or veracity of Mitford's allegations – as important to address. Her work stimulated the committee to think harder about the ethics of experiments involving prisoners.

36 Jessica Mitford, *Kind and Usual Punishment: The Prison Business* (New York: Knopf, 1973), in Chapter 9, "Cheaper than Chimpanzees," p. 164.

37 R. Marks, A.D. Pearse, A.P. Walker, "The effects of a shampoo containing zinc pyrithione on the control of dandruff," *British Journal of Dermatology*, Volume 112, Issue 4, 1 April 1985, Pages 415-422, https://doi.org/10.1111/j.1365-2133.1985.tb02314.x.

38 Sidney Riegelman, [Dr. Y], and Robert Upton, "Development of Prophylactic Anti-Fungal Preparations: Final Report," U.S. Army Medical Research and Development Command (October 1980). Online here.

39 Committee deliberations November 4, 1971. Minutes of CHR, in AR86-23, Box 1, Folder 7, Folio 116.

40 A full articulation of the committee's concerns in Leslie Bennett to [Dr. Y], November 9, 1971, UCSF Archives AR86-23, Box 1, Folder 5, folio 119.

41 David Arome and Enegide Chinedu, "The Importance of Toxicity Testing," *Journal of Pharmaceutical and Biosciences* 4 (2013), 146-148.

42 Jonathan Kimmelman, "Ethics at Phase 0: Clarifying the Issues," *Law, Medicine, and Ethics* 35:4 (2007), 727-733.

43 Allen Hornblum, *Acres of Skin: Human Experiments at Holmesburg Prison* (New York: Routledge, 1998).

44 C. Doose, J. Ranke, F. Stock, U. Bottin-Weber, and B. Jastorff, "Structure–activity relationships of pyrithiones – IPC-81 toxicity tests with the antifouling biocide zinc pyrithione and structural analogs," *Green Chemistry* (Royal Society of Chemistry), 6 (2004), 259-266.

45 Quoted in Julius Mastro, "The Pharmaceutical Manufacturers Association, The Ethical Drug Industry and the 1962 Drug Amendments: A Case Study of Congressional Action and Interest Group Reaction." New York University, Ph.D., 1965.

46 Suzanne Junad, "FDA and Clinical Drug Trials: A Short History," *FDLI Update* (2008): 55-76, on page 60.

47 David Cavers, "The Legal Control of the Clinical Investigation of Drugs:

Some Political, Economic, and Social Questions," Daedalus 98: 2 (1969), 427-448, p. 437 and reference 30 of that article.

48   Ibid, p. 447, n. 30.

49   Ibid, p. 429.

50   [Dr. Y] to CHE, November 10, 1971, in UCSF Archives, AR86-23, Box 1, Folder 5, folio 133.

51   Committee minutes, November 18, 1971, in UCSF Archives, AR86-23, Box 1, Folder 7, folio 109. The study was conditionally approved on December 2, 1971, following further revisions to the consent form and the provision that "a skin biopsy is described in lay language." Ibid, folio 101. A revised protocol was approved December 14, 1971, Leslie Bennett to [Dr. Y], in AR86-23, Box 1, Folder 5, folio 81.

52   [Dr. Y] to Leslie Bennett, November 10, 1971, UCSF Archive, AR86-23, Box 1, Folder 5, Folio 133.

53   Jay Katz, "Who's Afraid of Informed Consent?" *The Journal of Psychiatry & Law*, 4:2 (1976), 315-325. https://doi.org/10.1177/009318537600400213

54   Ruth R. Faden and Tom L. Beauchamp, *A History and Theory of Informed Consent* (Oxford: Oxford University Press, 1986), esp. Chapter 5, "The Development of Consent Requirements in Research Ethics."

55   In 1974, Frank Herch and Ruth Flower analyzed the historical context of prisoner experimentation, highlighting past abuses and the evolution of regulatory frameworks. They also discuss the challenges in obtaining truly informed consent from prisoners, considering the inherent power dynamics and potential for coercion within the prison environment. See Frank Herch and Ruth Flower. "Medical and psychological experimentation on California prisoners." *UCDL Rev.* 7 (1974): 351.

56   Jessica Mitford, *Kind and Usual Punishment: The Prison Business* (New York: Knopf, 1973), in Chapter 9, "Cheaper than Chimpanzees," p. 163.

57   This instruction is quoted from Leslie Bennett to [Dr. X], January 31, 1972, AR86-23, Box 1, Folder 003, folio 88.

58   Sidney Riegelman to Ad Hoc Committee on Human Experimentation, December 11, 1968, in MSS2023-09, Box 8, Folder 3, folio 5.

59 Committee on Human Experimentation, MSS 2023-09, Box 8, Folder 3, Folio 8 – ad hoc committee reviewer commenting on poor consent forms submitted by those working at CMF.

60 Stark, *Behind Closed Doors* (op. cit. n. 24), pp. 34-35.

61 Copies of CHE decisions in letters sent to PIs in 1971 onwards in UCSF Archives, AR86-23, Box 1, Folder 3, passim.

62 "Food and Drug Administration has recently required the written consent of the patient in all cases where investigational drugs are administered." See: *Food and Drug Regulation* § 130.37, as revised on June 20, 1967, and published in 32 Federal Register 8753.

63 *The PEOPLE, Plaintiff and Respondent, v. Howard Stanton LEWIS, Philip Thomas Brylke, and James William Jones*, Cr. 8439, 8444, November 7, 1963. FindLaw.

64 Philip T. Brylke, *Issues in Criminology* 7, no. 2 (1972): 130–31.

65 Leslie Bennett to John Bowers, November 23, 1971, in UCSF archives, AR86-23, 001, 003, f. 181.

66 "Selected Excerpts from the CHR Minutes," March 1983. Typescript in Box 12, IRB Office Archive.

67 CHE meeting January 13, 1972, in "Selected Excerpts from the CHR Minutes," March 1983. Typescript in Box 12, IRB Office Archive.

68 Office of Auditor General, State of California. *Operational Review of the Solano Institute for Medical and Pharmacological Research*, Report 712 (November 1977).

69 "Selected Excerpts from the CHR Minutes," March 1983. Typescript in Box 12, IRB Office Archive. Entry January 6, 1972. Bold type added to quotation.

70 "Selected Excerpts from the CHR Minutes," March 1983. Typescript in Box 12, IRB Office Archive. Entry November 29, 1971. Bold type added to quotation.

71 Letter from Leslie Bennett to [Dr. X], January 11, 1972, in UCSF Archives, AR86-23, Box 1, 003.PDF p. 125.

72 "Selected Excerpts from the CHR Minutes," March 1983. Typescript in Box 12, IRB Office Archive. Entry February 3, 1972. Bold type added to quotation.

73 Leslie Bennett to Henry Elliott, March 7, 1972, in UCSF archives, AR86-23, Box 1, 003.PDF, Box p. 44.

74   CHE Index Cards referencing study #150302, Expired August 31, 1973. UCSF Archives, IRB-CHR-1972-1997.

75   Robert Levine, "Changing Federal Regulation of IRBs: The Commission's Recommendations and the FDA's Proposals," *IRB: Ethics & Human Research* 1: 1 (1979), 1-3+12, on p. 2.

76   *Federal Register* 43 (No. 231): 56174-56198, November 30,1978, on 56181.

77   Marian Ratanoff and Justin Smith, "Some Legal Problems in Medical Treatment and Research, Human Laboratory Animals: Martyrs for Medicine," *Fordham Law Review* 4:36 (1968), 673-694, p. 694.

78   For example the interviews in *Corpus Christi Caller Times*, Aug 14, 1978, p. 18.

79   "Ethics Governing the Service of Prisoners as Subjects in Medical Experiments," in Irving Ladimer and Roger W. Newman, *Clinical Investigation in Medicine: Legal, Ethical, and Moral Aspects; an Anthology and Bibliography* (Boston: Law-Medicine Research Institute, Boston University, 1963), p. 464.

80   Robert Bradwell to "Institutional Review Board Members," March 1, 1979. Uncatalogued digital scan of document provided to UCSF Archives and Special Collections. Contact author for copy.

81   The three questions that Brylke had upon reading Dr. X's letter were put to Dr. X in a letter to him by Leslie Bennett dated January 5, 1972, which said that Brylke "will be in touch with you regarding elaboration of these points." Letter in UCSF Archives, AR86-23, Box 1, 003.PDF, f. 130.

82   CHE meeting February 15, 1973, in "Selected Excerpts from the CHR Minutes," March 1983. Typescript in Box 12, IRB Office Archive.

83   Carol Levine, "California Laws on 'Human Experimentation' and 'Experimental Drugs,'" *IRB: Ethics and Human Research* 1:2 (1979), 9-10. The Bill of Rights stated:

To be told what the study is trying to find out

To be told what will happen to me and whether any of the procedures, drugs, or devices is different from what would be used in standard practice

To be told about the frequent and/or important risks, side effects or discomforts of the things that will happen to me for research purposes

To be told if I can expect any benefit from participating and, if so, what the benefit might be

To be told the other choices I have and how they may be better or worse than being in the study

To be allowed to ask any questions concerning the study both before agreeing to be involved and during the course of the study

To be told what sort of medical treatment is available if any complications arise

To refuse to participate at all or to change my mind about participation after the study is started. This decision will not affect my right to receive the care I would receive if I were not in the study

To receive a copy of the signed and dated consent form

To be free of pressure when considering whether I wish to agree to be in the study

5

Self-Accommodation

Katherine Macfarlane*

Abstract

The reasonable accommodation mandate was intended to ensure access for people with disabilities. Yet some people with disabilities who are eligible for and in need of a reasonable accommodation choose to forego seeking one. Instead, they proceed unaccommodated, or they implement their own accommodation—taking on the accommodation's physical and financial burdens themselves. Focusing on the workplace, as well as health care and educational settings, this essay identifies the self-accommodation phenomenon and frames it as a civil rights failure. In so doing, it challenges the notion that people with disabilities who are eligible for accommodations but do not seek them are simply uniformed about the rights they enjoy. Instead, it contends that people with disabilities who self-accommodate are rational actors who reject what might be a futile, and humiliating, option. The essay proposes incentivizing people with disabilities to refrain from self-accommodation by making the accommodations process envisioned by the law more appealing, and effective.

Introduction

The reasonable accommodation mandate is a hallmark of federal disability law.[1] It embodies the Americans with Disabilities Act's ("ADA") commitment to the social model of disability, which views disability as the result of social barriers that must be dismantled.[2] Those barriers may be physical or imbued in policy that render physical spaces and experiences inaccessible to people with disabilities. Reasonable accommodations are the tools designed to tear the barriers down.[3] As Sam Bagenstos has explained, the reasonable accommodation requirement "is thought to be the ADA's

---

* Professor of Law, Director, Disability, Law and Policy Program, Syracuse University College of Law, and Senior Fellow, Burton Blatt Institute.

great innovation."[4] Yet some people with disabilities who are eligible for reasonable accommodations never ask for them.

Commentators have suggested that eligible people with disabilities do not seek accommodations because they do not know what their rights are.[5] If a lack of knowledge is the problem, then education and information-sharing is the solution to ensuring everyone who needs an accommodation receives one.[6] Yet even individuals who know their rights still may not seek the accommodations they are entitled to. Instead, they accommodate themselves.

To understand why, imagine the dilemma facing an employee with a disability eager to make a good impression at a new job. Imagine further that the new employee is a law firm associate with the invisible disability Lupus, an autoimmune disease that causes joint pain, stiffness, and swelling.[7] No one at the associate's law firm knows that she has Lupus.

On her first day of work, the associate is assigned to an office that contains a heavy, wooden desk and an executive chair with leather cushions and plastic armrests, that look something like the below:

In the United States, the design of office executive chairs is tied to outdated gender norms, which assume that executive chairs are for men and that therefore their dimensions should accommodate the largest male bodies.[8] The average American woman is 5 feet 3 ½ inches tall, whereas the average American man is 5 feet 9 inches tall.[9] Women's bodies, typically smaller than men's, experience "discomfort and even pain" when sitting in chairs that do not take their bodies into account.[10]

Our new associate is five foot three and a half. Lupus causes her to experience pain and stiffness in her joints. The executive chair's head cushion juts slightly forward, so that when the associate is seated in the chair, her head hits the cushion at an awkward angle, causing her to lean uncomfortably forward. The shape of her chair and the height of the desk force her body into a position that causes her pain, making it difficult to work.

By the end of her first day, the new associate realizes that she needs a different chair in order to work without causing her Lupus pain and stiffness to become exacerbated. Her law firm provides ergonomic chairs that are adapted to each individual's body size and shape on a first come, first served basis. The average wait time for such a chair is about three months. Ten employees, some of whom are partners, are already in line and waiting for their ergonomic chair. Without a reasonable accommodation, the associate will have to wait in line behind everyone else.

The associate has several options. First, she could disclose her disability and request a reasonable accommodation from her new employer, asking for a comfortable office chair that does not cause her pain. She might also request that it be provided to her as soon as possible. Second, she could work unaccommodated. And third, she could finance and implement her own accommodation.

The first option is not without cost. Disclosing disability requires disclosing intimate details about a person's identity and health.[11] Beyond identity disclosure, obtaining an accommodation requires disclosing a disabled person's need for assistance.[12] As Katie Guest Pryal has explained, she would never seek a reasonable accommodation at work because of "[t]he invasion of privacy, the stigma, the fear of ableism – the general blowback that seeking accommodations would have brought – all of that would have been too high of a price to pay for the paltry accommodations my institution would have granted me."[13]

Additionally, if the associate chooses to ask for an accommodation, she will be forced to disclose that she has Lupus, and potentially be subject to ableist stereotypes about her ability to work as a lawyer.[14] Further, as Nicole Porter has described, accommodated employees often face special treatment stigma.[15] When the associate's office chair arrives, it will be obvious to others that she somehow jumped the line. Anyone still waiting on their furniture may resent her, assuming that she received an unearned favor. Some of that resentment may come from her peers. But here, the new associate might also obtain a desired resource before others who are more senior to her, the very people who may later evaluate her for plum assignments or even partnership. They may perceive that she received special treatment and treat her less favorably in the future.

Moreover, her firm's reasonable accommodation process requires the new associate to obtain medical proof of disability, and that proof must be less than a year old. But the new associate has recently moved to a new town for her new position and has yet to establish care. Her new health insurance will not kick in until the end of her first month of work, and her first paycheck is still weeks away. The first available appointment with the specialist she needs to see requires a six month wait. As a result, seeking out a specialist who can document her disability presents its own challenges. The new associate also worries about taking time off for a medical appointment so soon after starting a new position.

The second option may seem like the path of least resistance. It certainly involves the least paperwork. But an employee with disabilities who needs an accommodation and attempts to work without one risks termination if they cannot perform each of their job duties without accommodation.[16] Will the associate be able to meet her billable hour requirements if she must complete her work in an office equipped with furniture that causes her significant pain? Given her experience after only one day of work, probably not.

The third option ensures that an employee's disabilities are accommodated and that as a result, she can perform each of her essential job functions. It also avoids disclosure of personal information about her health and avoids her colleagues' scorn. Still, there will be a cost. Though often inexpensive, accommodations are not free. If our new law firm associate purchases a new chair and second monitor she will be out several hundred dollars—at least. She will not benefit from any discount provided to employers who buy in bulk. To avoid missing work during regular business hours, she may need to move the new furniture and monitor into her office herself on a weekend. It might be physically painful to carry her new furniture and monitor from the workplace parking lot to her office. She may injure herself doing so.

Self-accommodation is often perceived as a poor choice made by people who simply do not know better. Yet people who self-accommodate have often weighed their options and made rational choices. Understanding self-accommodation in the workplace and beyond is critical to shaping our understanding of the reasonable accommodation mandate's success, and its shortcomings.

Following this Introduction, the essay proceeds in three parts. Part I defines and identifies self-accommodation in the workplace, health care settings, and higher education. Part II explores how self-accommodation runs counter to anti-discrimination law's decision to assign the cost of most accommodations to employers and businesses, and also explains how self-accommodation may give rise to discipline. Part III proposes how to reduce the likelihood that a person with disabilities who is eligible for reasonable accommodations self-accommodates. The essay then concludes.

I. Seeing Self-Accommodation

A. Work

Carrie Griffin Basas has defined self-accommodation in the workplace as the way people with disabilities "implement strategies and create reasonable accommodations on their own to be able to work or to work more effectively."[17] In her study of female attorneys with disabilities, Griffin Basas found that her subjects self-accommodated in three ways: "by doing the work of accommodation themselves by acquiring adaptive equipment or making physical space changes, by selecting jobs that are disability-friendly and flexible enough to be molded to fit their needs, and by becoming their own bosses through entrepreneurialism."[18]

Griffin Basas' qualitative research captured the experience of women with disabilities practicing law. She was interested in "the interaction of a high-status profession, such as being a lawyer, and a low-status, second- or even third-class position, such as being a woman with a disability."[19]

The first type of self-accommodation Griffin Basas identified took the form of purchasing adaptive equipment like a keyboard tray, ergonomic mousepad, or headset, or perhaps installing additional lighting for one's office. It might have involved physically moving furniture to make room for adaptive equipment. Outside of a law firm setting, this sort of self-accommodation might involve a cashier purchasing a stool to sit on during long shifts.

The second type of accommodation Griffin Basas identified, selecting jobs that are disability-friendly and flexible enough to be molded to fit a disabled person's needs, meant that her subjects sought out a specific type of employment rather than trying to make one particular job work. The third type of accommodation involved women becoming their own bosses through entrepreneurialism—such as starting their own law firm. Both of these forms of self-accommodation are likely only available to individuals with skill sets that help them negotiate effectively, and those with the financial security to leave one paying job in hopes that another will materialize. These kinds of self-accommodation are not a realistic option for most workers.

B. Health Care

Self-accommodation is not limited to the employment context. Though legally-mandated, obtaining accommodations in health care settings is also not simple. Patients with disabilities may be left with no choice but to engage in self-accommodation. In health care, people with disabilities may be entitled to accommodations under either the ADA, the Rehabilitation Act, the Affordable Care Act, or all three.[20] Accommodations might include providing patient records in a format accessible to screen readers, assigning patients with mobility impairments to an exam room that requires the least amount of walking to and from the reception area, or requiring that all staff, including health care providers, wears masks when interacting with a high-risk patient.[21]

Despite the prevalence of universal masking requirements at the earliest stages of the COVID-19 pandemic, health care settings have now largely abandoned masking measures. In most health care settings, patients and health care providers alike are no longer required to wear masks, and most providers do not do so even if they treat high-risk patients. Of course, high-risk people with disabilities are safer when two-way masking is in place: transmission is less likely when they wear a mask and the people around them do too. Ensuring that health care providers who interact face-to-face with their patients are wearing masks remains key. And asking a health care provider to wear a mask for a high-risk patient is a quintessential reasonable accommodation request.

Like an employee who needs to be accommodated with respect to her office furniture, a high-risk patient who needs those around her to wear a mask faces a difficult decision. First, a patient might identify and engage with the provider's formal reasonable accommodation process. Yet a health care provider, even a large medical center, may not provide any public infor-mation about how to obtain a reasonable accommodation, let alone with respect to an accommodation as politically-charged as masking. Though the legal soundness of requesting masking remains unchanged, some medical centers have communicated to patients that masking is optional and subject to each provider's discretion, suggesting that a masking accommodation is unavailable or unreasonable.

Second, a patient may simply forego any masking-related request. This option avoids conflict, but also creates the risk that a patient will contract

COVID-19 or another respiratory illness.

Third, the patient with disabilities who needs their health care providers to wear a mask may attempt to self-accommodate. What form does self-accommodation take here? Rather than filling out a form, a patient will be required to engage in a negotiation intended to result in their health care provider deciding to wear a mask. The patient may do so by asking the receptionist at the front desk if the doctor, nurse and/or tech will wear a mask while interacting with them. Given the lack of understanding surrounding the legitimacy of masking as a reasonable accommodation to a policy that does not otherwise require it, non-clinical staff may be unwilling to facilitate a patient's request. Or they may simply lack training regarding what constitutes a reasonable accommodation and how to evaluate and provide one, or fear a physician's angry reaction. Here, self-accommodation takes on another layer of complexity: the patient must negotiate masking with their health care provider directly.

As I have previously argued, policies that discourage patients' masking requests "create a conflict of interest by assigning the decision about whether a mask is legally necessary to the same person who decides whether they should wear one."[22] Moreover, "[s]ome doctors may refuse to mask because they believe that such a requirement violates their political beliefs, regardless of science" or that "the 'discomfort' of a mask is beneath them."[23] A patient who asks an unwilling health care provider to mask creates conflict in a situation in which patients have very little power. That conflict is not risk-free for the patient. "If patients persist in asking their doctors to mask after an initial refusal, care may be discontinued, on the grounds that the physician-patient relationship has broken down," and even though termination generally includes a 30-day notice period, "[g]iven nationwide physician shortages, a 30-day notice is generally insufficient to transfer care seamlessly."[24] "The possibility of discontinuation of care becomes a threat intended to ensure patient obedience,"[25] and renders the self-accommodation process even more fraught.

My own requests that my health care providers and their staff wear masks have been met with everything from a refusal to check me in for my appointment, the suggestion that I move out of state, an order that I "show [them] the studies" on two-way masking's efficacy, and, ultimately, termination of care. All of this occurred in connection with the care provided by a rheumatology office that prescribed me two potent immunosuppressants (Remicade and methotrexate). The individual who told me to show him the studies yelled his request at me in the hallway of his medical practice; he is a rheumatologist.

Debating a health care provider about their need to wear a mask also carries with it the risk of personal injury. Imagine a situation in which a high-risk patient asks an unwilling phlebotomist to wear a mask: "[t]he patient must have blood drawn so that tests can be run to determine if the patient's treatment is working," but "[n]ot all blood draws are alike—there are ways to make a blood draw more or less painful."[26] There, "[t]he power imbalance in that moment never favors the patient, who has to weigh the benefits of masking against the perils of a sharp needle in an angry hand."[27]

C. Higher Education

Colleges and universities must provide students with reasonable accommodations as a result of either the ADA, the Rehabilitation Act, or both. Accommodations may take the form of providing accessible dormitory housing, or receiving extended time on a test. Most higher education disability services offices require students to provide medical documentation of disability in order to obtain a reasonable accommodation, and may also set strict deadlines as to when an accommodation request must be received. For example, an accommodation related to end-of-semester testing may need to be made two months before the exam date itself.

Many universities require their professors to include information about how students can obtain accommodations in every syllabus the professors share with their students. As a result, a student may receive the information in question ten times each academic year. Accessibility offices and websites are often not difficult to locate. Though the information provided to students about accommodations may not encourage students to seek them, unlike other scholars, I contend that at least some information is out there and that all students see it.

There are other reasons that explain why students do not seek the accommodations they need. Students, like employees, face difficult options when deciding whether and how to obtain the accommodations they need. First, they might try to engage with a school's formal accommodation processes. Yet a student who has recently arrived on a college campus far away from home may be unable to obtain the detailed medical evaluation and medical records necessary to support an accommodation request required by the student's institution. That student may be unable to pay for an out-of-network provider, for example. Alternatively, a student's disability may manifest for the first time, or in a new fashion, long after the relevant formal accommodations deadline has passed.

Imagine a student who is disabled as result of generalized anxiety disorder. The student was diagnosed their freshman year of high school. Until the student entered university, their anxiety did not result in panic attacks, but midway through the first semester of their freshman year, the student begins experiencing multiple panic attacks each week. The student is worried about experiencing a panic attack during an exam administered by a professor who does not allow more than one five-minute bathroom break during the exam itself. The student needs permission to take several off-the-clock breaks should a panic attack occur during the professor's exam, which is less than three weeks away.

The student reviews their institution's formal reasonable accommodation policies, and realizes that because his documentation is now more than three years old, it will not suffice to support any accommodation request. Moreover, the deadline for exam-related accommodations passed several weeks before the student realized they would need an exam accommodation.

The student might choose the second option: take a test without any accommodation, or, as people with disabilities often phrase it, tough it out. To do so requires embracing cognitive dissonance about how a disability like anxiety is impacted by an upcoming stressful event such as a final exam. With a stressful test looming, going without any form of accommodation is never a real option for this student.

Third, the student might decide to self-accommodate. They could attempt to do so by making an office hours appointment with their professor and asking for permission to take, for example, no more than three off-the-clock breaks during the exam should the student experience a panic attack. The student might offer to provide the professor with evidence of their original diagnosis, explaining that they have not been able to update it. The professor, in turn, may refuse and refer the student back to the university's disability services office.

Given the documentation policy and the expired accommodation deadline, the student again decides that seeking a formal accommodation is not a viable option. Instead, they decide to make the most of the bathroom break provided by the professor. In order to avoid using the restroom during the exam for reasons unrelated to managing a panic attack, the student limits their liquid and food intake the day before and the day of the exam itself.

Predictably, the student experiences anxiety during the exam, and, sensing an oncoming panic attack, takes a bathroom break 30 minutes into the four-hour exam. The student is able to eventually control the panic attack and return to the room where the test is being administered after approximately ten minutes. However, after the exam concludes, the student is informed that they have received a failing grade due to violating the five-minute break policy.

Here, self-accommodation has failed.

II. The Law Against Self-Accommodation

A. The Duty to Accommodate

As Mark Weber has explained, the ADA is properly viewed as a "governmental intervention[,] but a modest one, [that shifts] some costs of disability to employers (in the form of reasonable accommodations), merchants (in the form of readily achievable removal of barriers for shop-keepers), and government itself (in the form of program accessibility)."[28]

Placing the burden of accommodation on employers and businesses, in the context of Title I and III of the ADA, "represent[s] a shift in congressional civil rights policy by mandating that employers and public accommodations (along with commercial facilities), respectively, bear the monetary cost of modifications," instead of state-funded benefits programs that place the costs of accommodation on the government and taxpayers.[29]

Congress could have, but did not, shoulder the entire cost of accommodations itself, nor did it elect to provide subsidies to businesses that modify their structures or policies to comply with the ADA.[30] Congress did so at least in part by identifying the least cost avoider. In the context of Title III, that entity is a company with "an economic incentive to spend wisely and reduce unnecessary costs when making modifications," but also one with "firm-specific knowledge about how and where to conduct modification projects and the requisite expertise, staff, and access to facilities," able to "reduce transaction and information costs that may result in a waste of resources in a tax-and-spend program."[31]

In the context of employment, the reasonable accommodation mandate recognizes that employers are best able to bear the costs of employing a person with disabilities. Self-accommodation redistributes the cost of accommodations to disabled people, despite the ADA's recognition that the burden of rendering workplaces accessible should be on employers.[32] Moreover, self-accommodation may require more than financial expenditures; it may force an employee to make changes to a physical space, without any assistance. Self-accommodation therefore also assigns additional uncompensated work and costs to employees with disabilities.

Self-accommodation is not a necessary rebalancing. Defendants against whom failure-to-accommodate claims are brought can already avail themselves of powerful defenses, including defenses that demonstrate that an accommodation is unreasonable, would create an undue burden, or would fundamentally alter the nature of a business or educational program.

B. Self-Accommodation as Punishable Insubordination

Self-accommodation creates risk for people with disabilities. Employees who self-accommodate may risk workplace discipline. For example, two-way masking may still be necessary for employees who are high-risk for COVID-19, but some employers have instructed employees to refrain from asking their co-workers to wear a mask. An employee who self-accommodates by attempting to negotiate masking with their co-workers may be disciplined, or even terminated. Though an employer may not retaliate against an employee who engages in protected activity, requests that an employee makes on their own behalf outside of a formal accommodation process may not be shielded from workplace consequences.

Similarly, an employee who self-accommodates by moving furniture around may suffer physical injury and violate an employer's safety rules, risking termination. An employee who self-accommodates by taking on physical labor that their body cannot manage may be deemed a direct threat subject to termination.

A patient who self-accommodates risks compromising the patient-provider relationship, creating conflict that limits access to competent care, or results in termination of care. Termination of care by a specialist can jeopardize a patient's wellbeing. Though state laws often require thirty days of notice before care is officially terminated, providers who have decided to terminate care often provide no assistance during the thirty-day notice period, effectively advancing the termination of care date to the date of notice. Moreover, when the specialty in question suffers from a provider shortage, it may take six months or even a year to establish new care. In the meantime, patients go without treatment.

A student who self-accommodates may violate an institution's policies regarding how and to whom disability may be disclosed. As a law school student, I experienced this consequence myself. My legal research class included an assignment that required students to find hard-copy sources in the library in a limited amount of time (as I recall, we were given about thirty minutes to complete the assignment). Students who could move around the library quickly, or without impediment, were at an advantage as they would be able to locate more sources. At the time, I was experiencing rheumatoid arthritis flares that caused my knees to swell. Moving quickly was either painful or simply impossible.

I contacted my school's accommodations officer about the assignment, and learned that he was out of town. Fearful that the assignment would happen before the accommodations officer returned, I spoke to my legal research professor about my concerns. That is, I attempted to self-accommodate. The professor was kind and encouraged me to reach out to the accommodations officer again.

When I finally met with the accommodations officer, he informed me that I had violated the school's honor code by disclosing my disability to my professor, and threatened me with disciplinary action. I feared that I would fail the class, or be expelled. The accommodation ultimately suggested to me by the accommodations officer was carrying a small stool around the library during the assignment. Carrying a stool was, of course, an unsuitable solution for someone with a joint disease, and did nothing to help me manage how physical disability impacted my ability to complete the assignment. Throughout my decade in legal academia, I have heard from other law students that they too have been threatened with similar discipline and informed that they have violated a school's honor code when they shared details about their disability.

III. Reducing Self-Accommodation

This essay has argued that self-accommodation is a rational choice. However, it is also one that undermines the accommodation mandate, a hallmark of U.S. disability law. To render self-accommodation less common, the circumstances that lead to self-accommodation must change.

First, self-accommodation should not be treated as a problem that arises out of ignorance. When a lack of information is perceived as the problem, providing disabled people with more information becomes the only solution—even though it is often no solution at all. For example, consider how most universities require instructors to include a statement in their syllabi about how a student can obtain a reasonable accommodation. The information that is inserted into a syllabus is standardized, and is often characterized by bold, all caps text. If a student takes five classes in a given semester, they receive the same accommodations information five times over.

Accommodations are a frequent subject of conversation, and vilification, on university campuses. Students who experienced disability before college may have also had Individualized Education Programs or Section 504 Plans in connection with their disabilities, and aware of at least the notion that some protection would continue in college. Disability requires so much self-advocacy and self-learning that it is odd if not illogical to assume that students are not requesting accommodations because they do not know they are entitled to them. A student who flips through at least one syllabus throughout their undergraduate career will know that accommodations are available. A contrary suggestion patronizes people with disabilities.

Of course, some students who experience disability for the first time in college do need guidance. They may be unaware that help is available. But an accommodations system could still support those students while tackling the larger issue of how inhumane the accommodations process has become.

Limiting a person with disabilities' resort to self-accommodation first requires making the accommodation process more attractive. In the employment context, strengthening confidentiality protocol regarding both an employee's underlying disability and the fact that an employee receives an accommodation would lessen concerns about disclosure. The ADA treats information about job applicants' and employees' medical conditions and history as presumptively confidential. Interpreting those provisions broadly would provide greater protection for information that gives rise to stigma and scrutiny, and render the fear of disclosure less of a barrier to seeking an accommodation. Moreover, information that an employee receives an accommodation often reveals that an employee is disabled, and how. For example, a cashier who asks for a stool to sit during a long shift is disclosing that they have difficulty standing for the duration of the shift. That itself is the disclosure of an impairment related to standing (or mobility). The protections afforded the medical records justifying the employee's need for the stool should be extended to information about the fact that the stool is being provided as an accommodation.

Another way to render the accommodation process more attractive is to eliminate the conflicts of interest current processes create. At work, an individual who does not supervise the employee requesting the accommodation should be charged with reviewing a request for reasonable accommodation. Because workplace accommodations require an interactive process, and involve some negotiation, or at least an attempt at negotiation, an employee should not be forced to negotiate the terms of their accommodation with the same person who determines whether they receive a raise or promotion. Accommodation procedures should also be made transparent, both during employment and during the interview and onboarding process. Onerous documentation standards should be revised or eliminated.

Accommodation procedures in higher education are long overdue for an overhaul. Many colleges and universities require students to deliver "accommodation letters" to their professors, disclosing the students' accommodation needs and often their underlying disability in one fell swoop. However, most professors do not need to know about their students' accommodations. For example, if a student is accommodated with a notetaker, all a professor needs to know is that a notetaker will be present in their classroom—not who the notetaker is there for. If the notetaker is a member of the class, the professor arguably needs to know nothing about that particular accommodation. Professors who do not proctor their own exams do not need to know who is receiving additional testing time.

The use of accommodation letters, and other standardized accommodation notification processes, are often employed because they are administratively convenient. Students take on the free labor of assisting in the administration of their own accommodations, though the law does not require them to do so. Forcing a student to communicate to their professor that they are receiving an accommodation may also unintentionally empower a reluctant professor to refuse to implement an accommodation. A professor may feel emboldened to refuse a student, but would not refuse a university employee. The student whose accommodation is refused must then also take on the labor of communicating and overcoming the professor's refusal. When reasonable accommodations are accompanied by this much work, self-accommodation, or no accommodation at all, looks like the better option.

What about healthcare? This particular setting does arguably suffer from an information deficit, but, it is not people with disabilities who need to be educated. Rather, everyone from a practice's receptionist to a large hospital's patient relations department should be trained in facilitating the accommodation process. Telling patients that doctors are no longer required to wear masks in response to a patient's request that their doctor do so, for example, miscommunicates the law. An accommodation may require changing a general policy. A masking request made in a healthcare setting is very easily identifiable as a request intended to accommodate a disability. In healthcare settings, a patient needs the care they have signed up to receive, and cannot risk angering a provider by negotiating something as politicized as a masking request. The entity subject to the federal law that requires that accommodations be made must develop a system that supports patients and takes on the burden of evaluating and implementing those accommodations that are deemed to be reasonable.

In the workplace, as well as in health care and higher education settings, accommodating people with disabilities should be treated as a necessary and beneficial aspect of the status quo rather than as a burdensome departure from the norm.

Conclusion

This essay has described how people with disabilities self-accommodate at work, in health care settings, and in higher education. It has argued that their choice to do so is not a result of ignorance, but rather a rational choice informed by their knowledge of how the accommodations process functions, and fails. It has also described how self-accommodation is a civil rights failure. The accommodation mandate is an integral aspect of the integration the ADA was designed to bring about. Self-accommodation is a solution, but when a person with disabilities chooses it over a reasonable accommodation provided, civil rights law has failed to reach the very individual it was designed to assist. It also represents an unintentional rejection of the social model, embraced by the ADA, through which society, and not the individual experiencing disability, is tasked with dismantling barriers. In that sense, self-accommodation violates the spirit of the law.

People with disabilities who choose to accommodate place themselves at risk—of discipline or retaliation. Reducing self-accommodation requires overhauling the accommodations process, rendering it less fraught with disclosure anxiety, less burdensome with respect to documentation standards, and less discriminatory. Once legal accommodation becomes more appealing, self-accommodation will abate.

The second Trump Administration has focused a spotlight on all employees who may be perceived to have received a hiring advantage related to their difference. President Trump has suggested that unqualified people with disabilities have been hired by the federal government, and that their lack of qualification may be to blame for the failures that resulted in a recent plane crash at a Washington D.C. airport. Of course, federal disability law only protects employees with disabilities who are qualified for their positions, and does not protect those who pose a direct threat to others as a result of their presence in the workplace. Nevertheless, because all forms of identity-based difference are currently the subject of potential scrutiny, people with disabilities may be even less inclined than before to identify themselves as disabled, or to ask for accommodation as a result of their disability. As a result, for the near future, self-accommodation may persist.

Endnotes

1   *See* Karla Gilbride, *Evolving Beyond Reasonable Accommodations Towards "Off-the--Shelf Accessible" Workplaces and Campuses* (2022), 30 Am. U. J. Gender Soc. Pol'y & L. 297, 297–98; Samuel A. Marcosson, *Of Square Pegs and Round Holes: The Supreme Court's Ongoing "Title VII-Ization" of the Americans with Disabilities Act* (2004), 8 J. Gender Race & Just. 361, 389–90.

2   *See* Samuel R. Bagenstos & Margo Schlanger, *Hedonic Damages, Hedonic Adaptation, and Disability* (2007), 60 Vand. L. Rev. 745, 780 (stating that the social mo-

del "directs attention not at the individual with a disability but at the array of social choices that create most of the disadvantage attached to disability" and that the ADA, "with its broad requirements of physical accessibility, reasonable accommodation, and antidiscrimination, is a paradigmatic social-model policy response to disability"); Shirley Lin, *Bargaining for Integration* (2021), 96 N.Y.U. L. Rev. 1826, 1827–28 (describing the origin and purpose of the reasonable accommodation mandate); James Leonard, *The Equity Trap: How Reliance on Traditional Civil Rights Concepts Has Rendered Title I of the ADA Ineffective* (2005), 56 Case W. Res. L. Rev. 1, 34 (stating that "social construction provides a theoretical justification for Title I's integrationist goals, as manifest in the reasonable accommodations mandate").

3   Katherine A. Macfarlane, *Disability Without Documentation* (2021), 90 Fordham L. Rev. 59, 65.

4   Samuel R. Bagenstos, *The Future of Disability Law* (2004), 114 Yale L.J. 1, 23–24.

5   *See* Heidi H. Liu, *The Proactive Process: An Empirical Study of Disparities in Workplace Accommodations* (2024), 56 Ariz. St. L.J. 225, 243–44 (describing knowledge deficits and lack of cultural capital as factors that may influence whether a person with disabilities seeks accommodation); *see also* Gleb Tsipursky (2024), *Many government workers don't realize they can use disability law to work from home*, The Hill, https://thehill.com/opinion/technology/4704248-many-government-workers-dont-realize-they-can-use-ada-to-work-from-home/ (stating that "[d]espite the clear legal framework, few government employees are aware of their rights under the ADA" and "many may not realize they can request remote work as an accommodation for mental health conditions"). Some of these critiques do not consider the underlying law. *See, e.g.*, Kate Jones and Jeong IL Cho, J. of the Scholarship of Teaching and Learning, Vol. 24, No. 3, Sept. 2024 (criticizing students with disabilities' lack of self-advocacy and self-determination and concluding that those failures unnecessarily limit students' access to accommodations). Jones and Cho contend that "college students with disabilities often do not discuss their needs with professors due to the fear of negative reactions to this disclosure" and that ""[t]his lack of communication and in-

volvement in interactions with fellow students and professors keeps them from practicing their self-advocacy skills, receiving appropriate accommodations (e.g., testing in a quiet place, preferential seating, large-letter handouts, and assistive technology devices), and achieving their maximum educational potential." The self-advocacy Jones and Cho envision requires disclosure of information that the law would otherwise treat as confidential. The disclosure proposed also invites the sort of discrimination that confidentiality protections are intended to avoid. Moreover, institutions, and not individual professors and classmates, are legally obligated to implement accommodations. What Jones and Cho have observed is not necessarily a problematic lack of self-advocacy, but rather a recognition of what disclosure carries with it, and more significantly, an awareness of the identity of the real accommodations decisionmakers. Jones and Cho also attribute students' failure to obtain needed accommodations to their lack of knowledge regarding the ADA. The ADA is a complex civil rights law that lawyers and judges struggle to understand. Expecting students with disabilities to have a sophisticated understanding of their legal rights is an unreasonable expectation, or at least one that should not be used to shift the blame for accommodation failures onto people with disabilities themselves.

6   *See* Liu, *The Proactive Process*, 233 (suggesting that the employers should "take the first step in offering accommodations to new employees" to "reduce ambiguity about *how* to request accommodations, thus responding to knowledge barriers").

7   *Lupus*, Mayo Clinic, https://www.mayoclinic.org/diseases-conditions/lupus/symptoms-causes/syc-20365789. Lupus affects more women than men. Corinna E. Weckerle & Timothy B. Niewold, *The Unexplained Female Predominance of Systemic Lupus Erythematosus: Clues from Genetic and Cytokine Studies* (2011), Clinical Revs. in Allergy & Immunology, Vol. 40, pages 42–49.

8   *See generally* Jennifer Kaufman-Buhler, *If the Chair Fits: Sexism in American Office Furniture Design*, J. of Design History (2019), Vol. 32, No. 4, pp. 375-91.

9   *Body Measurements*, Nat'l Center for Health Statistics, https://www.cdc.gov/nchs/fastats/body-measurements.htm.

10   Kaufman-Buhler, *If the Chair Fits*, 388.

11   *See* Katherine Macfarlane, *Accommodation Discrimination* (2023), 72 Am. U. L. Rev. 1971, 1986 (stating that "[o]btaining reasonable accommodations requires disabled employees to disclose personal information nondisabled employees can keep to themselves," rendering the accommodations process invasive, stressful and intrusive).

12   Macfarlane, *Accommodation Discrimination*, 1979.

13   Katie Rose Guest Pryal (Blue Osprey Books, 2017), Life of the Mind Interrupted: Essays on Mental Health and Disability in Higher Education 111.

14   *See generally* Peter Blanck, Fitore Hyseni & Fatma Altunkol Wise, *Diversity and Inclusion in the American Legal Profession: Discrimination and Bias Reported by Lawyers with Disabilities and Lawyers Who Identify as LGBTQ+* (2021), 47 Am. J.L. & Med. 9; *see also* Michael Waterstone, *A New Vision of Public Enforcement* (2007), 92 Minn. L. Rev. 434, 473–74 (describing the survey results and anecdotal information about qualified lawyers with disabilities denied legal work as a result of stereotypes); Wm. T. (Bill) Robinson III, *Lawyer + Disability = Lawyer Time to Reject Perception That Disabilities Are Barriers to Productive Legal Careers*, ABA J (2012), 10 (stating that "[b]ias, stereotypes and assumptions continue to impede the hiring, retention and promotion of lawyers with disabilities. Employers are too often skeptical that they can deliver high-quality work in a timely manner").

15   *See* Nicole Buonocore Porter, *Special Treatment Stigma After the ADA Amendments Act,* (2016) 43 Pepp. L. Rev. 213.

16   The ADA protects "qualified" individuals with disabilities. 42 U.S.C. § 12112(a) (stating that "[n]o covered entity shall discriminate against a qualified individual on the basis of disability in regard to job application procedures, the hiring, advancement, or discharge of employees, employee compensation, job training, and other terms, conditions, and privileges of employment"). An individual with a disability is qualified if they "possess the requisite skill, education, experience, and training for his position" and can "perform the essential job functions, with or without reasonable accommodation." *Ehlers v. Univ. of Minnesota*, 34 F.4th 655, 659 (8th Cir. 2022).

17   Carrie Griffin Basas, *The New Boys: Women with Disabilities and the Legal Profession* (2010), 25 Berkeley J. Gender L. & Just. 32.

18   Basas, *The New Boys*, 59-60.

19   Basas, *The New Boys*, at 50.

20   Though also referred to as reasonable modifications in the health care setting, I use the term "accommodation" throughout this essay.

21   A person who is high-risk for death or serious illness from COVID-19 may be entitled to accommodations as a person with disabilities. *See, e.g., Transcript of March 27, 2020 Outreach Webinar*, U.S. Equal Emp. Opportunity Comm'n, https://www.eeoc.gov/transcript-march-27-2020-outreach-webinar#q17.

22   Katherine A. Macfarlane, *A Patient's Right to Masked Health Care Providers* (2023), Petrie-Flom Center at Harvard Law School Bill of Health Blog.

23   Id.

24   Id.

25   Id.

26   Katherine A. Macfarlane, *Personal Crusades for Public Health*, Petrie-Flom Center at Harvard Law School Bill of Health Blog (2023).

27   Katherine A. Macfarlane, *Personal Crusades for Public Health*.

28   Mark C. Weber, *Disability and the Law of Welfare: A Post-Integrationist Examination* (2000), 2000 U. Ill. L. Rev. 889, 907–08.

29   Kevin J. Coco, *Beyond the Price Tag: An Economic Analysis of Title III of the Americans with Disabilities Act* (2010), Kan. J.L. & Pub. Pol'y, 58, 90–91.

30   Coco, *Beyond the Price Tag*, 91.

31   Id.

32   *See EEOC v. BNSF Ry. Co.*, 902 F.3d 916, 926 (9th Cir. 2018) ("The ADA requires *employers* to pay for reasonable accommodations unless it is an undue hardship—it does not require employees to procure reasonable accommodations at their own expense" because "[o]therwise, people with disabilities would face "costly barriers to employment.").

6

Disabling Torts

Beth Ribet*

Abstract

Torts damage arguments in injury claims have long been attached to a conception of disability as a cruelly inflicted tragedy. This discussion proposes the possibility of "disabling torts," modeled loosely after Robert Rabin's conception of "enabling torts," to prospectively introduce a more complex conception of disability into torts doctrine. A "disabling tort" is one in which a tortfeasor who has created or has escalated substantial and/or permanent disability might be held further liable for making the tort victim foreseeably vulnerable to disability discrimination or disability subordination by third parties. This model invites attention to prospects for using torts doctrine to address "disablement," defined to include physical and mental disabilities that have been created or escalated by exposure to patterns of violence, exploitation or inequity. The chapter also considers some obstacles to advancing a "disabling tort" argument successfully in court, and reviews prospects for working through such barriers. The analysis concludes with consideration of the prospects for using "disabling torts" arguments to at least partially challenge systemic racial, gender and economic inequities currently operationalized through torts damage claims.

Introduction

In popular film and television representations of torts litigation, the plaintiff in a torts claim is stereotypically a person who is visibly and obviously embodying some form of disability. She/he/they may be using a wheelchair, wearing a neck collar, or displaying a cast and crutches, or may be made up to represent proximity to terminal illness and premature death. Disability, in our collective imagination, can be the drastic outcome of a

* Beth Ribet is the director and co-founder of Repair, a Health & Disability Justice Organization. She also lectures at UCLA, UC Law San Francisco and Tulane University School of Law. She can be reached at: beth.ribet@gmail.com

tortious act. The "damage" to a body is the most compelling evidence of the harm committed by a tort-feasor. The more tragic, devastating, pitiable, or heart-rending the disability, the more compelling the narrative of harm, whether the villain is a drunk driver, a greedy insurance carrier denying valid medical benefits claims, a corporation poisoning the water supply of a neighborhood or town, the manufacturers of Teflon, or a perpetrator of domestic violence. Popular representation has real-world implications of course, in both embodying and shaping the perceptions of jurors, judges, and other legal actors, and in turn, the types of narratives likely to gain traction in legal proceedings.[1]

In torts practice, though the representations of disability are not as consistently simplistic or stereotypical, and though practice will typically lack the glamor and drama of popular representation, the fundamental association between disabling harm and the legal viability and value of a claim has meaningful import.[2] Medical evidence and plaintiff testimony regarding the experience of becoming physical or mentally injured, impaired, or ill as the result of the negligence or malice of another party serves as a vital element in torts claims, for instance in the sub-fields of medical malpractice, product liability, some intentional torts, and broadly, a variety of other claims proceeding under personal injury doctrine. In torts litigation narratives, disability demonstrates the severity or degree of devastation associated with tortious harms, and thereby helps to determine the value or economic worth of a torts claim.[3] That is, the greater the purported damage associated with a disabling act or dynamic, the more profitable or valuable a corresponding damage award can prospectively be. Disability – in such torts claims – is an inflicted harm, originating in the wrongful act(s) of another party, and translating, when successfully represented, into economic reparation.

Disability civil rights and human rights laws generally operate with radically different conceptual premises.[4] Whereas in torts claims, the emphasis is on the representation of disability as an inflicted harm and experience of resulting damage, disability rights law is grounded in a number of underlying aims advanced by the disability rights movement, including de-stigmatization of disability, removal of structural and ideological barriers to social and economic participation for people with disabilities, and maximization of equal opportunities.[5] The tragedy or wrong postulated in Western disability rights law rests not in disability itself, but in the social reaction to disability. That is, the disability rights movement has told us, and disability rights law at least partially echoes the message, that people with disabilities are not fundamentally or organically burdened or troubled by our own bodies or psyches, but rather are only or primarily harmed by inaccessibility, discrimination, and prejudice, all dynamics which emerge after or when a disability is present.[6] Disability rights law is not presented as a remedy or response to the origination of disability itself, but rather as a corrective mechanism intended to remedy injustice or inequity in response to disability, regardless of its origin.[7] Disability, in civil and human rights legal frames, is a basis for protected class membership, and is vested in broader legal promises related to freedom from discrimination in civil society.[8]

There is an obvious tension between the utilization of disability as evidence that a person is damaged in torts legal doctrine, and the efforts of the disability rights movement to operationalize disability civil rights in order to combat the associations between disability and representations of tragedy, damage or defect, or deficiency. For example, in a journalistic intervention, disability scholars Heidi L. Janz and Michelle Stack recently articulated a social constructionist view of disability, stating: "Think disability is a tragedy? We pity you."[9] In the ensuing discussion, although the authors were not specifically engaging law, they proceeded to describe and define precisely the sorts of premises that are normatively operating in conventional torts doctrine as an ideological expression of "ableism" – or oppression and discrimination based on disability.[10] The field of Disability Studies in the last two decades has generated a host of literature analyzing and decrying traditional medical conceptions of disability that presume disability as a defective or deficient state, as compared to supposed constructs of normal bodies and psyches.[11] In this framework, the presumption or assertion that disability is a tragic or negative experience, as opposed to a benign, albeit stigmatized social variation, is understood as a disability-based prejudice, which inflicts harm on persons with disabilities through the deployment of flat stereotypes inviting pity, blame or contempt, and by underestimating the many capacities and potentials that people with varying disabilities possess.

It should therefore not be surprising that normatively, disability-related claims in torts doctrine (at least those in which disability exists or has been escalated as a consequence of a tortious act or fact pattern) and disability rights claims grounded in civil rights doctrine commonly operate in separate spheres. When discussing torts framing of disability with colleagues engaged in disability rights advocacy or work, whether in law and social service spheres, I have repeated heard the ideologies about disability manifest in torts doctrine described in energetically critical terms such as "disgusting," "exploiting the worst images of disability," or "horrifying." These references particularly pinpoint the common practice by plaintiffs' counsel of describing disability in the most catastrophic or tragic terms, in order to maximize the evidentiary value of medical facts related to an injury, impairment or illness. While my identification with disability communities is strong, personally and intellectually, my purpose in this paper is not to engage in reflexive finger-pointing at torts practitioners for utilizing stigmatizing language, or to under-estimate the ways in which the current structure of contemporary torts litigation often presupposes and mandates arguments within precisely such stigmatizing frames.

Even among practitioners who may be particularly friendly to disability rights epistemologies and agendas, or empathically connected to clients struggling with disability stigma, it would likely be ineffective, and in the worst instances legal malpractice, to advance a torts claim related to a disabling event or harm, and to simultaneously argue that the resulting disability is in fact *not* a harmful experience. That is, despite their many compelling aims, it would be reasonable to state that, at least at present, mainstream disability rights frameworks focusing on the de-stigmatization and normalization of disability apparently have little to offer plaintiff-side torts practitioners, as the emphases on removing stigma and acknowledging the positive and benign elements of disability hardly strengthen legal actions that rest in part on demonstrating that disability is persuasive evidence of damage and harm. This dichotomy, in which one cannot simultaneously advocate for positive conceptions of disability and pursue meaningful remedies for harms that are disabling, should be understood as part of a larger legal landscape in which complexity or the wholeness or integrity of experience are too often inarticulable.[12]

One response to the tension between torts and civil rights frames might be to simply accept that each has fundamentally different premises and ideological foundations, and nevertheless both have functioned for decades in advancing their respective purposes, notwithstanding their irreconcilable elements. It is not novel, after all, for varying areas of legal doctrine to embody incompatible or dissonant principles, and to nevertheless continue to operate in their own spheres.[13] While the differing frames may be theoretically interesting, beyond comparison as an intellectual exercise, why does engaging this tension matter? I have two responses to this question.

First, representing a client's disability and its economic and social implications can implicate professional responsibility. While many attorneys may reflexively consider a client's "interests" strictly in terms of the client's attachment to a favorable legal outcome or a "win," it is vital to note that standards of professional conduct encourage attorneys to provide "counsel" as needed, in a broader sense. As a simple example, the American Bar Association Model Rules of Professional Conduct delineate the role of an attorney as an "Advisor," and state that: "In rendering advice, a lawyer may refer not only to law but to other considerations such as moral, economic, social and political factors, that may be relevant to the client's situation."[14]

Having one's disability rendered in comparatively catastrophic or stigmatizing terms will predictably have at least some psychological and social consequences for many plaintiffs. On balance, some clients may be fully able to manage those consequences, and may also be thoroughly capable of making an informed choice to prioritize particular positive legal outcomes over other social-psychological considerations. However, it can readily be argued that whether or not any shift in legal strategy ultimately results, plaintiffs' attorneys have some ethical obligation to consider the psycho-social consequences associated with representing disability in a torts claim, and to provide counsel informed by that consideration, among the various factors bearing on client's interests.[15] That is, the frames and considerations that tend to typify disability civil rights doctrine, while not eclipsing the existing traditions, precedents and norms operative in torts claims, should not truly be understood as presumptively separate from or irrelevant to torts litigation. Robust application of legal standards of professional conduct can mandate that in at least some cases, the social and legal meanings of disability need to be contemplated from multiple vectors.

My second response to the question of whether and why to integrate equity-based conceptions of disability into torts practice constitutes a primary project in this paper. My supposition is that there is an under-explored opportunity to draw on conceptions of disability prevalent in disability movements, inclusive of disability rights, and also disability justice movements.[16] Doing so can enhance, rather than detract from the viability and material value associated with torts claims related to many forms of disabling injury or harm. Advancing this thought experiment, and ideally making it the basis for an analysis with practical utility, involves several theoretical elements and tools. First, in order to explore how a critical disability analysis might strengthen a torts claim, I engage the concept of "disablement." Disablement is a term primarily located in critical disability theory, and in its varied definitions, consistently implicates the social contexts that shape disability.[17] After introducing and explaining the concept, I reflect on its prospects for productively informing plaintiff-side legal strategy in torts claims related to one or more disabling conditions.

This project also draws on the work of Robert Rabin, and his now classic analysis in "Enabling Torts."[18] Rabin's analysis of gun manufacturer liability essentially proposes that in assessing tortfeasor culpability, "the enabler" – referencing a person or entity who takes actions that sets the stage for the tortious act of another – can be subject to damages for creating a risk that would not have existed or would not have been as severe, but for their actions.[19] Rabin's analysis complicated the field of torts scholarship in order to better capture the complexity of liability involving successive causation.

My analysis similarly engages successive causation in torts claims, and essentially moves in a different direction. Rabin's analysis takes the tortious act as an endpoint, and then focuses on the relationships between and choices made by actors who played different roles in bringing that tort to fruition.[20] In contrast, I take a tortious act as a beginning point, and consider how the infliction of a disabling injury can make the tortfeasor prospectively liable for increasing the risk of plaintiff vulnerability to a range of present or future harms and legal claims, including but not limited to disability civil rights violations by third parties. This intervention is meaningful. The approach allows for the articulation of legally cognizable damage without exclusively relying on the framing of all disabilities as a medically defined tragedy. That is, by disabling a plaintiff, a tortfeasor has certainly created some illness, injury or impairment to which torts doctrine traditionally accords varying "value" based on medical consequences or outcomes. But in addition, I propose that the tortfeasor can face liability based on social definitions and responses to disability drawing directly on (though not necessarily limited to) conceptions of disability present in contemporary disability civil rights doctrine.

In instances where the disabling damage is, in medical terms, moderate, ultimate economic damages might nevertheless be higher based on arguments about vulnerability to discrimination and other social risks associated with disability. Rabin's argument is a vital foundation for this frame, because he does the crucial work of conceptualizing and articulating how one actor may bear some torts liability for enabling the action of another.[21] As noted however, because we are exploring different axes of liability, an analysis of disablement and torts claims must engage some different questions. One of the more formidable challenges embedded in this analysis involves establishing liability for potential harms that may not yet have occurred at the time of legal action, but that are likely and foreseeable. In subsequent discussion, I explore some pathways by which this type of advocacy can occur.

Disablement: An Introduction to the Concept

An initial conception of "disablement" was piloted in 2001 by Marta

Russell and Jean Stewart, as a contribution to the interdisciplinary field of Disability Studies, and as an adjunct to related disability activism and advocacy.[22] As Russell and Stewart advanced the term, "disablement" refers to the set of processes that undergird and limit the social status of "person with a disability."[23] A salient feature of disability in Russell and Stewart's paradigm is its social meaning, and the set of economic, structural and political constraints imposed on people with disabilities by our social world.[24] In this analysis, a physical or psychological impairment, illness or injury may exist in its own right, and may or may not pose an innate hardship or organic experience of deprivation or suffering. However, the socio-political subordination of people with disabilities should be understood as a substantial, if not the primary reason why people with disabilities are truly "disabled." That is, disablement references the institutions, norms, restrictions, inequities and structural dynamics that result in people with disabilities being disproportionately impoverished, often excluded from multiple areas of community or political participation, stigmatized, and disproportionately institutionalized or incarcerated.[25]

The oppression or harm caused by "disability" in this schematic is not primarily located in a (supposed) defect or weakness in individual bodies or psyches, but rather in the dehumanization, punishment and marginalization experienced by people with disabilities at the hands of the state.[26] This epistemological relationship to disability is consistent with the "social constructionist" critique in Disability Studies. Critical disability theorists have posited a dichotomy between social vs. medical conceptions of disability, with the latter embodying traditional notions of disability commonly deployed in medical professions, and also incorporated in U.S. law and policy.[27] Although there are varying elements of the social constructionist critique, the core message consistent through most of its applications challenges the presumption that disability is an objective, medical or psychiatric fact, unmediated by the social response to illness and impairment, and the social location – including the racial, gender and class identities – of an individual with a disability.[28] In this theoretical intervention, the "problem" of disability is vested entirely, or at least substantially, in medical, legal, economic, and other structural responses to disability, rather than in the body or psyche of an individual with a disability.[29]

Introducing Another Dimension of Disablement

I generally adopt and appreciate Russell and Stewart's conception of disablement. Although in this and prior work, I use a partially redefined version of the term "disablement," my agenda in deploying the word is an expansion of, rather than a critique of, Russell and Stewart's original framework.[30] I have previously proposed and illustrated a second (and compatible) definition of disablement.[31] Specifically, in addition to adopting Russell and Stewart's meaning, I utilize the term disablement to describe the imposition of injuries, illnesses and impairments as a direct consequence of exposure to subordination and inequity.[32] That is, "disablement," in my academic and community work, describes the processes by which subordination based on race, gender, class, sexuality, religion, citizenship and age can operate to damage, sicken, injure, and sometimes break bodies and minds, with long-term disabling consequences.[33] Whereas Russell and Stewart focused on the social interpretation and process of subordination based on perceived or actual illnesses, injuries or impairments, my second conception of disablement foregrounds the ways in which subordination – based on race, gender, class, sexuality, age, religion, immigrant status, or any related form of social vulnerability – can generate new injuries, illnesses and impairments, which then, as new or escalated "disabilities" become the target of further subordination.[34]

This compound definition of disablement deliberately encompasses a very wide range of social dynamics and their physical and psychological consequences. For instance, racial justice and environmental advocates have delineated the practice of dumping industrial waste or other toxic by-products in low-income neighborhoods, disproportionately comprised of poor people of color, as an example of "environmental racism."[35] The documented consequences of such practices include development of asthma, certain cancers, and other diseases related to toxic exposure from air or groundwater.[36] To the extent that such conditions can be understood as "disabilities" – and in most instances under contemporary U.S. disability law they can – the development of disease as a result of vulnerability to environmental racism can also be understood as one example of "disablement."

Disablement can also be the consequence of exploitation or violence.[37] For instance, widespread phenomena such as gender-based and domestic violence have well-documented medical and disabling consequences. These can include the infliction of a range of potential physical injuries, some of which may be permanent, and also normatively and routinely include the generation of post-traumatic stress disorder, as well as other prospective psychiatric disabilities such as anxiety disorders and clinical depression.[38] Similarly, labor exploitation, for instance in "sweatshops" or among migrant or day laborers, when continuing over any substantial length of time, commonly results in physical ailments associated with overwork or exposure to brutal or unsafe working conditions, including an increased risk of heart disease.[39] Mass or state violence, including through torture, or among civilian populations exposed to ethnic cleansing, genocidal violence[40], or other acts categorized as "war crimes" also has documented medical, psychiatric and disabling consequences, for those who survive.[41] In each of these instances, a social vulnerability, whether based on gender, class, immigration status, ethno-racial group membership, or a combination can precipitate or maintain exposure to harmful conditions. That vulnerability, when it results in lasting or prolonged medical or psychiatric damage cognizable as "disability," is a basic element of "disablement" as I utilize the term.

The prior examples involve obviously aggressive or at least negligent actions by a concrete entity, actor, or set of actors. However, disablement can also be the product of mass systemic deprivation, originating in very diffuse social institutions, and evolving over generations. For instance, exposure to poverty can generate an additional range of prospectively devastating medical consequences, whether through malnutrition, housing insecurity, deficits in access to clean water, deficits in healthcare access and quality, and over-exposure to the elements, as well as by decreasing options to avoid violent, dangerous or exploitative conditions in work, neighborhoods, and schools.[42] The medical conditions associated with poverty (and with the racial and gender inequities that commonly undergird poverty in the U.S.), are a well-recognized basis for the prevalence of "health disparities" as articulated in the fields of medicine, public health, and related social scientific spheres.[43] In mental health scholarship and clinical practice, the role of poverty in generating anxiety, depression, disruption of sleep, and severe psychological stress is also acknowledged, and linked to physical as well as psychological deterioration later in life, as psychological stress depresses immunity, neurological function, and cellular health.[44] When these analyses and sources of data are linked to contemporary legal definitions of disability, there is little difficulty or intellectual leap needed to make the case that poverty is a social determinant of health, and moreover that poverty is often and normatively "disabling" in its embodied impact.[45]

Are all disabilities the result of disablement?

To synthesize, "disablement" in my conception rests on two integrated dynamics:

1.   The generation of new or escalated injuries or illnesses and impairments as a result of a systemic pattern of racial, economic, and gender inequity or vulnerability.[46]

2.   The socio-political, economic and structural discrimination that a person who is injured, ill, or impaired then faces as a "disabled" person.[47]

It should be noted that only the second dynamic would apply relatively universally to all persons with disabilities generally, or among torts plaintiffs. That is, not all disabilities are the product of inequity, or caused by "disablement." Disability may occur as a result of normative and relatively healthy aging, as a result of random accidents, or as a result of arguably voluntary risk-taking (e.g. riding a motorcycle, initiating a fight, or engaging in physically intensive recreation).[48] In many instances, whether vulnerability to inequity or subordination is at issue takes some analysis. For instance, the infliction of disabilities is very high among military personnel, contributing to the high rates of disability among veterans.[49] It would be easy to argue that, absent a draft, since military service is generally "voluntary," disabilities resulting from military service are not a clear example of "disablement," with the implication that inequity is not at issue. However patterns of enlistment in the United States support the insight that military service is common among working-class and poverty-class young people, who are disproportionately people of color, as a response to the relative lack of economic and higher educational opportunities.[50] Therefore, one result of economic and educational disparities in the U.S., for at least some racially and economically vulnerable populations, is the increased likelihood of becoming disabled during military service. In this sense, at least for some service-people and veterans, disablement is directly at issue in the risks inherent in many military settings for military personnel, in addition to the many disabling harms present for civilian victims or targets of military violence.

Another illustrative example involves disabilities present at birth, some of which are commonly termed "birth defects."[51] Disabilities present at birth can happen within any demographic or family, and it would therefore, again be easy to assume that the conception of disablement – describing injuries, illnesses and impairments generated by inequity or subordination – are automatically never at issue. However, ample data documents the correlations between gender, racial, and economic inequities, and threats to the possibility of healthy pregnancies, potentially resulting in maternal illness and mortality, and in fetal or infant mortality, or disability.[52] Moreover, disabilities that are genetic or biological in origin are not presumptively always separable from a context of inequity. Parental genetics or biology can be profoundly influenced by social conditions, including for instance, exposure to toxins, unsafe medications, and to extreme stressors, and each of these can potentially originate in inequitable or subordinating conditions.[53] So for instance, a child born with illness or impairments related to a parent's exposure to harmful chemicals as a migrant farmworker, or in other conditions involving unsafe and exploitative uses of vulnerable labor, would fit within this frame of "disablement," because labor and immigrant exploitation was a factor in fetal exposure to toxins, that then generated disability. The growing study of "epigenetics" particularly indicates that the social conditions experienced by a given person can create genetic changes, which are then heritable, and can in some instances be harmful.[54] That is, exposure to stress, damage, trauma, and deprivation, particularly for prolonged periods, can ultimately shape biology and genetics over generations.[55] Therefore, while not all disabilities grounded in genetics or present at birth are necessarily a consequence of "disablement," for populations and communities experiencing severe harms over time, inequity may often be a significant contributing factor to the development of disabilities based on biological or genetic variations.

In essence, the first dynamic – the creation or aggravation of injuries, illnesses and impairments as a result of vulnerability to subordination or inequity – is at issue with many, but not all disabilities, including but not limited to those that become at issue in torts litigation. The second dynamic – the subjection of persons who are injured, ill or impaired to disability discrimination, subordination, or inequity – is potentially at issue with virtually all disabilities, including but not limited to those at issue in torts litigation.

Why would thinking of (some) disabilities within the frame of "disablement" potentially be significant in torts claims?

One might argue that while disablement as a phenomenon is interesting, a disability-conscious approach to torts claims need not focus on disablement per se. After all, liability for making someone vulnerable to present and future disability discrimination could happen negligently and generate liability, whether or not the cause of disability was specifically rooted in inequity or exploitation. Having an analysis of torts liability based on making someone vulnerable to disability discrimination can be somewhat productive regardless. I want to acknowledge that some readers might indeed choose to use this analysis for clients who are not the victims of disablement, but who have suffered disabling injuries, and can still benefit from a basic disability rights conscious analysis. However, it is my priority in this paper to advance an argument that can begin to use torts law differently, and hopefully innovatively. I propose that torts law might function – albeit imperfectly – to challenge systemic patterns of action that tend to distribute disabling harm, often collectively, in ways that are inextricable from structural racism, gender, and economic stratification. In this project, an analysis of disablement is of course essential. In the ensuing analysis, I advance discussion of "disabling torts" in terms that need not be strictly limited to litigating disablement, but that are attentive to that possibility.

Enabling Torts: Foundations for Understanding Successive Causation and Shared Liability

In his classic analysis of prospective liability for enabling the actions of a tortfeasor, Robert Rabin engages the notion of "negligent entrustment" in torts legal tradition, as a partial basis to propose that in the presence of sufficiently negligent behavior, a party may be held responsible for actions that support or strengthen the tortious behavior of another.[56] Rabin proposes that where corporate irresponsibility "puts a potentially dangerous product in the hands of criminal actors with malevolent intentions, ultimately leading to the injury of innocent victims," then attaching some liability to the irresponsible corporation can be an appropriate remedy.[57] He uses multiple examples, including an instance where an individual who paid for the cost of a car for a relative who was grossly negligent behind the wheel was found to be culpable for the injuries that relative caused. Similarly, he discusses an instance where a train traveler was not able to exit at her stop due to the train conductor's error, and then had to attempt to get home through a dangerous area, where she was raped twice.[58] In this latter instance, the negligence of the transit staff was a basis for liability for the physical and sexual harms she suffered.[59] Rabin also acknowledges that some aspects of his "enabling" paradigm can apply or appear to apply, though not as readily or cleanly, to circumstances in which there is not a clear third party "criminal" actor or an "innocent" individual victim.[60] He discusses government health cost reimbursement suits against the tobacco industry as an example.[61]

My aim in this discussion is not to suggest that Rabin's paradigm of enablement generally captures the scenarios at issue in thinking about liability for making victims of torts vulnerable to disability subordination. Rabin's analysis is useful however, for several reasons. First, he outlines how liability may attach for creating a circumstance which can be understood as "inviting" tortious behavior, or creating danger or risk.[62] Second, he highlights that the danger or risk is both significant and foreseeable.[63] Third, he acknowledges policy and practical imperatives for holding corporate actors accountable for serially creating significant dangers to public health and safety.[64] While a "malevolent" actor may take advantage of the risk that a gun company creates, Rabin recognizes that the manufacturer has played a role in enabling a tortious act without which the act might never have occurred.[65] That is, at least some gun violence would not occur "but for" the irresponsible actions of the gun industry. This dynamic can be understood as a policy issue because the actions of the industry function as an "underlying cause" of gun violence, which – proponents argue – must be addressed in order to reduce the incidence of gun-related crimes.[66] How might this analysis support a conception of "disabling" torts? In the subsequent section, I unpack how Rabin's model can be helpful.

Disabling Torts: A New (or Expanded) Direction for Legal Advocacy?

To explore the utility of a "disabling tort," and potentially to integrate analysis of "disablement" into torts practice, it is helpful to consider the elements that might be at issue. This project is complicated by the complexity of the concept of "disability." The term includes a very wide range of physical and mental conditions, variations in degree or severity of conditions on life activities and experience, and variations in the degrees to which and instances in which conditions make a person a target for disability discrimination.[67] This complexity is not unique to conceptions of disability in torts practice; the meanings of disability continue to evolve and shift in a variety of social and legal spheres. Without attempting to meaningfully explore the broader definitions of disability, I acknowledge this complexity as a factor in analysis of a prospective "disabling tort," which may affect the applicability of some elements. I elaborate below.

Proposed Elements of a Disabling Tort

Terms like "elements" or "factors" are typically used in legal practice and scholarship to describe the considerations that courts take into account when assessing whether a particular claim is fully applicable, or to consider how it should be decided. Since this analysis is hypothetical, and also aspirational (i.e. I hope that it will eventually materialize in practice), I use the term "element" in somewhat fluid terms. I discuss proposed elements that might (or might not in some instances) eventually manifest more formally in torts doctrine, but also acknowledge them as bases for consideration that a torts practitioner can informally consider in assessing the potential arguments to make in order to advance an argument about liability for creating a new or enhanced risk of disability discrimination or subordination.

Creating or Escalating Disability

The first element of a "disabling tort" involves liability for creating an injury, illness or impairment, or for significantly escalating an existing injury, illness or impairment. That is, a tortfeasor must be wholly or partially culpable for a tortious act, and that act must be explicitly tied to the creation of disability or the expansion or increased severity of disability-related symptoms. Note here that traditional torts litigation already addresses the impact of disabling symptoms relative to pain and suffering, and to various kinds of resulting physical difficulties. Therefore, this element is necessary, but – on its own – insufficient to advance an analysis of further liability for imposing the risk of discrimination or subordination.

Foreseeability (and the Limitations in Current Legal Responses to Disability)

A second element involves foreseeability of social consequences. Echoing Rabin's analysis of the creation of risk, the attachment of liability would generally be predicated on the fact that the tortfeasor was reckless, negligent, or intentional in making a person vulnerable to the social harms that U.S. society attaches to having a disability.[68] This analysis is complicated by a few considerations. As noted, disabilities can vary significantly relative to the degree to which they are detectable by others, and the degree to which they are the targets of legally cognizable discrimination. As a result, this element will require some analysis of the foreseeable likelihood of disability-related discrimination or other related harms. Note that the fact that many disabilities can be "hidden" does not necessarily preclude meeting this element. As in torts law (which focuses more heavily on negligent, as compared to intentional torts), disability discrimination law does not formally, and should not consistently, require that discrimination always be intentional, admitted, or conscious on the part of a defendant.[69] Further, ignorance of legal requirements under federal or state statutes or doctrine is generally not a viable defense to a charge of disability discrimination.[70] People with hidden disabilities can experience discrimination because they make themselves known in order to pursue a disability accommodation or because they are open about having a disability identity, or because the discrimination is built into the structure of a given setting, and does not need to be targeted at individuals who are known to have disabilities in order to have a discriminatory impact.[71] Similarly, I would suggest that a tortfeasor's sensitivity to disability issues or awareness of statistics about disability discrimination need not be essential to determining that the likelihood of social consequences is foreseeable, provided that the incidents at issue (or prospectively at issue in future) are ones which could reasonably have been anticipated.

However, there are circumstances in which a foreseeability argument would be more likely to fail. For instance, there are many aspects of "disability subordination" or "oppression" as articulated in fields such as Disability Studies and within disability communities that cannot presently be fully articulated using our U.S. civil rights model.[72] I preface the next part of this discussion with the qualification that the example I am about to articulate is not exhaustive or representative of all instances in which either foreseeability or the challenges embedded in the articulation of experience in a legal context would be in question. However, as one important example: the U.S.

civil rights model diverges from the international disability human rights model captured in the United Nations Convention on the Rights of Persons with Disabilities (CRPD).[73] The CRPD calls generally on state signatories to implement "universal design" in a range of possible spheres.[74] Universal design emerged first in the field of architecture as a way to describe efforts to build spaces that would be organically accessible, without later modification, for wheelchair users, and for some other people with physical disabilities.[75] The notion of building accessibility into "spaces" become a larger concept, applicable to a range of spheres including but not limited to workplace norms and policies, educational settings, and social policy. In simple terms, a difference between universally designed spaces, policies, and programs, and the U.S. civil rights model is that universal design more rarely burdens individuals with having to ask for or negotiate receipt of "accommodations," "modifications," or accessibility, because institutions are responsible for creating enough options and flexibility to generate accessibility to the extent possible, without the need for an individual request.[76]

Much of the current U.S. civil rights model, including, for instance, the use of "interactive processes" in employment and some other settings, becomes typically irrelevant when universal design is a requisite and actualized policy approach. However, the United States has not ratified the CRPD, preferring our current civil rights model which allows for substantial institutional inaccessibility, so long as at least some individual exceptions are made for some recognized persons with disabilities. I note that the increased burden on plaintiffs to ask for accessibility embodied in the U.S. civil rights model has racially and economically disparate effects.[77] Access to white privilege and social and economic resources bears both on the likelihood that individuals will be aware of and empowered to negotiate access to disability accommodations and modifications, and that the institutional response will be relatively receptive.[78]

I raise the question of universal design relative to "foreseeability" because it is likely foreseeable that some persons with disabilities would sometimes suffer due to the absence of universal design in employment, educational and/or social spheres. However, part of the element of foreseeability goes beyond knowing of the likelihood of an outcome.[79] In this context, the outcome would generally also be one that would predictably generate a legal remedy. Rabin's model of an enabling tort focused primarily on third party liability for crimes committed by malevolent others.[80] That is, he addressed instances in which the question of legal accountability was tied to well-established criminal categories that courts consistently recognized. It is at least conceivable but substantially less likely that a U.S. court would be willing to hold a tortfeasor accountable for exposing a person to the absence of universally designed options to live, work, or learn when the right to universal design is not otherwise recognized by almost all federal or state civil rights instruments.[81] Legally cognizable experiences of disability discrimination are also the subject of more empirical study, and therefore tend to be attached to a much wider range of existing data.[82] As a result, classical experiences of discrimination are, at least in some instances, more likely to be supported by the possibility of introducing empirical evidence needed to successfully advance a claim for related damages.

U.S. disability civil rights as such captures and can remedy a limited subset of the ways in which people experience disabling harm and disability discrimination. We might ask the question: does torts doctrine actually have to be bound by the current limitations of the U.S. civil rights approach? Why not push for more recognition or a wider conception of discrimination in a different area of law? While it is at least conceivable that torts doctrine could become far more expansive in its recognition of the experiences people with disabilities have than contemporary civil rights doctrine, it seems more likely that torts courts would, at least initially, recognize vulnerability to legal examples of "discrimination," rather than holding tortfeasors accountable for a wider range of harms to people with disabilities than the U.S. legal system otherwise tends to recognize. I use the term "subordination" here to recognize the broader category of disability-related harms that include, but are not limited to discrimination. Plaintiff-side torts attorneys can be creative in their arguments, and my aim is not to foreclose possibilities (even presently unlikely ones). It may be helpful in assessment of this element to consider the extent to which plaintiffs and their attorneys are prepared to be daring in their approach or arguments, or to couple such arguments with less daring ones that may survive even if an argument about a legally nebulous harm fails. It is also important to note that disability civil rights and human rights are evolving areas, and frameworks that are on the "fringe" or are unenforceable now, may have more traction in time – for instance if the U.S. Congress did eventually vote to ratify the CRPD.[83]

Policy, Fragmentation and Time

A third element involves a policy issue: essentially the articulation of a problem that a court can address, and that is not otherwise already fully captured in either existing torts doctrine, or in any area of disability law. Unlike torts doctrine – disability civil rights models in the U.S. tend not to conceive of the origin of disability as relevant to the applicability of civil rights doctrine.[84] Let us imagine a hypothetical where an employer is responsible for creating or escalating a worker's disability. While liability for that harm may result in a workers compensation claim or personal injury claim, it has relatively minimal bearing on the application of disability civil rights law in the future.

So, for instance, if an employee received temporary workers compensation benefits after being injured at work, and – maybe – some torts damages for the medical costs, stress and pain associated with the injury as well, torts and labor law would be understood as having fulfilled their functions. If the following year, or a few years later, the employer terminated this same employee based on an argument that it was an undue hardship to cover the cost of providing the employee with disability accommodations related to the disability it caused, the fact that the employer had created the disability at issue would likely not negate the viability of that undue hardship argument, because the origin of the disability is not a factor that disability civil rights law acknowledges.[85] Similarly, if, after a few years, that employer argued successfully that the employee was no longer able to perform their essential job functions because of the disability, that employee would likely no longer be protected under Title I of the Americans with Disabilities Act, notwithstanding the fact that the employer caused, created, or escalated the disability in question.[86]

In theory, torts law could be reliably available to address the origin of (or escalation of) disability. However, given: (a) inequitable access to legal counsel for many workers,[87] (b) statutes of limitation and (c) the unpredictable aspects of disabilities over time, scenarios like these are readily part of the landscape of disability in employment. In other work, I have talked about the abilities of employers to essentially "use up" (i.e. injure or sicken) and "throw away" (i.e. stop employing) vulnerable workers through labor exploitation without incurring either significant torts or civil rights liability.[88] A substantial aspect of the policy import involved in exploring "disabling torts" involves essentially making the causation of harmful and predictable injuries substantially less cost-effective, in employment, and other spheres.

Disability legal scholarship refers to the problem of "fragmentation" within disability rights law, in that different aspects of disability rights and needs are partially captured in different laws, leaving gaps in which the fulfillment or delivery of rights is no one's responsibility.[89] To my knowledge, the concept of fragmentation has not previously been applied to describe this particular nexus of disability civil rights and torts law. However, the concept fits well here, as a way to understand how torts and disability civil rights doctrine both fail to fully remedy disabling harm in its social context. A question in analyzing the viability of enhancing torts damages can be essentially – is there a meaningful option to argue for damages related to present or future social consequences associated with disability discrimination? This third element invites us to consider: is this particular torts claim one in which the long-term impact of disability is or was likely to be under-recognized in torts practice and in damages? If so, can that lack of recognition be remedied?

It bears noting that arguments about torts liability for creating vulnerability to disability discrimination (or for subordination) can sometimes focus on discrimination that occurred after the tortious act but began before the onset of legal action. In these cases, the analysis is closer to that envisioned by Rabin in "Enabling Torts," in that it considers the role of one party (a tortfeasor) in enabling the harmful actions of an identified second party (who might for instance, be violating civil rights law).[90] In such cases, the actions for which damages are sought, and the parties responsible are likely more clear. However, a disabling tort might also encompass claims – such as that posited in the hypothetical above – in which the aim is to argue for the harm done by making a tort victim vulnerable to future disability discrimination which has not yet commenced, and where the perpetrator(s) might or might not yet be known. Therefore, part of this analysis is about time or timing. A vital strategic question prospects for advancing a claim for damages that will be predicated on the ability or receptivity of courts to recognize the risk of future discriminatory (or subordinating) acts as stemming from a disabling tort. If the answer to this question is affirmative, it may be higher risk or require more empirical evidence, though it may nevertheless be quite viable.

Disablement

While this fourth element is not one that applies to every prospective disabling tort, it is a helpful one to analyze, both in individual and class-based claims. I do not claim to have imagined all of the ways it may ultimately become relevant. Arguments about "disablement" may in time lend persuasive strength to assertions about the deterrent value associated with higher damage awards, and may eventually drive new statutory protections. As discussed earlier, we should understand "disablement" as referencing disabilities that are in essence created or exacerbated by violence, inequity and/or exploitation.[91] The concepts of "violence" and "exploitation" may be interpreted broadly to include interpersonal, economic/commercial, structural, and systemic forms of violence and exploitation.[92] In beginning to imagine deeper remedies for disablement within torts law, it is helpful to think about disablement as built into the power relations and structural inequities in our society.[93] In other words, the social justice imperative that drives my analysis involves imagining how to make it more costly, rather than easy and without substantial consequence, for those with power to injure vulnerable people.[94]

In analyzing whether disablement is at issue, at least two questions are relevant. First, in what ways (if any) was the plaintiff socially vulnerable? Answers to this question can involve and are not limited to socio-economic status, gender, race, ethnicity, nationality, sexuality, immigrant or citizenship status, age, (pre-existing) disability, veteran status, trauma history, incarceration history, physical appearance, and/or marital or family status.[95] Second, was that vulnerability such that it either caused all or part of the plaintiff's experience of tortious harm, or escalated the impact of the tortious harm, or both? The fact that a plaintiff is very vulnerable does not in itself always suffice to make any disabling harm an example of disablement. In addition, in some instances, disablement may be present, but it may be difficult to apply culpability for the dynamics of disablement to any person(s) or individual entity. That is, "poverty" is not a plausible defendant in a torts claim. This fact does not negate the analysis. Not every tortfeasor need be a sweatshop owner, a brutal police officer or prison warden, a corporate CEO who engages in union busting, a human trafficker, a white nationalist, a perpetrator of intimate partner violence, or an exploitative landlord in order for an analysis of disablement to be meaningful. The complexity of disablement can, however, complicate that analysis. For the moment, it is meaningful to note that the defendant in a torts claim need not bear responsibility for all or even for any of the plaintiff's circumstances or vulnerability, but may have some liability for foreseeable harms related to disablement. This recognition potentially matters in the formulation of damage arguments and claims, in proposing that the defendant has not just made the plaintiff vulnerable to disability discrimination, but that the discrimination will worsen and interact with existing dynamics of subordination.[96]

Application of the Elements

While the notion of expanding torts advocacy and bridging currently disparate notions of disability is compelling, certain challenges must be engaged in order to move the prospect of such an expansion from the purely conceptual into potential practice. I consider the broad category of "accidental torts due to negligence," as an entry point to examine how we might conceive of disablement in an accidental torts action.[97] Much of this analysis however, could also apply to intentional torts.

An accidental tort has four recognized elements: duty, breach, causation and damages.[98] I propose a hypothetical plaintiff who has suffered multiple disabling injuries, resulting in the need to use a walker for the foreseeable future, which she/he/they did not use before. In this hypothetical, the tortfeasor has been or will be found liable for duty and breach, for causing the injuries, and for damages corresponding to resulting physical pain and suffering, and medical costs. We can also imagine that this is a solo plaintiff, rather than a member of a class.

I will not spend more time discussing duty and breach, as these elements bear on whether a defendant is liable for having behaved negligently in such as a way that they might be liable for having done harm.[99] Since this hypothetical involves a plaintiff who has a good cause of action for an injury, we can assume that these elements are met. Causation is more complicated. While the defendant has been or will be found liable for having caused the injury, in a disabling tort, the question here is also whether by causing the injury, the defendant(s) may be liable for making the plaintiff vulnerable to disability discrimination. Similarly, damages are also complex. We know that the plaintiff is owed damages related to pain and suffering and medical costs. But if they are vulnerable to disability discrimination (or related forms of subordination) as a result of the injuries, how might that vulnerability be argued and monetized? While I do not aim to fully answer this question in this paper, I propose that the answers to the question may be helpful in significantly categorizing and increasing damage awards for lost income (not simply related to disability, but specifically for employment discrimination), for losses related to social opportunities and networks (including recreational options), and for health consequences predictably associated with subordination-related stress. For the most part, analysis related to disabling torts will fit this model, in that an analysis of a "disabling" tort becomes relevant at the stages of causation and damages, once a defendant clearly is culpable for duty and breach.

I proceed now to consider the proposed elements of a disabling tort, as they might help inform and enhance analysis of causation and damages in an unintentional tort that has caused injury. In this hypothetical, the first element of a disabling tort can again, be understood as having been met, because the defendant has created disability. The second element is foreseeability (of discrimination or subordination). Because the plaintiff's injury is readily detectible (i.e. people will see the plaintiff using a walker), there is somewhat less work to do to determine whether the plaintiff will encounter discriminatory treatment or other disability-related harms, though as noted earlier, discrimination against people with hidden disabilities will often still be readily foreseeable. But what discrimination or subordination is at issue?

Answers to this question can of course vary significantly. Traditional torts doctrine relies essentially on a medical as opposed to a social conception of disability, in which demonstrated and foreseeable outcomes are assessed based on a supposedly objective set of consequences and symptoms associated with a diagnosis.[100] We can of course cherry pick individual cases which demonstrate creative arguments related to social outcomes associated with the infliction of disability. For instance, some cases related to the infliction of burn scars will overtly acknowledge and calculate the stigmatized social response to physical "disfigurement" as a basis for damages.[101] While often not as overtly calculable, plaintiff testimony about the challenges in navigating the world can also surface in negotiations and other trial processes as part of the broader framing of disability as life-altering and tragic. It is not that social discrimination is never raised. However, for the most part the traditional calculation of harm treats social discrimination and the broader landscape of disability subordination as mostly distinct from contemplation of the tortfeasor's responsibility. Changing that norm can certainly draw in some instances on plaintiff testimony based on their experiences interacting with the world after the tortious harm has occurred. However, not all plaintiffs will be able to meaningfully advance this work through experiential testimony. In beginning to build this type of argument, empirical evidence, coupled with expert testimony needed to translate social scientific and health-related data to courts will be vital.[102]

Relative to our instant hypothetical, empirical data can demonstrate that a substantial portion of public spaces still fail to comply with the basic architectural requirements of the Americans with Disabilities Act, such that the use of a walker will make entry to and navigation of some public spaces a hardship.[103] The more challenging part of the argument involves charting out how interpersonal discrimination related to the use of a walker tends to manifest, in spheres including but not limited to employment, friendship, community leadership, religious participation, voting, recreation, transportation and travel, romance and sexuality, and housing. As the interdisciplinary field of Disability Studies has developed in recent decades however, resulting scholarship has actually provided a relatively robust set of materials that can advance this argument.[104] Public health analyses, for instance, of the social consequences of isolation related to disability, can meaningfully advance arguments for damages related to areas of social life that might otherwise be left entirely out of conventional torts damage calculations.[105]

It is notable here that the development of an empirical literature about disability discrimination and subordination is relatively new, with major growth in the last three decades since the passage of the Americans with Disabilities Act.[106] U.S. torts doctrine, in contrast, is grounded in part in pre-Revolutionary War British Common Law, and reflects generations of legal doctrine in which the notion of "disability discrimination" did not truly exist in the sense that it does now. Given this context, it is in some respects unsurprising that torts doctrine and disability civil rights law reflect major dissonances. However, the opportunity to essentially update torts doctrine to better capture contemporary conceptions of disability is supported now in ways that it could not have been before the present era.

Relative to the third element (on policy, fragmentation, and time), again, reliance on empirical data is likely to be helpful in many instances in advancing arguments based on compensation for harms associated with discrimination or other related forms of subordination that have not yet occurred, but that are a foreseeable and very likely consequence of disabling a tort victim. Damages for future harms are hardly unprecedented in torts damage calculations (for instance, for loss of income, home renovations, and medical costs), so the stretch in this instance is to prepare courts to more readily accept that the risk of discrimination for instance, is not either too nebulous or too disconnected from the tortious harm to reliably predict a basis for concrete damages. Relative to this hypothetical, the question of whether there is an under-realized area for pursuit of damages is reasonably straightforward. As long as the argument that being permanently disabled and using a walker will reliably generate disability discrimination can be supported through a combination of witness or expert testimony and empirical data, then this element prospectively supports advancing a related argument for damages.

Finally, the element of disablement can be, but does not have to be applied to this hypothetical in order to advance a disabling tort. Whether disablement has occurred will depend on additional facts, including the social status of the plaintiff, the dynamics involved in the tort, and the impact of the tort relative to existing and future vulnerability to complex subordination. If disablement is at issue, resulting arguments may take a number of possible forms, For instance, let us suppose that in this hypothetical, the plaintiff was violently injured through police brutality or by gender violence (or both.) "Impact litigation" – referencing trials that are intended to shift an area of legal doctrine – in the realm of torts practice commonly focuses on recognizing new bases for liability or sometimes novel evidentiary approaches.[107] But acknowledgment of disablement, even when representing a single plaintiff, opens up the possibility of making policy arguments that challenge dynamics of racial and gender inequity, and call on courts to intervene to disrupt broader dynamics, not just through the award of damages to individual plaintiffs, but through injunctive relief. Recognizing disablement also invites a different discourse and deeper approach to storytelling through court processes.[108] Rather than viewing a tort as an analysis of the value of an injury, disablement discourse can invite courts to consider how tortious harm interacts with broader power dynamics, and changes the life course of individuals who are already being harmed by subordination.

Conclusion

Many areas of the law remain under-explored as avenues available to achieve the ends of equal protection before and under the law – these

lofty equality-enhancing aspirations are not the exclusive domain of
constitutional and civil rights laws.

– Camille Nelson[109]

In her essay, "Of Eggshells and Thin Skulls," Critical Race Theorist
Camille Nelson advanced a conception of torts doctrine that could comprehend liability for the damage that tortfeasors do when harming the mental
health of Black women, who are always/already enduring white supremacy
and patriarchy.[110] Her powerful argument partially inspired this essay, and
essentially imagined how a traditional doctrine might be reconfigured
to support socially just, anti-racist and feminist outcomes. Nevertheless,
Nelson's challenge to the doctrine has been mostly unanswered since
publication in 2006.[111]

An acknowledged problem in torts damage calculations involves
significant racial and gender disparities in damage awards, favoring white
and male plaintiffs.[112] The structural basis for the disparity is not hard to
identify. Doctrinal conventions essentially allow tort victims who become
disabled due to a tort to recover for lost wages (in instances when injuries
make it medically impossible to work at all, or to work full-time).[113] Racial
and gender stratification of wages in the U.S. do the rest of the work in
strengthening this inequity.[114] White men are statistically likely to be eligible
for greater damage recovery, because they are statistically likely to be paid
more, and therefore the infliction of disabilities is "worth" more relative
to loss of income.[115] In some instances, the likely devaluation of damage
awards prevents prospective plaintiffs from getting legal counsel (who are
typically taking such cases on contingency) at all. Disrupting this dynamic
requires statutory and doctrinal interventions, which most states have been
slow to explore.[116]

In developing more equitable outcomes in the torts field, sensitizing
torts practitioners and courts to better understand, argue, and remedy
social consequences of tortious harm can at least begin to serve as a partial
remedy for these entrenched dynamics. An indigenous, Black or Latina
female (cisgendered or transgender) plaintiff may earn substantially less than

her white and male counterparts. Rather than devaluing harm to her, courts should be challenged to better understand how deeply she has been injured through the addition of vulnerability to intersectional disability subordination to her life course, as she is already struggling economically. The fact that she is underpaid could be understood as contributing to the argument that she is more vulnerable to the social dynamics that accompany her disability, as compared to a white, male plaintiff who, in medical terms, is similarly injured.

Fundamentally, torts doctrine will likely continue to manifest certain core problems. It is a field that translates pain, injury, loss and trauma into monetized damages.[117] In essence, torts practice can invite desensitization to loss and harm, can objectify the experiences of vulnerable people and populations, and often also can serve to mask or erase aspects of experience that are difficult to articulate in legal terms.[118] Moreover, while a partial shift in emphasis from "disability as presumptive tragedy" towards recognition of disability subordination as a basis for torts damages is a positive step in reducing the dissonances between torts and civil rights law, it would be naïve to imagine that torts doctrine will not continue to reproduce at least some of its familiar tropes about disability, or to imagine that this shift alone would be a sufficient remedy. Nevertheless, imagining, articulating, and establishing legal doctrine about "disabling torts" is needed. Such a shift brings with it the possibility of advancing more powerful responses to disablement, an area that is currently poorly recognized in both torts and civil rights doctrine, and that is nevertheless deeply significant in many of our lives.

Endnotes

1   Robert A. Kagan "How Much Do Conservative Tort Tales Matter," 31:3 Law and Social Inquiry 711 (2006).

2   Adam M. Milani, "Living the World: A New Look at the Disabled in the Law of Torts," 48 Cath. U. L. Rev. 323 (1998-1999).

3   University of the Pacific, McGeorge School of Law, Edited and Excerpted

Transcript of the Symposium on Injury as Cultural Practice, 28 Pac. McGeorge Global Bus. & Dev. L.J. 69 (2014); Sagit Mor, "The Meaning of Injury: A Disability Perspective," *Injury and Injustice: The Cultural Politics of Harm and Redress* 27 (2018).

4   Laura Rothstein, Disability Discrimination Statutes or Tort Law: Which Provides the Best Means to Ensure an Accessible Environment, 75 OHIO ST. L.J. 1263 (2014) [hereinafter Rothstein].

5   Ibid.

6   Richard K. Scotch, "Politics and Policy in the History of the Disability Rights Movement," 67:2, *The Millbank Quarterly* 380 (1989) [hereinafter Scotch].

7   Beth Ribet, "Surfacing Disability Through a Critical Race Theoretical Paradigm," 2 *Geo. J. L. & Mod. Critical Race Persp.* 209 (2010) [hereinafter Ribet].

8   Scotch Supra note 6.

9   Heidi L. Janz & Michelle Stack, "Think Disability is a Tragedy? We Pity You," *The Conversation*, http://theconversation.com/think-disability-is-a-tragedy-we--pity-you-82047

10   Ibid.

11   Lennard J. Davis, *The Disability Studies Reader* (2013) [hereinafter Davis]; Nirmala Erevelles, *Disability and Difference in Global Contexts: Enabling a Transformative Body Politic* (2011); Kim Q. Hall, *Feminist Disability Studies* (2011) [hereinafter Davis].

12   As one example, Martha Minow's work on law and difference engages with this point. Martha Minow, *Making All the Difference: Inclusion, Exclusion and American Law* (1990).

13   H. Russell Cort & Jack L. Sammons, The Search for Good Lawyering: A Concept and Model of Lawyering Competencies, 29 CLEV. ST. L. REV. 397 (1980).

14   Ibid.

15   The American Bar Associations Model Rules of Professional Conduct partially addresses this question, indicating: "In rendering advice, a lawyer may refer not only to law but to other considerations such as moral, economic, social and political factors, that may be relevant to the client's situation." ABA Model Rules of Professional Conduct, 2:1 Advisor, available at: https://www.americanbar. org/groups/professional_responsibility/publications/model_rules_of_profes-

sional_conduct/rule_2_1_advisor/

16   Davis supra note 11; Patricia Berne, Aurora Levins Morales, David Langstaff & Sins Invalid, "Ten Principles of Disability Justice," 46:1&2 *Women's Studies Quarterly* (2018).

17   Ribet supra note 7; Marta Russell & Jean Stewart, "Disablement, Prison & Historical Segregation," *Monthly Review* (2001) [hereinafter Russell]

18   Robert L. Rabin, "Enabling Torts," 49 DePaul L. Rev. 435 (1999) [hereinafter Rabin]

19   Ibid.

20   Ibid.

21   Ibid.

22   Russell supra note 17.

23   Ibid

24   Ibid

25   Ibid

26   Ibid

27   Steven R. Smith, "Social Justice and Disability: Competing Interpretations of the Medical and Social Models," *Arguing About Disability* (2008).

28   Ibid.

29   Ibid. It also bears noting that at least some Disability Studies scholars have become more critical of the "medical/social dichotomy" and of the rather glowing adherence to social constructionist frames in mainstream disability theory. See for instance, Tom Shakespeare, *Disability Rights and Wrongs Revisited* (2013).

30   Ribet supra note 7

31   Ibid.

32   Ibid.

33   Ibid.

34   Ibid; Russell supra note 17.

35   Ribet supra note 7; Ryan Holifield, "Defining Environmental Justice and Environmental Racism," 22 *Urban Geography* 78 (2001).

36   Ibid.

37   Ribet supra note 7.

38   Ibid; Deborah M. Capaldi et al, "Official Incidents of Domestic Violence: Types, Injuries, and Associations with Non-Couple Aggression," 24:4 *Violence & Victimization* 502 (2009).

39   Helen Meekosha, "Contextualizing Disability: Developing Southern/Global Theory," Keynote Address, 4th Biennial Disability Studies Conference, Lancaster U. (2008); Ribet supra note 7.

40   In "Palestine is Disabled" (2024), Leah Lakshmi Piepzna-Samarasinha explains that in the context of current Israeli genocidal practices directed at Gaza and its people, and relative to the broader history of ethnic cleansing affecting the people of Palestine, essentially no Palestinian people have been spared from developing some forms of disability. For instance, she describes disabling consequences of starvation, bombing, and destruction of healthcare systems relative to heart disease, strokes, and other destructive consequences, and also acknowledges post-traumatic stress disorder and suicidal ideation as deeply destructive to Palestinian health. The critical point she makes is that in the context of mass violence, no Palestinian people can escape disabling harm, and further, disabling harms are nearly impossible to fully recover from absent vital deficiencies and losses in social and healthcare systems. Leah Lakshmi Piepzna-Samarasinha, "Palestine is Disabled," The Disability Visibility Project (2024) last visited May 18, 2025, https://disabilityvisibilityproject.com/2024/01/26/palestine-is-disabled/. For helpful related discussion, see also, Lena Obermaier, "Disabling Palestine: The Case of Gaza's Great March of Return," 65:3 *Race and Class* (2023)

41   Ibid; Laura Jaffee & Kelsey John, "Disabling Bodies of/and Land: Reframing Disability Justice in Conversation with Indigenous Theory and Activism," 5:2 *Disability and the Global South* 1407 (2018).

42   Jennifer Pokempner and Dorothy E. Roberts, "Poverty, Welfare Reform, and the Meaning of Disability" 62 Ohio St. L. J. 425 (2001); Ribet supra note 7.

43   Ibid; James H. Price, Jagdish Khubchandani & Fern J. Webb, "Poverty & Health Disparities: What Can Public Health Professionals Do?" 19:2 *Health Promotion Practice* 170 (2018); Ribet supra note 7.

44   Crick Lund, "Poverty and Mental Health: A Review of Policies and Practices," 2:3 *Neuropsychiatry* 213 (2012).

45   Ribet supra note 7.

46   Ibid.

47   Ibid; Russell supra note 17.

48   Ribet supra note 7.

49   Maureen Murdoch et al, "Racial Disparities in VA Service Connection for Posttraumatic Stress Disorder Disability," 41:4 *Medical Care* 536 (2003).

50   Amy Lutz, "Who Joins the Military? A Look at Race, Class and Immigration Status," 36:2 *J. of Political & Military Sociology* 167 (2008).

51   Beverly Patterson et al, "Co-occurrence of Birth Defects and Intellectual Disability," 21:1 *Paediatric & Perinatal Epidemiology* 65 (2007); Julian Aguon, *What We Bury at Night: Disposable Humanity* (2008)

52   Ibid; Ribet supra note 7.

53   Ibid.

54   Connie J. Mulligan, "Systemic Racism Can Get Under Our Skin and into Our Genes," 175:2 *Amer. J. of Biological Anthropology* 399 (2021).

55   Ibid; Ribet supra note 7.

56   Rabin supra note 18.

57   Ibid at 449.

58   Ibid.

59   Ibid.

60   Ibid.

61   Ibid.

62   Ibid at 452.

63   Ibid.

64   Ibid.

65   Ibid.

66   Ibid.

67   Stephen F. Befort, "Let's Try This Again: The ADA Amendments Act of 2008 Attempts to Reinvigorate the Regarded as Prong of the Statutory Definition of Disability," 2010 Utah L. Rev. 993 (2010).

68   Rabin, supra note 18.

69   Mark C. Weber, "Accidentally on Purpose: Intent in Disability Discrimination Law," 56 Boston College L. Rev 1417 (2015). To avoid over-simplifying this

point, it is helpful to acknowledge that Weber's analysis acknowledges that even though intent requirements are not generally formalized in disability-related statutes, courts may still impose an expectation that plaintiffs with disabilities should produce evidence of defendant intent, notwithstanding an absence of any statutory requirement.

70   Dan M. Kahan, "Ignorance of Law in an Excuse– But Only for the Virtuous," 96 Mich. L. Rev. 127 (1997)

71   Adam Cureton, "Hiding a Disability and Passing as Non-Disabled," *Disability in Practice: Attitudes, Policies and Relationships*, eds. Adam Cureton & Thomas E. Hill Jr. 18 (2018)

72   Ribet supra note 7.

73   The United Nations Convention on the Rights of Persons with Disabilities, available at: https://www.ohchr.org/en/instruments-mechanisms/instruments/convention-rights-persons-disabilities [hereinafter CRPD]

74   Ibid.

75   Aimi Hamraie, *Building Access: Universal Design and the Politics of Disability* (2015)

76   Molly Follette Story, "Maximizing Usability: The Principles of Universal Design," 10:1 *Assistive Technology* 4 (2010).

77   Ribet supra note 7.

78   Ibid.

79   Benjamin C. Zipursky, "Foreseeability in Breach, Duty & Proximate Cause," 44 Wake Forest L. Rev. 1247 (2009).

80   Rabin supra note 17.

81   As one partial exception, universal design is at least referenced, though with limited enforceability, in some K-12 and higher education disability rights law in the United States. For related critical discussion, see Lina Zhang, Richard Allen Carter, and Nicholas Hoekstra, "A Critical Analysis of Universal Design for Learning in the U.S. Federal Education Law," 22:4, *Policy Futures in Education* (2023)

82   See e.g. Christine Joffs & J.J. Prescott, "Disaggregating Employment Discrimination: The Case of Employment Discrimination," National Bureau of Economic Research (2004).

83   It is important to acknowledge that the fact of ratification does not firmly pre-

dict how a UN member nation will interpret its obligations under a UN Convention, or how strictly it will comply with that interpretation. In the event that the U.S. Congress were to ratify the CRPD, the interpretation of the Convention's call to implement or at least be influenced by the principles of universal design might fall along a wide spectrum of possibilities, such that the impact on the U.S. civil rights model could be dramatic, very minimal, or anywhere in between. For the moment however, it is helpful to note that ratification of the CRPD would create a potential (though not a guarantee) for a more robust framework for accessibility in the United States; CRPD supra note 72.

84   Ribet supra note 7.

85   Ibid.

86   Ibid; Beth Ribet, "Emergent Disability and the Limits of Equality: A Critical Reading of the UN Convention on the Rights of Persons with Disabilities," 14 *Yale Human Rights & Dev. L. J.* 101 (2011). [hereinafter Ribet2].

87   Kevin Dahaghi, "Uneven Access to Justice: Social Context and Eligibility for the Right to Counsel," 71:2 *Social Problems* 455 (2024).

88   Ribet2 supra note 86.

89   Ani B. Satz, "Overcoming Fragmentation in Disability and Health Law," 60 Emory L. J. 277 (2010-2011).

90   Rabin supra note 18.

91   Ribet supra note 7.

92   Ibid.

93   Ibid.

94   One question that this strategy raises for me involves the potential effectiveness of attempting to make subordination "costly." While I won't take up the broader work of unpacking this question carefully in this paper, I want to acknowledge that the question is ultimately vital to this type of project, namely attempting to move our existing legal doctrine to serve an economically and racially just purpose, despite and in response to the histories of racialized commodification and property that typify U.S. jurisprudence. I am indebted to Cheryl Harris for enhancing my attention to U.S. law as it is fundamentally grounded in racialized objectification. Cheryl I. Harris, "Whiteness as Property," 106:8 Harvard L. Rev. (1993). Naomi Klein's attention to the relationship

between economic justice and climate justice is also important to this broader conversation, and invites us to imagine a future in which very deep changes to social institutions, including law, are not just possible, but essential to any possibility of an environmentally sustainable and livable future. Naomi Klein, *Hot Money* (2021). It is helpful to at least recognize that the context in which torts law operates may change radically. I readily acknowledge that I do not know whether such changes will render much of this paper either irrelevant, or relevant but lacking adequate social imagination needed to thoroughly advance vital changes.

95 Ribet supra note 7.

96 Ribet2 supra note 86.

97 For background, see e.g. Thomas C. Grey, "Accidental Torts," 54 Vand. L. Rev. 1225 (2001).

98 Ibid; Keith N. Hylton, "Duty in Tort Law: An Economic Approach," 75 Fordham L. Rev. 1501 (2006-2007).

99 Ibid.

100 Rothstein supra note 6.

101 See e.g. Donna Lee Hawley, "Assessment of Damages for Permanent Incapacitating Injuries," 13 Alta. L. Rev. 430 (1975).

102 For related discussion on the critical utility of empiricism in law, see Osagie Obasogie, "Foreword: Critical Race Theory and Empirical Methods," 3 UC Irvine L. Rev. 183 (2013).

103 Americans with Disabilities Act of 1990, as Amended, Title 42, Chapter 126.

104 Davis supra note 11.

105 See e.g. Eric Emerson et al, "Loneliness, Social Support, Social Isolation and Wellbeing Among Working Age Adults With and Without Disability: Cross-sectional Study," 14:1 *Disability and Health J.* 1 (2021).

106 See e.g. Davis, supra note 11.

107 Deborah R. Hensler, "The New Social Policy Torts: Litigation as Legislative Strategy – Some Preliminary Thoughts on a New Research Project," 51 DePaul L. Rev. 493 (2001-2002).

108 Ribet supra note 7; For background on narrative conceptions of legal engagement (in Critical Race Theory), see Rachel F. Moran & Devon W. Carbado,

Race Law Stories (2008).

109 Camille A. Nelson, "Of Eggshells and Thin-skulls: A Consideration of Racism-Related Mental Illness Impacting Black Women," 29:2 *International J. of L. & Psychiatry* 113 (2006).

110 Ibid.

111 Earlier in this paper, I discussed the social/medical dichotomy relative to the meanings of disability, and identified that medical conceptions of disability have generally informed U.S. law. Although I respect some of the critiques of medical conceptions of disability advanced by critical disability theorists, and appreciate the critical, social constructionist approach embodied in Russell & Stewart's conception of disablement (Russell supra note 16), one of the embedded themes in this discussion involves problematizing the social/medical dichotomy. While doing so is not my primary project in this paper, it is helpful to acknowledge that Nelson's work is a compelling example of Black feminist disability legal scholarship that cannot fit either end of this dichotomy. One side (the medical model) stigmatizes disability as a presumptive tragedy based on supposedly objective medical criteria. Nelson's critiques of racist and sexist disabling harm are of course disruptive to this model and its supposed scientific validity, both in centering (rather than objectifying) the experiences of Black women, and in countering the notion that disability is merely a physically generated occurrence, rather than an element of structural subordination. However, one of the premises of the social model is that "disability is only disabling when it prevents someone from doing what they want or need to do" (Sarah Buder & Rose Perry, "The Social Model of Disability Explained," last visited May 18, 2025, https://www.thesocialcreatures.org/thecreaturetimes/the-social-model--of-disability). In this framework, being harmfully disabled by racism is sexism is likely to be poorly understood at best, because the primary measure of disabling harm is not the ease in which the violent infliction of disability occurs or the failure to remedy that violence or its structural origins, but whether the society is sufficiently accessible to the person who has been disabled. While accessibility matters, Nelson's approach is intentional about imagining how torts law can become responsive not just to the social consequences of disability, but also to the social origins of disability, and the inherent resulting harms. In use-

ful related discussion contained in her work on the meanings of disability in the Global North vs. South, Helen Meekosha delineates the discursive and practical differences between colonial conceptions of disability focused on (formal) equality of opportunity, and global southern conceptions of disability focused on access to water and other basic questions embedded in disabling damage in fundamentally violent and hierarchical societies. Helen Meekosha, "Decolonizing Disability: Thinking and Acting Globally," 26:6 *Disability & Society* (2011).

112 Martha Chamallas & Jennifer B. Wriggins, *The Measure of Injury: Race, Gender & Tort Law* (2010) [hereinafter Chammallas].

113 Ibid.

114 Ibid; Sydney Dhue, "Social Thinking and Pay Inequities," 16:5 *McNair Scholars Res. J.* 15 (2023).

115 Chamallas supra note 112.

116 One arguably helpful development in this area is California's "S.B. 41," which took effect on January 1, 2020. The legislation prohibits reductions of torts damages for future earnings based solely on race and gender. Although this is moderately useful in itself, it does not actually fundamentally address how earnings are shaped by race and gender, or provide any remedy for low-income people who are only eligible for reduced damages due to their actual income, which has already been shaped by racial and gender stratification. The legislation would be meaningful for instance if a child of color was violently disabled, and defense attorneys were prohibited from reducing damage calculations based on the child's race. However, it would have more limited application (if any) for working-class plaintiffs who are attempting to address loss of income from low-paying jobs. CA Civ Code § 3361 (2024).

117 For critical discussion on torts law and opportunities to shift current dynamics, see e.g. Martha Chamallas, "Social Justice Tort Theory," 14:2, *J. Tort Law* 309 (2021).

118 Ibid.